IMAGES
of America

MAINE'S JEWISH HERITAGE

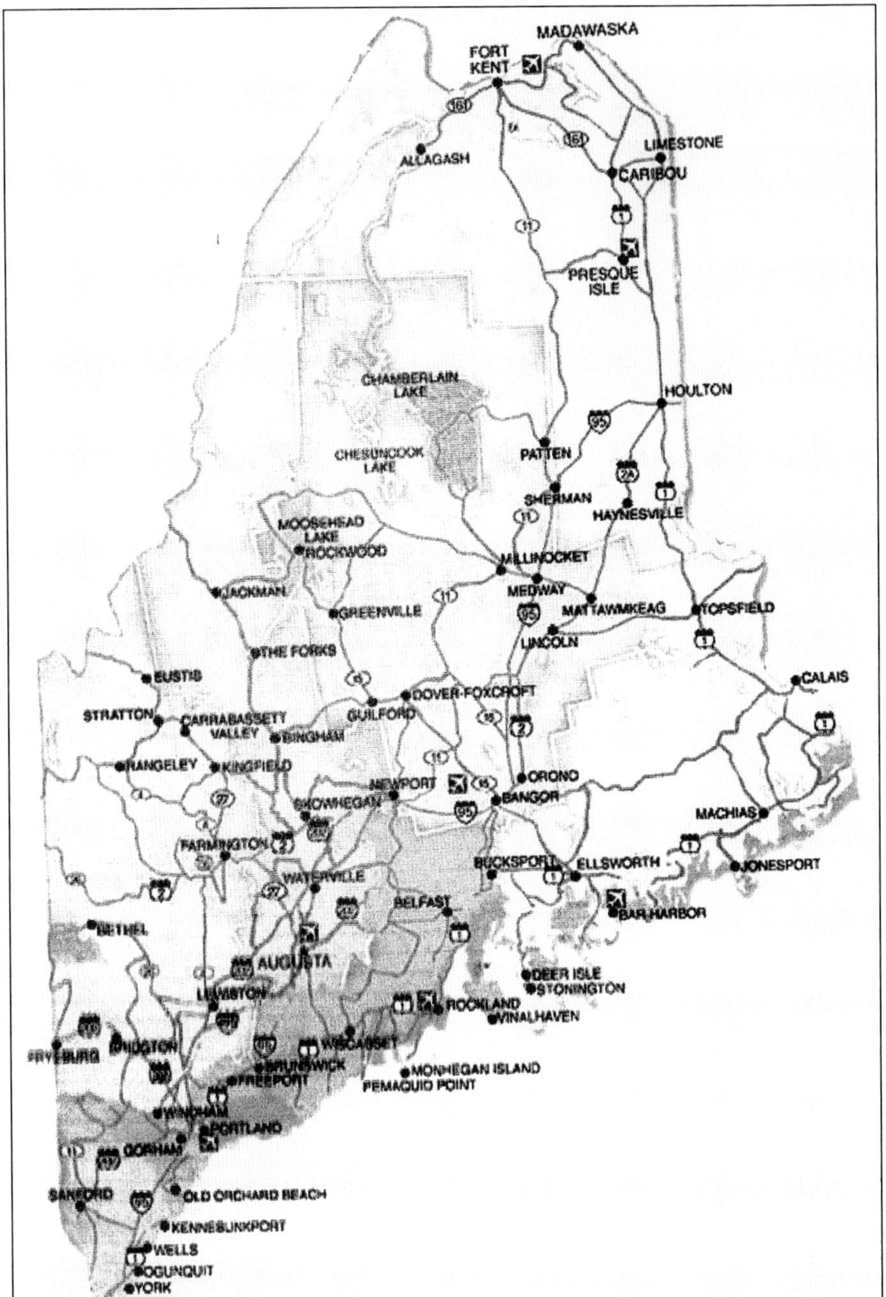

Maine is big, bigger than all the other New England states put together, but its population is only just over a million. Currently, Maine is home to about 10,000 Jews, most of whom live in or around the southern half of the state.

On the cover: Congregants from Bangor's Beth Israel marched with their new Torah scrolls into their building around 1930. Across the street from Beth Israel is the Beth Abraham Synagogue; both were Orthodox synagogues at the time. Beth Israel became a Conservative temple in 1969. (Courtesy of the Bangor Public Library.)

IMAGES
of America

MAINE'S JEWISH HERITAGE

Abraham J. Peck and Jean M. Peck

ARCADIA
PUBLISHING

ISBN 978-0-7385-4965-1

Published by Arcadia Publishing
Charleston, South Carolina

Printed in the United States of America

Library of Congress Catalog Card Number: 2006935916

For all general information contact Arcadia Publishing at:
Telephone 843-853-2070
Fax 843-853-0044
E-mail sales@arcadiapublishing.com
For customer service and orders:
Toll-Free 1-888-313-2665

Visit us on the Internet at www.arcadiapublishing.com

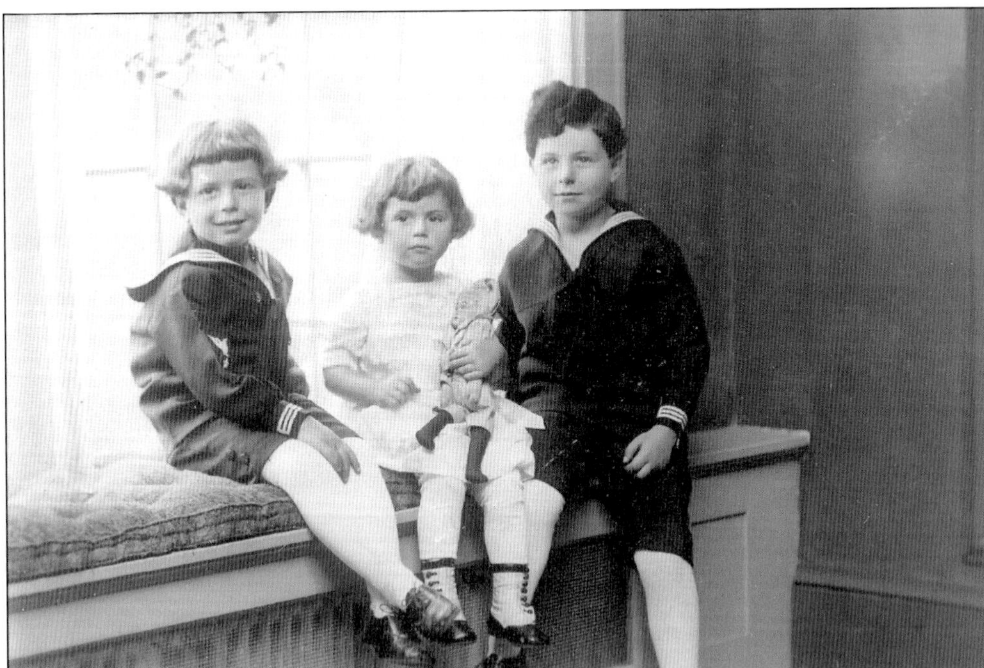

From left to right, Harry, Anna, and Myer Marcus pose for this picture in the early 1920s. Myer Marcus, at age 92, is now the oldest practicing attorney in Maine. This book is for our children, Abby and Joel, and for our loving family, all of whom are blessed with their Jewish heritage and Maine roots. (Courtesy of Anna Marcus Stillman.)

Contents

ACKNOWLEDGMENTS

The challenge of doing a history, photographic or otherwise, of an entire community in a state as large as Maine is an awesome one.

Thank goodness that a number of individuals and institutions responded to our constant pleas for assistance with generosity and, usually, good humor.

We are grateful to the entire rabbinic community of Maine. Each and every rabbi responded to our requests by sending materials, contacting a staff member to help, or by asking a congregant to send information. We are grateful to Rabbi Carolyn Braun of Temple Beth El; Rabbi Alice Dubinsky of Congregation Bet Ha'am; Rabbi Moshe Wilansky of Chabad Maine and David Bergman, president of Congregation Shaarey Tphiloh, all of Portland; Rabbi Hillel Katzir of Temple Shalom Synagogue-Center, Auburn; Rabbi Susan Bulba Carvutto of Temple Beth El, Augusta; Rabbi Amita Jarmon of Adas Yoshuron Synagogue, Rockland; Cantor Daniel Leeman of Beth Israel Congregation, Bath; Rabbi Raymond Krinsky, Beth Israel Congregation, Waterville; Rabbi Fred Nebel, Beth Abraham Synagogue; Rabbi David Cantor, Congregation Beth Israel; and Rabbi Dara R. Lerner, Congregation Beth El, all of Bangor.

The following individuals were immensely helpful: David Andreasen and Susie Bock of the Sampson Center for Diversity, Portland; Bill Berry, Nick Noyes, Gabrielle Daniello of the Maine Historical Society, Portland; Richard Lindemann and Caroline Moseley of the George J. Mitchell Dept. of Special Collections and Archives, Bowdoin College Library; former colleagues Kevin Proffitt and Camille Servizzi of the Jacob Rader Marcus Center of the American Jewish Archives, Cincinnati; Dr. Carole Kolker, Maryland; Mary Wierzbicki, Portland; Professor William Small, Bangor; Jennie Aranovitch, a fine historian of the Biddeford/Saco Jewish experience, Biddeford; Bill Cook, Bangor Public Library; Laura Carlson and Todd Reynolds of the Portland tax assessor's office; Donald Silver, Portland; Eber Weinstein, Old Orchard Beach; Myrtle McKenna, Rumford; Sr. Rita Mae Bissonnette, Roman Catholic Diocese, Portland; Raphael Gribetz, Presque Isle; Justin Schair, Portland; Phil, Nancy, and Ken Levinsky of Portland; Claire Connell, Portland; and Kenny Nelson, Portland, for his sage advice.

If we have failed to mention anyone, we are grateful to them nonetheless. Any other errors of omission or commission are ours alone, although we hope they are few in number.

Introduction

Within the long sweep of American Jewish history, several overarching themes have emerged that characterize the three-and-a-half centuries of Jewish life in the United States (1654–2006): a belief in the promise of America; faith in the pluralistic nature of America; a quest for economic and professional success; and a commitment to the survival of the Jewish community.

Although never more than 10,000 strong, Maine's Jewish community has always reflected these particular themes. Maine Jewry has sought to balance its American social contract, the notion of being a good American, with the understanding that it was part of a holy community, whose essential purpose was to be "a light unto the nations." Beginning in the 1840s, a small number of Jewish peddlers, tailors, and dry goods merchants from German-speaking lands came to Bangor, "the Queen City." By 1849, they had established a synagogue and a cemetery. Neither the peddlers nor the synagogue remained very long, and both were gone by the late 1850s.

For those few German Jewish immigrants and those who began to come to Maine from Eastern Europe in the 1860s (many of them to escape from the oppression of Czarist Russia), the state seemed a reassuring haven. When Portland celebrated its centenary on July 4, 1886, Barnard Aaronson, designated to speak for the small Jewish community of the time, observed, "We number sixty families, and over the majority portion being of the middle or poorer class, yet content with their lot . . . The form of religion is Orthodox, and yet [we] are thoroughly liberal in thought and action." In looking back at the 20 years since the great Portland fire of 1866 had attracted a group of Jewish merchants and peddlers to help the city's efforts in rebuilding, Aaronson could only find a positive relationship to his Christian neighbors: "our city fathers have in the past fully merited the good will and affectionate esteem in which they are held by us."

Aaronson's optimism was not an illusion. Unlike Jewish life in Europe, where Jews were by far the most visible and persecuted minority over a 2,000 year period, Jews in Maine could be comforted in the knowledge that other groups, especially Roman Catholics, often stood ahead of them as victims of religious and sometimes racial intolerance.

That good will and affectionate esteem belied the fact that for nearly a century, many places of lodging and certain social clubs were closed to the Jewish community of Maine. A kind of 9-to-5 atmosphere existed even between Jewish and non-Jewish business and professional partners, and neither group was eager to cross the lines of social interaction after the close of the business day.

The contentment and optimism of which Barnard Aaronson spoke were reflected in the fervent pursuit of study, learning, and pious synagogue worship, a piety that earned Portland Jewry the nickname of "The Jerusalem of America," or "The Jerusalem of the North," a designation that could also apply to the Orthodox communities of Bangor, Lewiston, Biddeford, and Old Orchard, among others.

The Jews who came to America from the various parts of the Russian Empire in the years between 1882 and the early 1920s, nearly 2.5 million of them, came with a certain chip on their shoulders. They carried little nostalgia for the *blotte shtetlach* (villages filled with mud streets) they had left, but those who came with a desire to keep Judaism alive, as they knew it in the Old Country, were prepared to beat back any efforts to change what they had always known and believed. Religious change came slowly to the Jewish communities of Maine and the Conservative movement did not develop until the late 1940s, and the Reform movement not until the 1980s.

The decades of the 1920s through the 1940s were tumultuous ones in American and in Maine Jewish history. The 1920s marked the resurgence of the national Ku Klux Klan (KKK), and Maine suffered through a decade of KKK activities. Because there were so few African Americans in the state, KKK activities focused on threats and cross burnings against Roman Catholics, but recorded at least one case of intimidation against a Portland Jewish shop owner.

The noxious presence of the KKK in Maine for nearly a decade may have been the driving force behind the creation of Portland's Interracial Fellowship of America. The group was founded in 1930 by Judge Max Pinansky, who, by the fellowship's founding, had become only the second Jew in history appointed to the Maine bench.

The Interracial Fellowship of America was devoted to the "need of some organization of or at least the recognition of the different nationalities represented in this city." Especially important to the existence of the group was the participation of numerous Protestants and Catholics, including both the Roman Catholic and Episcopal bishops of Portland and Maine.

For the most part however, Maine's Jewish communities and their synagogues focused on developing their economic status and in building communal organizations that would better serve the young. Both Portland and Bangor created Jewish community centers (also known as JCCs) in the 1930s, institutions that were essentially designed to increase social activities for Jewish adults and young people. The JCCs promoted Jewish education, adult and children's programming, and even social action, and took them from a religious to a secular location.

The 1940s, 1950s, and 1960s were momentous times in the history of Maine Jewish life. The destruction of six million Jewish lives and the creation of a 2,000 year-old Jewish dream, the State of Israel, all occurred within less than two decades.

Maine's Jewish congregations, like all of American Jewry, were traumatized by the one event and electrified by the other. The years after 1945 saw a slow but clear shift in the needs of Maine's Jewish congregations: women began to demand a greater voice in the affairs of synagogue life, from participation in religious services to leadership positions on congregational boards and finally, to ordination as rabbis and cantors. The era of civil rights and social action and the movement to break down the doors of exclusion to certain Christian-only clubs and lodging establishments went ahead full force and with much success.

Women began to lead congregations in Maine in the 1990s and soon were the spiritual leaders of Reform, Conservative, and Reconstructionist synagogues and temples as they struggled to understand the new issues facing their congregations and their communities, including intermarriage, assimilation, interreligious dialogue, and basic institutional survival. Yet no matter what their denominational status, all of Maine's Jewish congregations continue to adhere to the notion of being a light unto the nations.

Serving as a light unto the nondemocratic nations of the world has also been an important watchword of the American republic. Both visions have seen Judaism and America lead by example in a divine and in a temporal sense. Each vision has asked its community to work towards a time of redemption and a future of peace and freedom.

Yet it has not been easy being a light unto the nations; indeed it is an awesome responsibility—both a blessing and a burden. Clearly the task has been made easier by the existence of America and its own, sometimes difficult, vision as a second light unto the

One

Religious Life

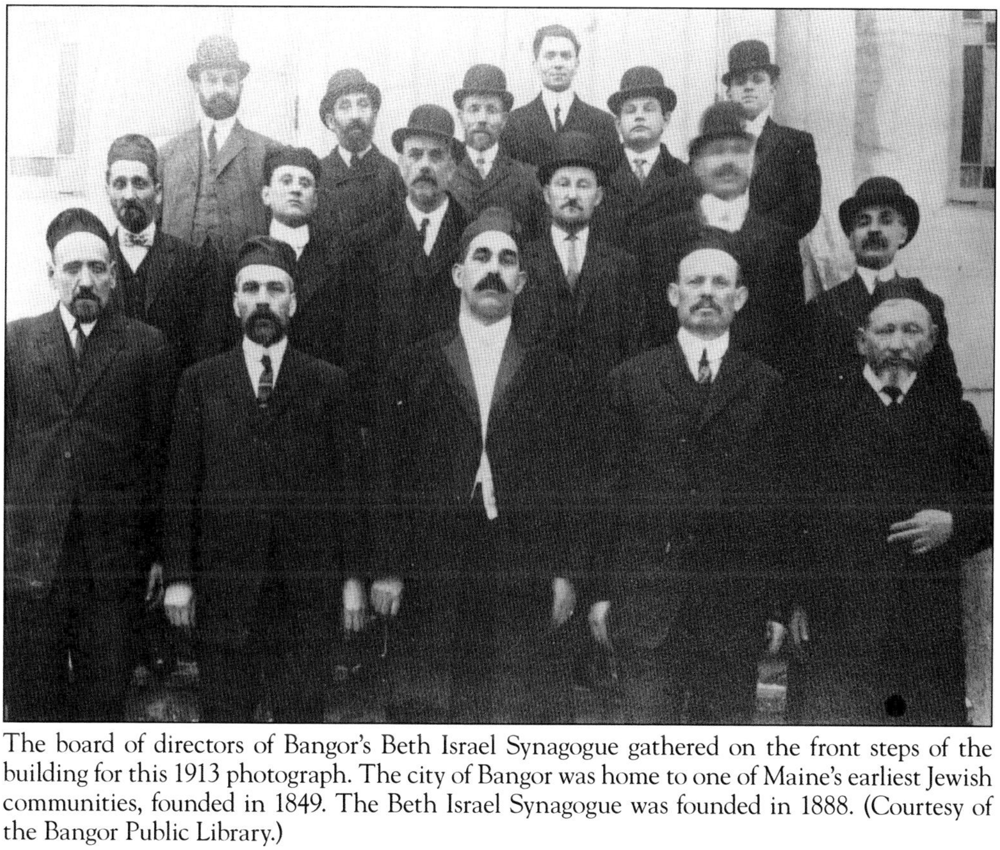

The board of directors of Bangor's Beth Israel Synagogue gathered on the front steps of the building for this 1913 photograph. The city of Bangor was home to one of Maine's earliest Jewish communities, founded in 1849. The Beth Israel Synagogue was founded in 1888. (Courtesy of the Bangor Public Library.)

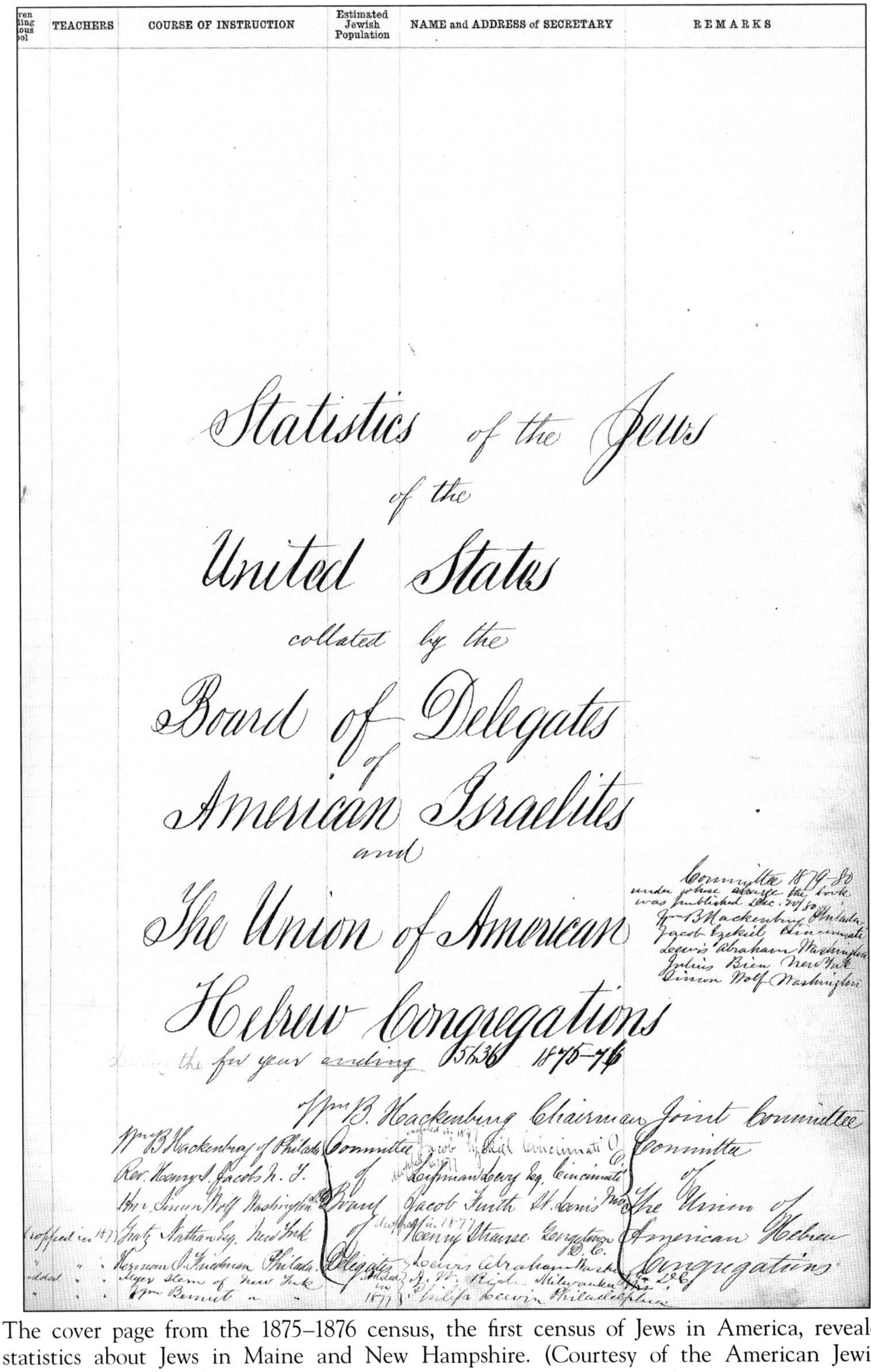

The cover page from the 1875–1876 census, the first census of Jews in America, revealed statistics about Jews in Maine and New Hampshire. (Courtesy of the American Jewish Archives, Cincinnati.)

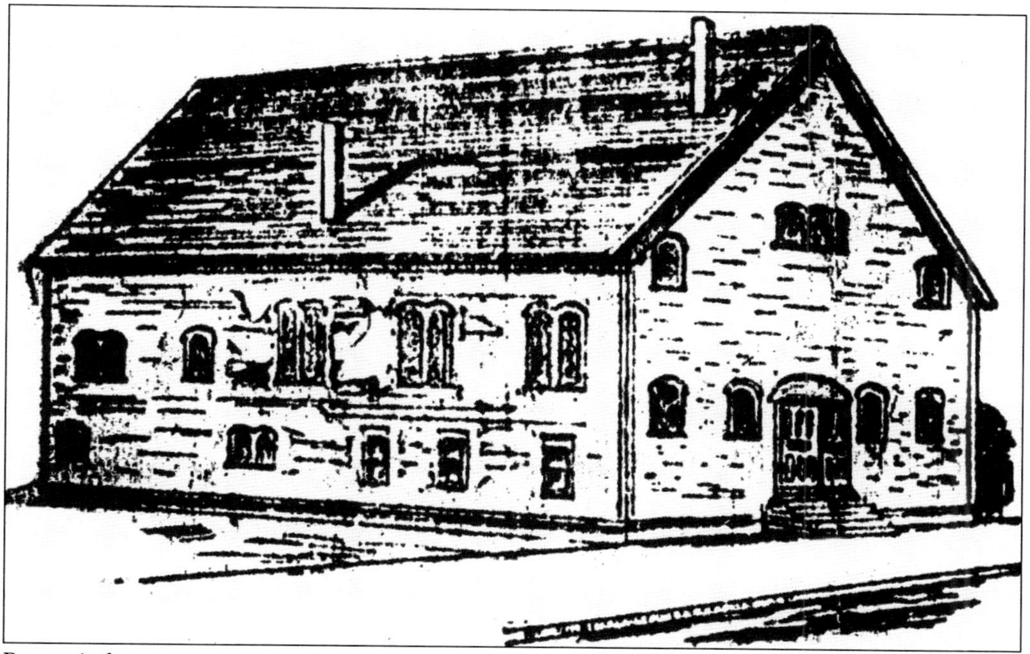

Bangor's first synagogue, Beth Israel, was completed in 1897. This drawing by Victor Hodgins appeared in the *Bangor Daily Commercial.* (Courtesy of the Bangor Public Library.)

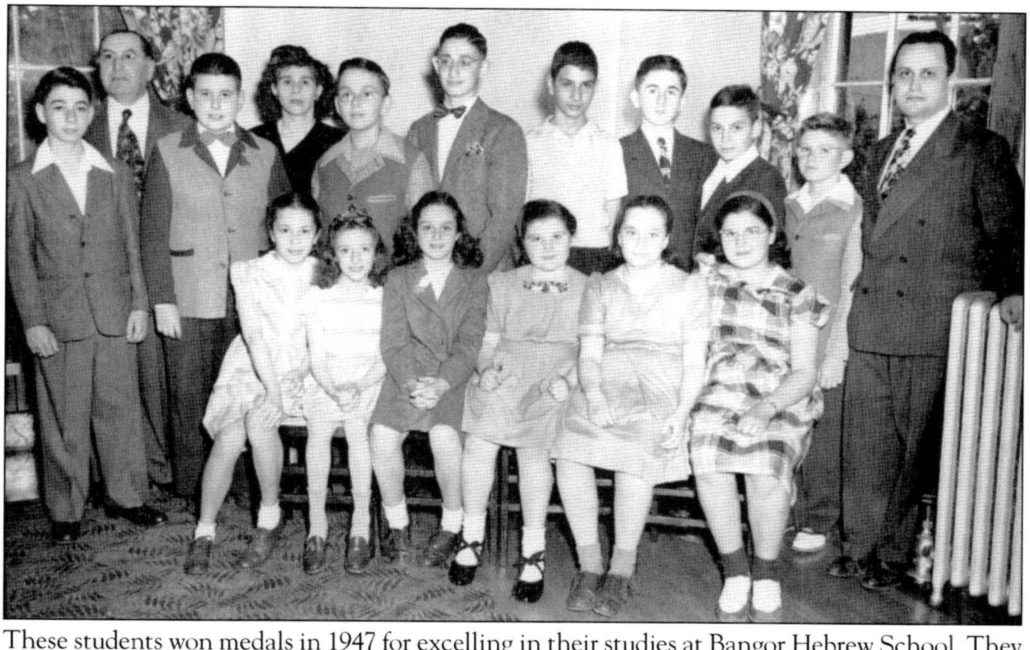

These students won medals in 1947 for excelling in their studies at Bangor Hebrew School. They are, from left to right, (first row) Ruth Schair, Nancy Ashmond, Nurith Fish, Joanne Kopelow, Beverly Segal, and Sybil Miller; (second row) Stephen Podolsky, Mr. Brown, Melvin Gotlieb, Mrs. Fish, Howard Silver, Harvey Leavitt, Jerry Cooper, Murray Leavitt, Sanford Gass, Sandy Podolsky, and Mr. Fish.

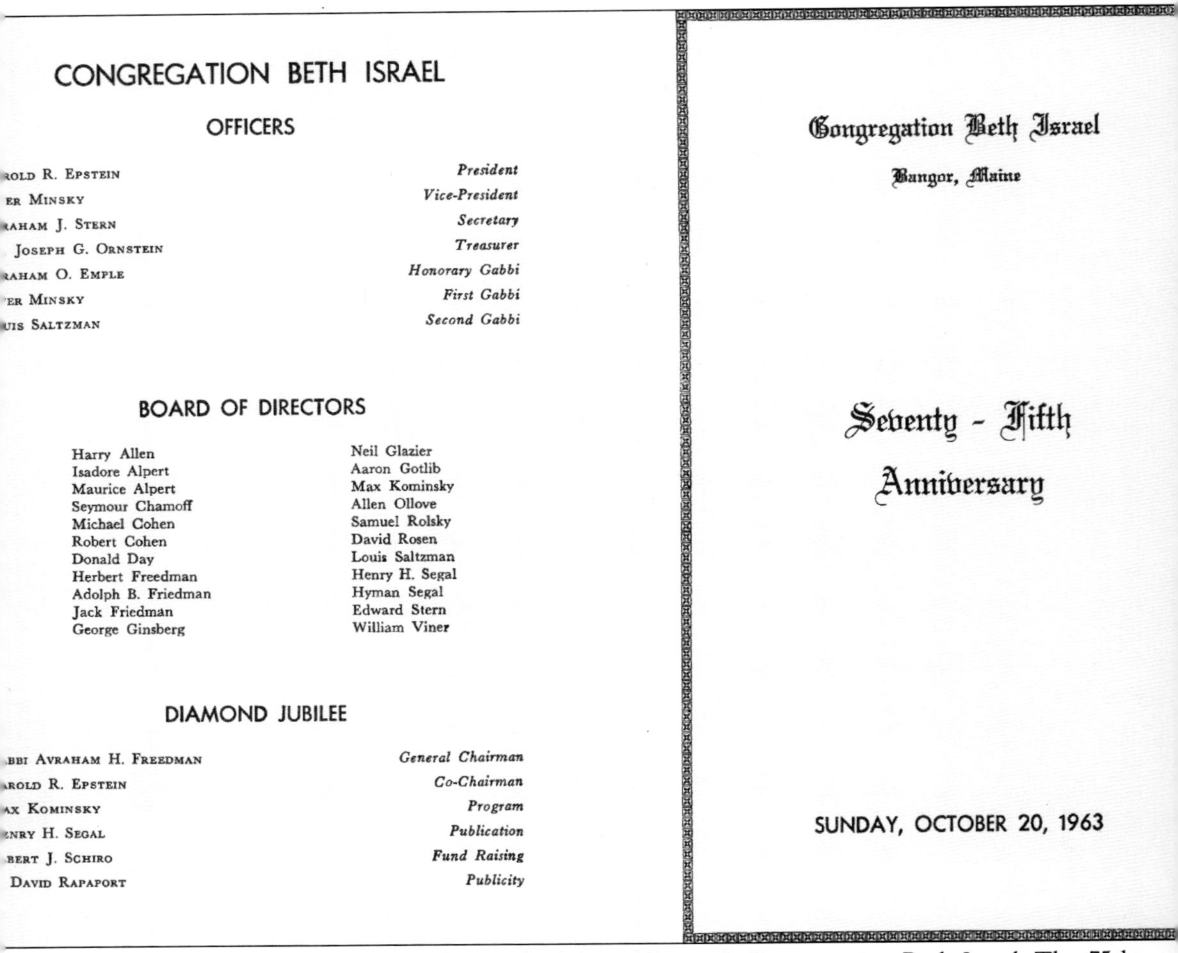

CONGREGATION BETH ISRAEL

OFFICERS

ROLD R. EPSTEIN	*President*
ER MINSKY	*Vice-President*
RAHAM J. STERN	*Secretary*
JOSEPH G. ORNSTEIN	*Treasurer*
RAHAM O. EMPLE	*Honorary Gabbi*
ER MINSKY	*First Gabbi*
UIS SALTZMAN	*Second Gabbi*

BOARD OF DIRECTORS

Harry Allen	Neil Glazier
Isadore Alpert	Aaron Gotlib
Maurice Alpert	Max Kominsky
Seymour Chamoff	Allen Ollove
Michael Cohen	Samuel Rolsky
Robert Cohen	David Rosen
Donald Day	Louis Saltzman
Herbert Freedman	Henry H. Segal
Adolph B. Friedman	Hyman Segal
Jack Friedman	Edward Stern
George Ginsberg	William Viner

DIAMOND JUBILEE

BBI AVRAHAM H. FREEDMAN	*General Chairman*
AROLD R. EPSTEIN	*Co-Chairman*
AX KOMINSKY	*Program*
ENRY H. SEGAL	*Publication*
BERT J. SCHIRO	*Fund Raising*
DAVID RAPAPORT	*Publicity*

Congregation Beth Israel

Bangor, Maine

Seventy - Fifth

Anniversary

SUNDAY, OCTOBER 20, 1963

This program celebrated the diamond jubilee of Bangor's Congregation Beth Israel. The 75th anniversary was honored on October 20, 1963. (Courtesy of the Bangor Public Library.)

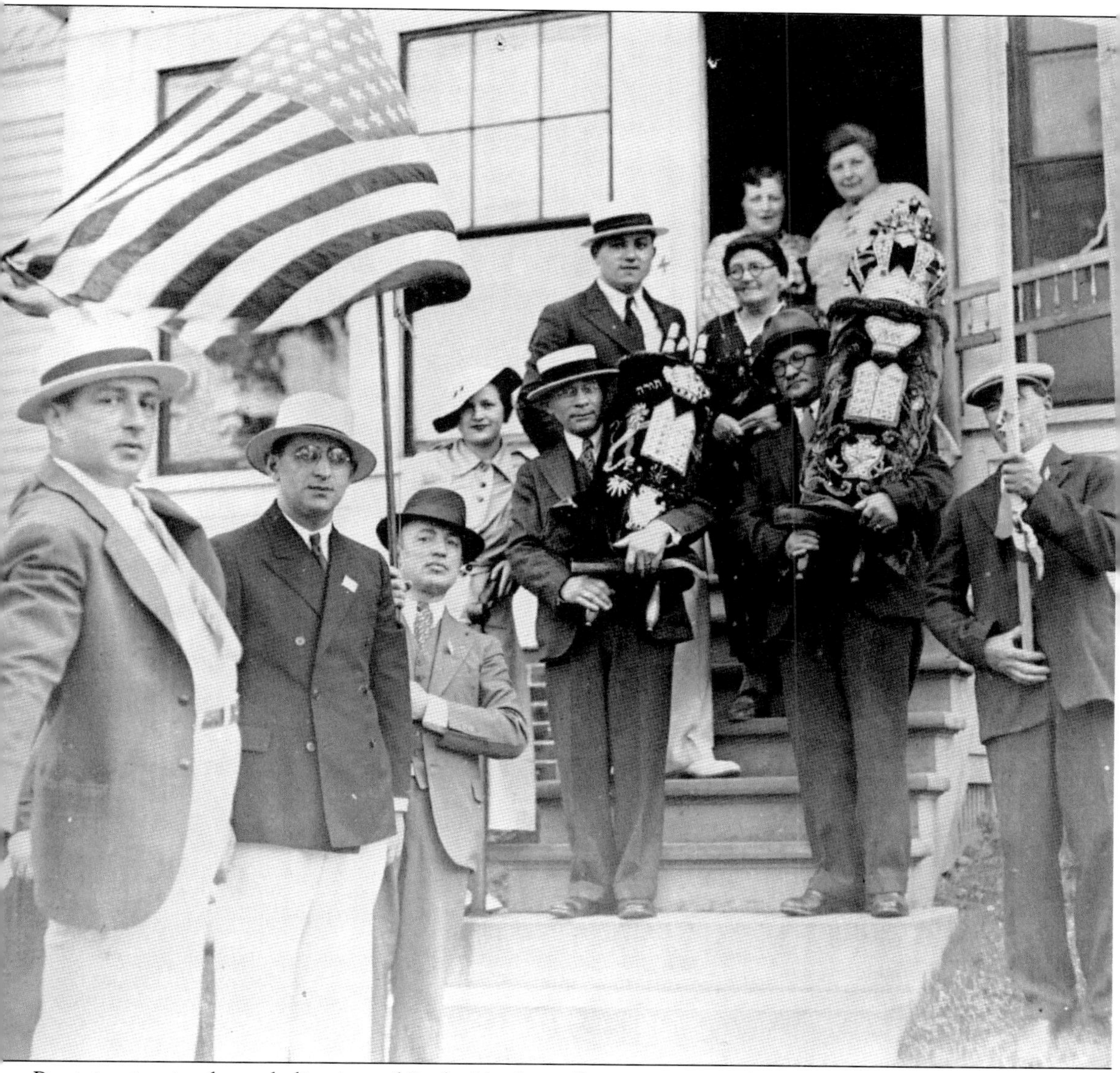

Participating in the rededication of Beth Abraham Synagogue in 1933 were Sam Less, Harry Rabin, Abraham Berg, Ida Striar, Barney Cooper, Joseph Cooper, Barney Striar, Harry Cohen, Sarah Striar, Martha Cooper, and Rebecca Cohen. The silver crown, which was rescued a year earlier when the original structure burned down, is atop the Torah on the right. (Courtesy of the Bangor Public Library.)

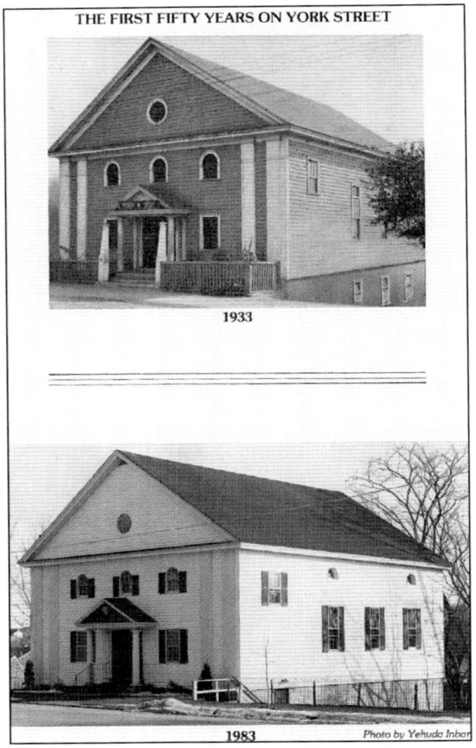

Two views show the old rebuilt Congregation Beth Abraham in 1933 and a renovated Beth Abraham 50 years later.

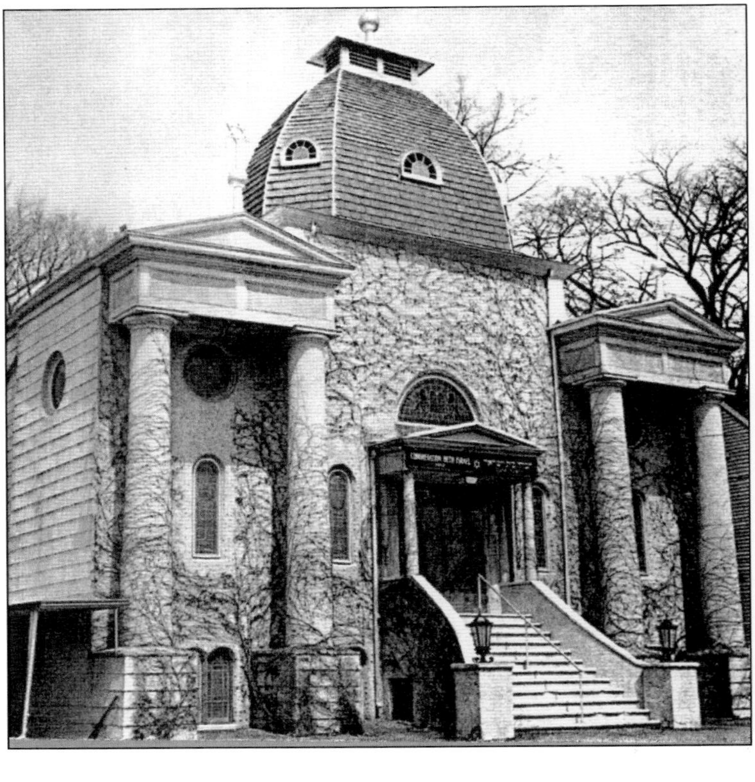

The exterior of Bangor's Congregation Beth Israel is shown here as it looked in 1913. (Courtesy of the Bangor Public Library.)

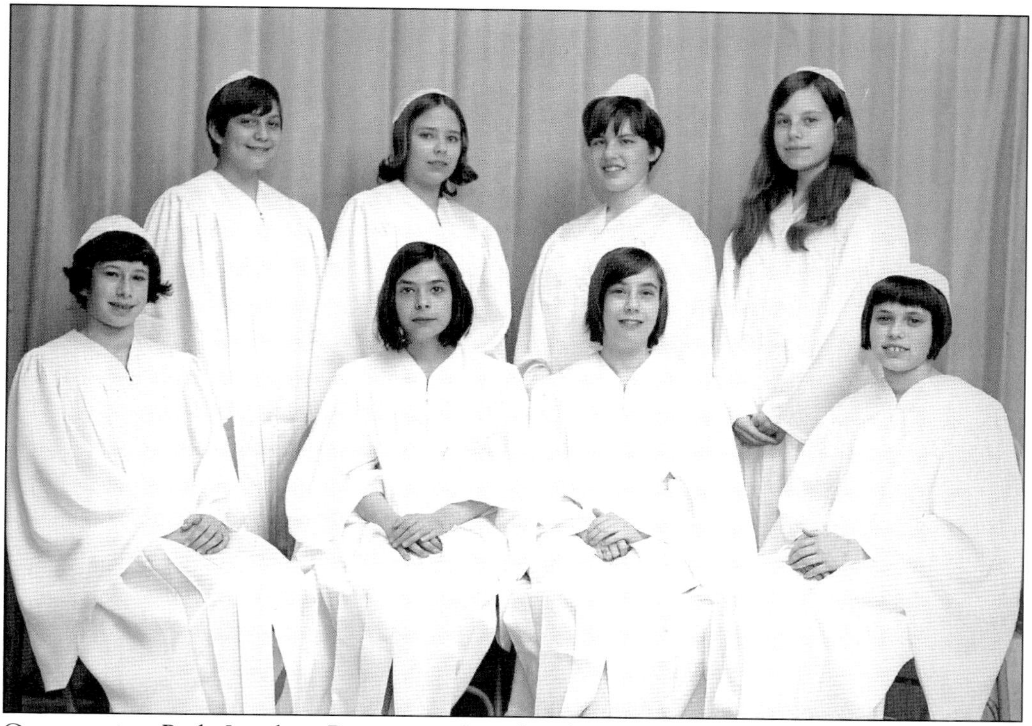

Congregation Beth Israel in Bangor confirmed eight girls. The photograph is undated, but appears to be from the 1960s. (Courtesy of Bangor Public Library.)

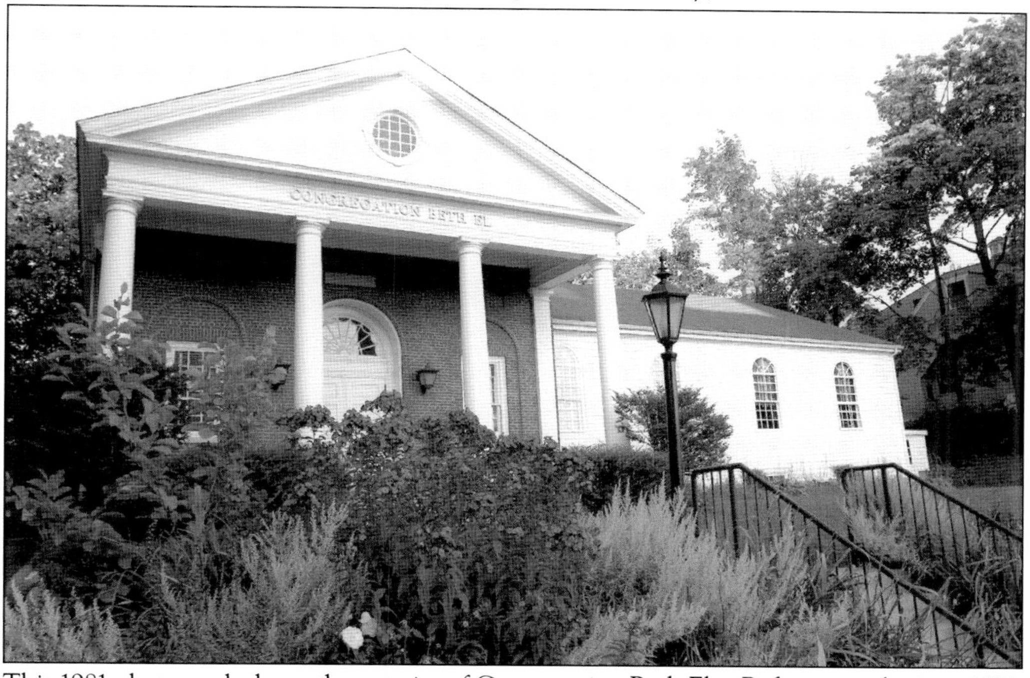

This 1981 photograph shows the exterior of Congregation Beth El, a Reform temple since 1981. (Courtesy of Ira Weissman, Bangor.)

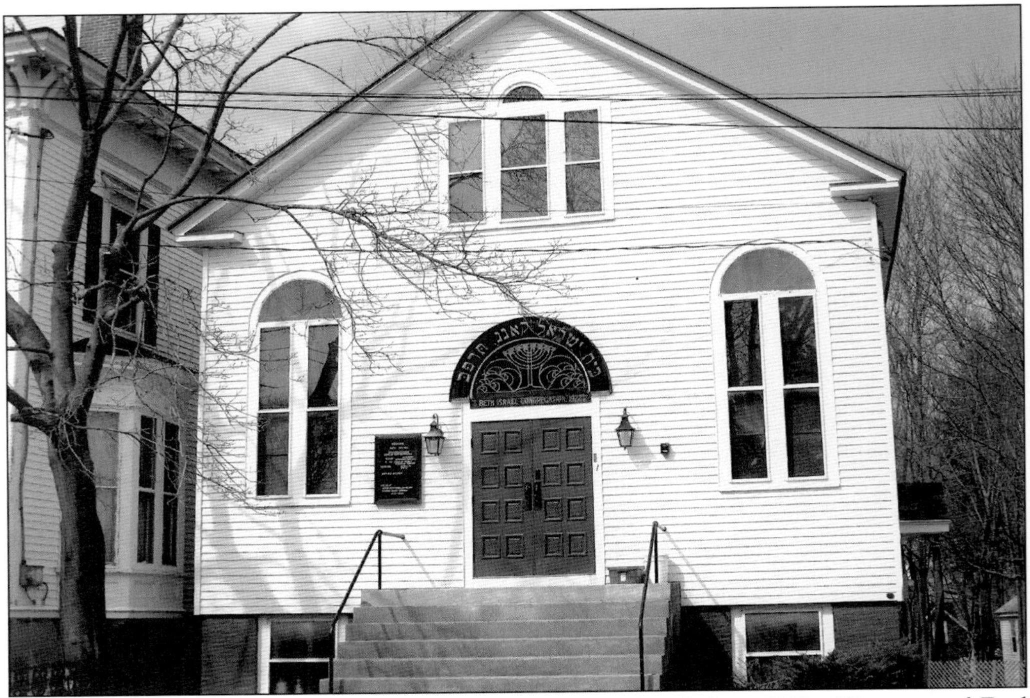

The Conservative synagogue, Beth Israel in Bath was founded in 1922. (Courtesy of Fred Weisberg, Bath.)

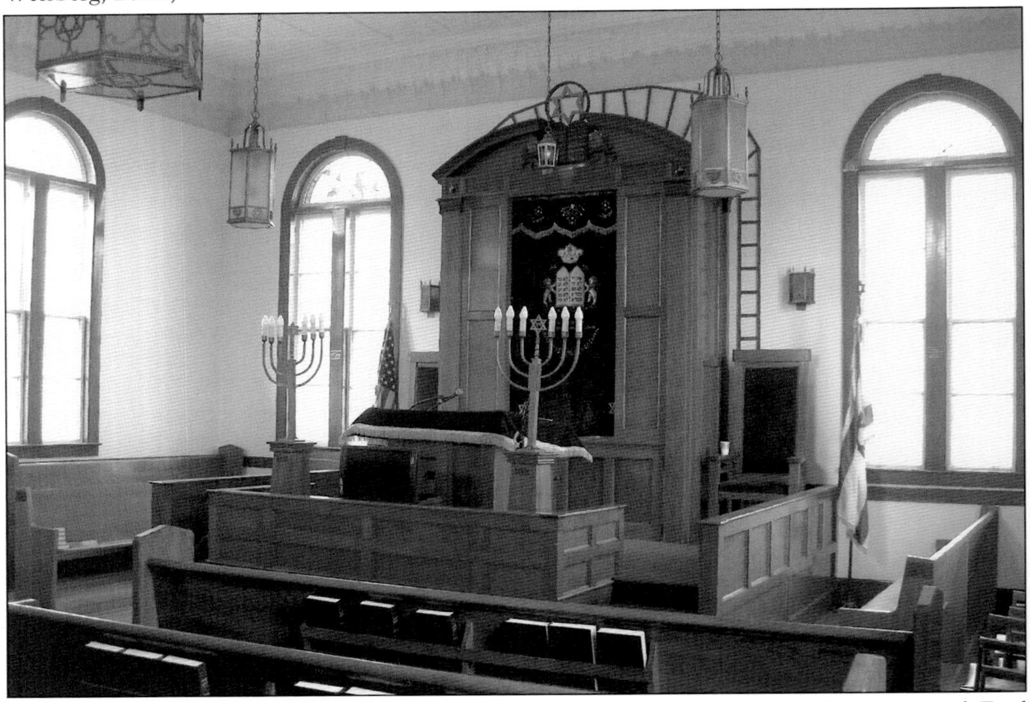

Seen here is the main sanctuary of Beth Israel Synagogue in Bath. (Courtesy of Fred Weisberg, Bath.)

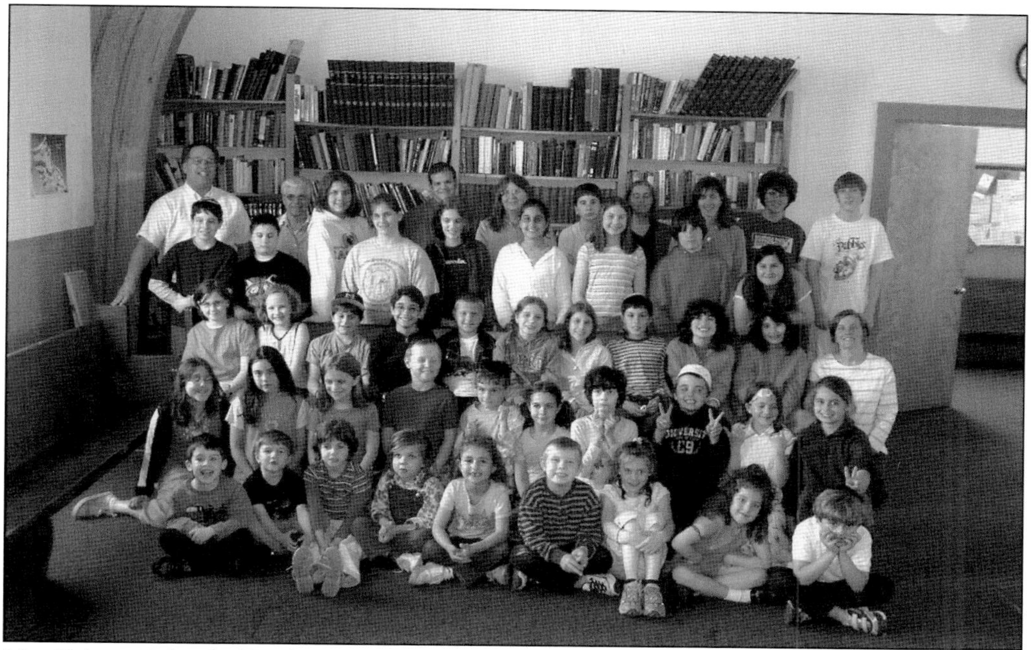

The Hebrew School of Bath's Beth Israel Synagogue serves children of all grades. Cantor Daniel Leeman is in the top row, at left. (Courtesy of Cantor Daniel Leeman, Bath.)

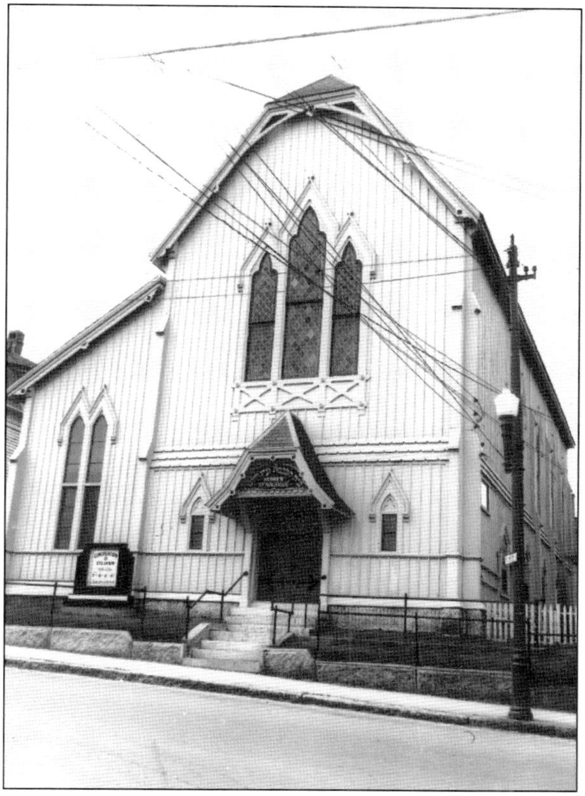

Etz Chaim, founded as an Orthodox congregation in Biddeford, is located on Bacon Street. (Courtesy of the McArthur Library, Biddeford.)

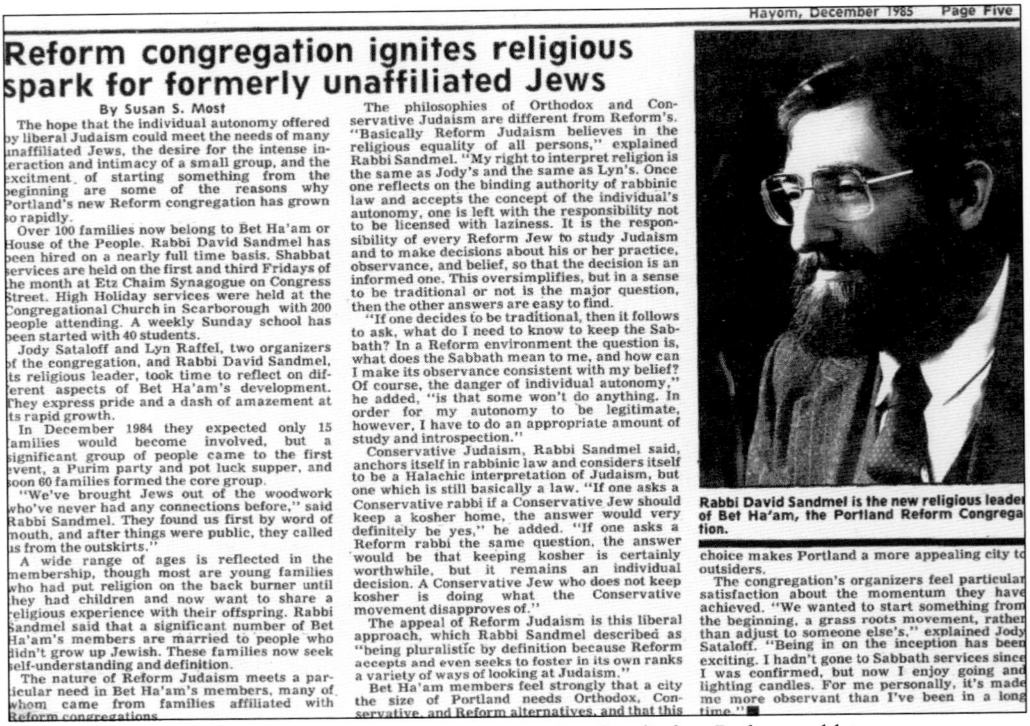

Hayom, December 1985 Page Five

Reform congregation ignites religious spark for formerly unaffiliated Jews

By Susan S. Most

The hope that the individual autonomy offered by liberal Judaism could meet the needs of many unaffiliated Jews, the desire for the intense interaction and intimacy of a small group, and the excitment of starting something from the beginning are some of the reasons why Portland's new Reform congregation has grown so rapidly.

Over 100 families now belong to Bet Ha'am or House of the People. Rabbi David Sandmel has been hired on a nearly full time basis. Shabbat services are held on the first and third Fridays of the month at Etz Chaim Synagogue on Congress Street. High Holiday services were held at the Congregational Church in Scarborough with 200 people attending. A weekly Sunday school has been started with 40 students.

Jody Sataloff and Lyn Raffel, two organizers of the congregation, and Rabbi David Sandmel, its religious leader, took time to reflect on different aspects of Bet Ha'am's development. They express pride and a dash of amazement at its rapid growth.

In December 1984 they expected only 15 families would become involved, but a significant group of people came to the first event, a Purim party and pot luck supper, and soon 60 families formed the core group.

"We've brought Jews out of the woodwork who've never had any connections before," said Rabbi Sandmel. They found us first by word of mouth, and after things were public, they called us from the outskirts."

A wide range of ages is reflected in the membership, though most are young families who had put religion on the back burner until they had children and now want to share a religious experience with their offspring. Rabbi Sandmel said that a significant number of Bet Ha'am's members are married to people who didn't grow up Jewish. These families now seek self-understanding and definition.

The nature of Reform Judaism meets a particular need in Bet Ha'am's members, many of whom came from families affiliated with Reform congregations.

The philosophies of Orthodox and Conservative Judaism are different from Reform's. "Basically Reform Judaism believes in the religious equality of all persons," explained Rabbi Sandmel. "My right to interpret religion is the same as Jody's and the same as Lyn's. Once one reflects on the binding authority of rabbinic law and accepts the concept of the individual's autonomy, one is left with the responsibility not to be licensed with laziness. It is the responsibility of every Reform Jew to study Judaism and to make decisions about his or her practice, observance, and belief, so that the decision is an informed one. This oversimplifies, but in a sense to be traditional or not is the major question, then the other answers are easy to find.

"If one decides to be traditional, then it follows to ask, what do I need to know to keep the Sabbath? In a Reform environment the question is, what does the Sabbath mean to me, and how can I make its observance consistent with my belief? Of course, the danger of individual autonomy," he added, "is that some won't do anything. In order for my autonomy to be legitimate, however, I have to do an appropriate amount of study and introspection."

Conservative Judaism, Rabbi Sandmel said, anchors itself in rabbinic law and considers itself to be a Halachic interpretation of Judaism, but one which is still basically a law. "If one asks a Conservative rabbi if a Conservative Jew should keep a kosher home, the answer would very definitely be yes," he added. "If one asks a Reform rabbi the same question, the answer would be that keeping kosher is certainly worthwhile, but it remains an individual decision. A Conservative Jew who does not keep kosher is doing what the Conservative movement disapproves of."

The appeal of Reform Judaism is this liberal approach, which Rabbi Sandmel described as "being pluralistic by definition because Reform accepts and even seeks to foster in its own ranks a variety of ways of looking at Judaism."

Bet Ha'am members feel strongly that a city the size of Portland needs Orthodox, Conservative, and Reform alternatives, and that this choice makes Portland a more appealing city to outsiders.

The congregation's organizers feel particular satisfaction about the momentum they have achieved. "We wanted to start something from the beginning, a grass roots movement, rather than adjust to someone else's," explained Jody Sataloff. "Being in on the inception has been exciting. I hadn't gone to Sabbath services since I was confirmed, but now I enjoy going and lighting candles. For me personally, it's made me more observant than I've been in a long time."

Rabbi David Sandmel is the new religious leader of Bet Ha'am, the Portland Reform Congregation.

David Sandmel served Congregation Bet Ha'am as Portland's first Reform rabbi.

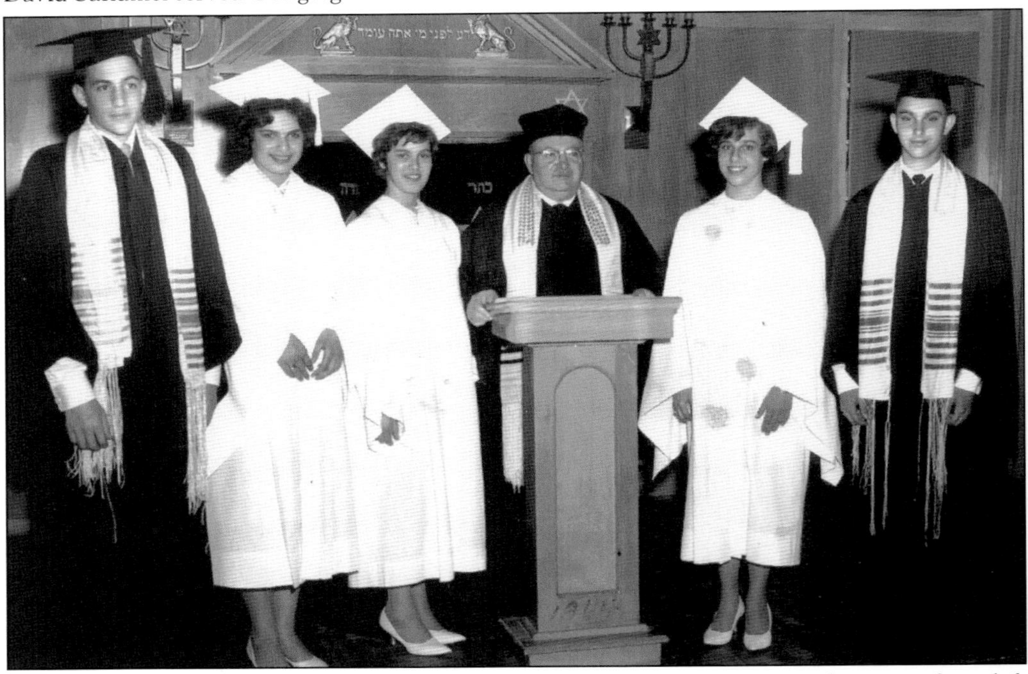

In 1964, Congregation Beth Jacob of Lewiston graduated its seniors. Seen here are, from left to right, Andrew Ross, Geri Marcus, Ronnie Wilner, Rabbi David Berent, Diane Leitman, and David Hurwitz. (Courtesy of Phyllis Graber Jensen and Tim McCall, Lewiston.)

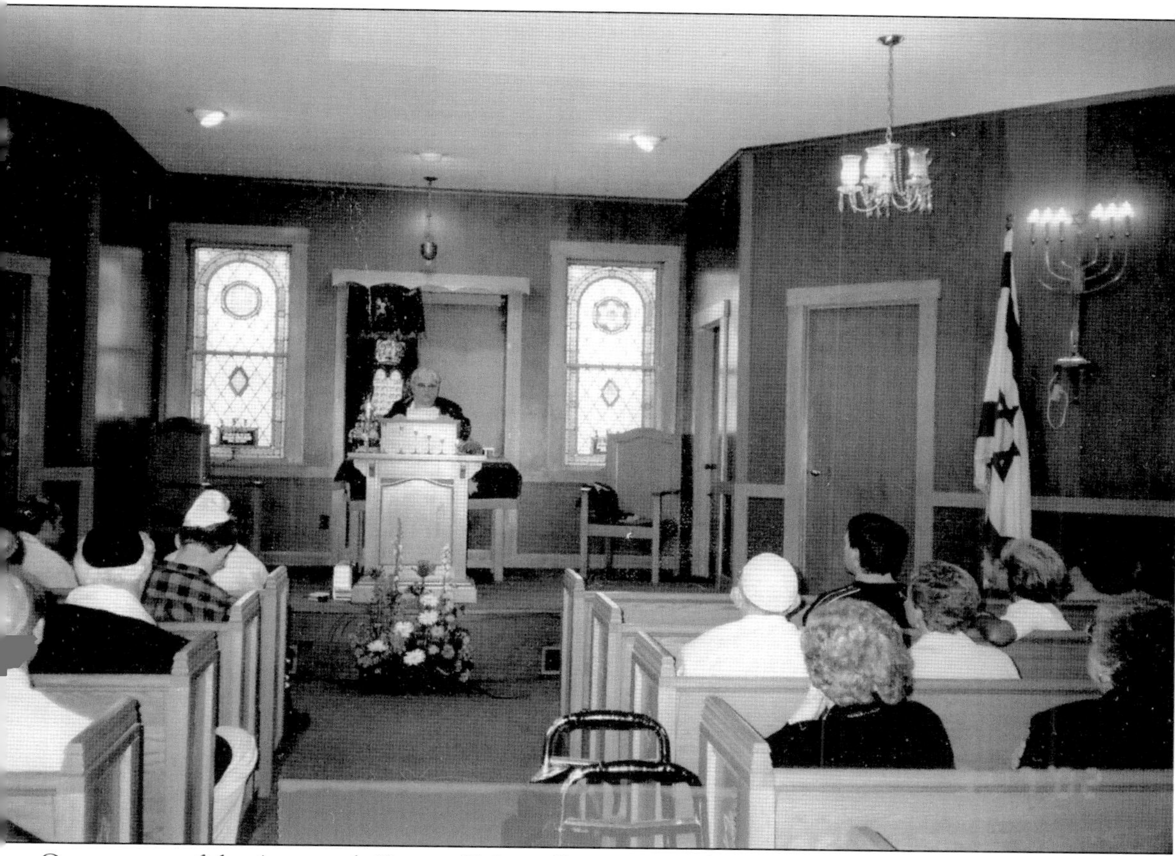

Congregants of the Aroostook County Hebrew Community of Presque Isle prepare for services. (Courtesy of Raphael and Naomi Gribetz.)

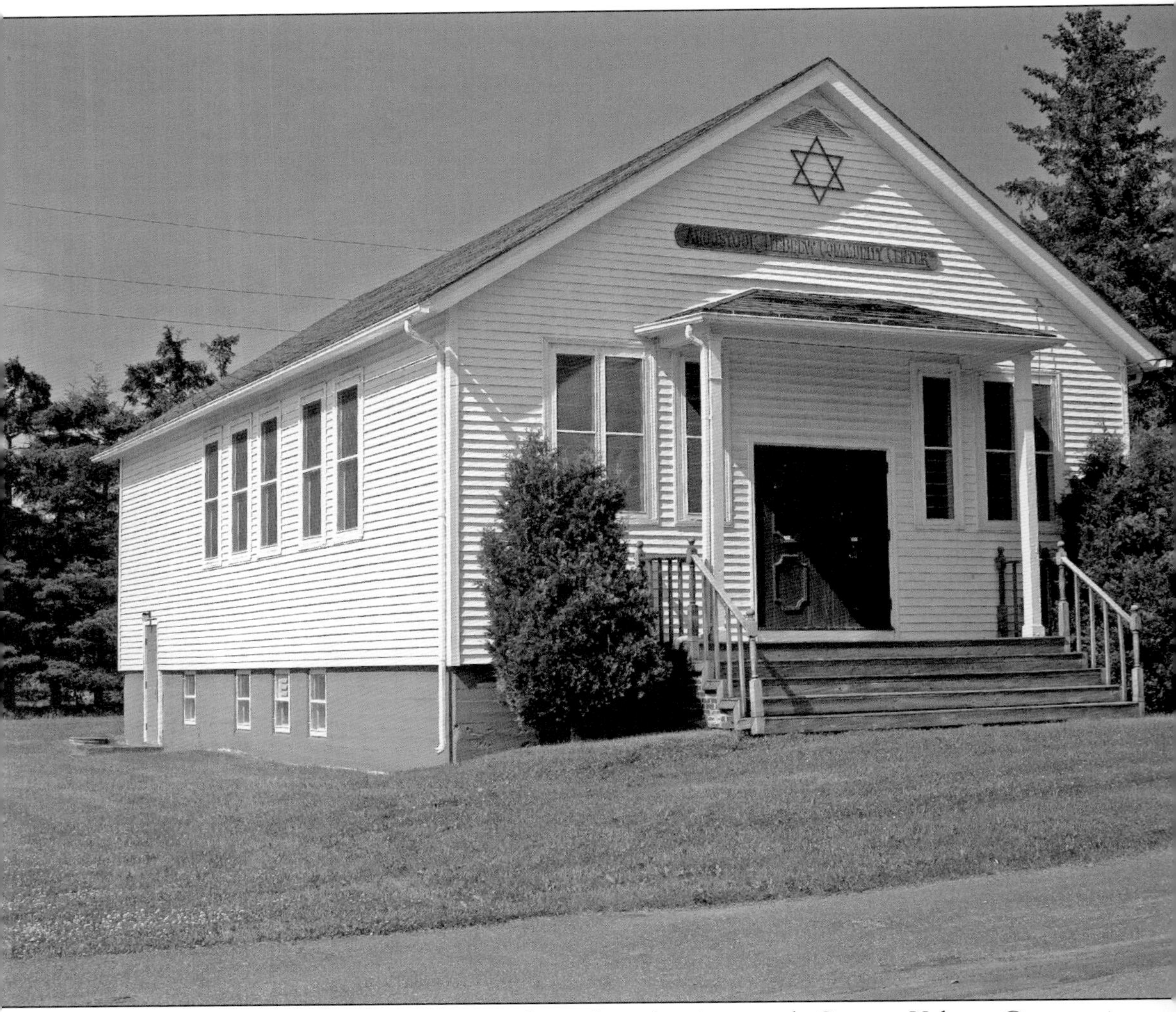

The Jews of Aroostook County worshipped at the Aroostook County Hebrew Community Center. Before the congregation moved to this building, members gathered above Green's Department Store in Presque Isle. (Photograph by Paul S. Hamlin, Presque Isle.)

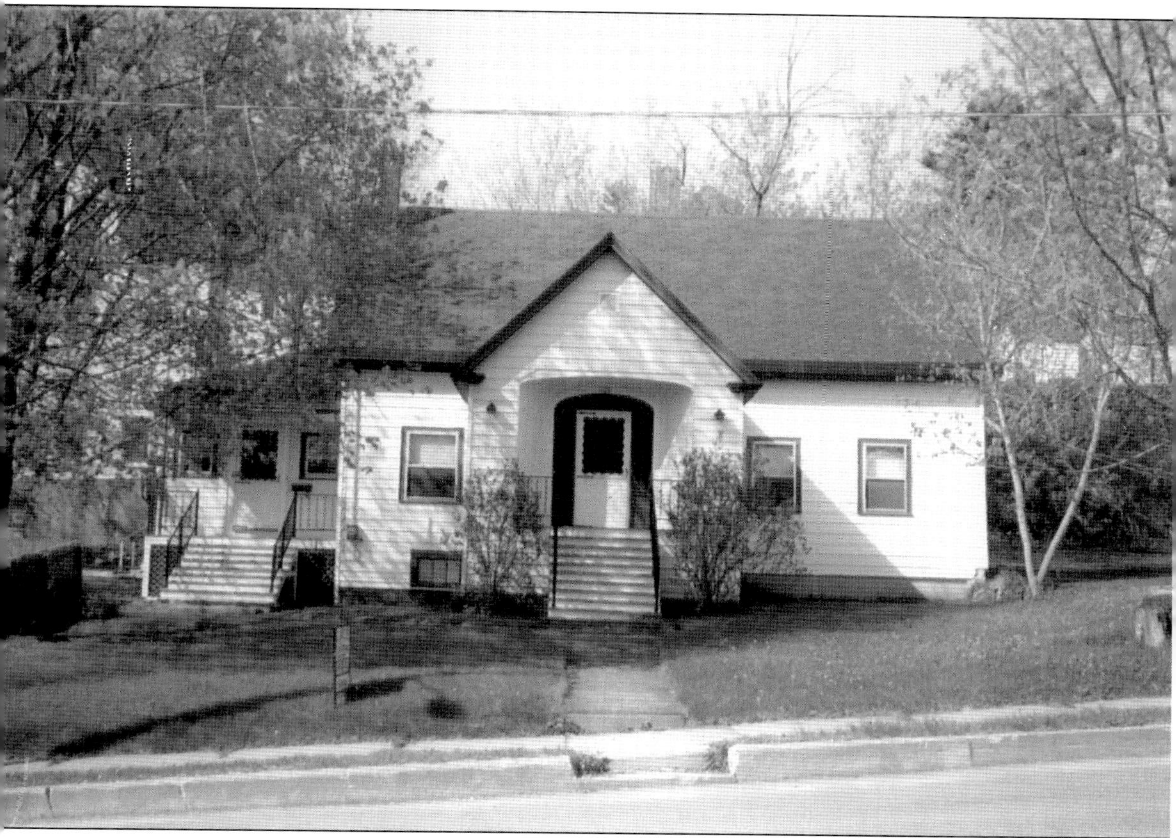

Temple Israel, Rumford, served as the Jewish community synagogue from 1937 to 1967, when it closed for lack of membership. (Courtesy of Rumford Historical Society.)

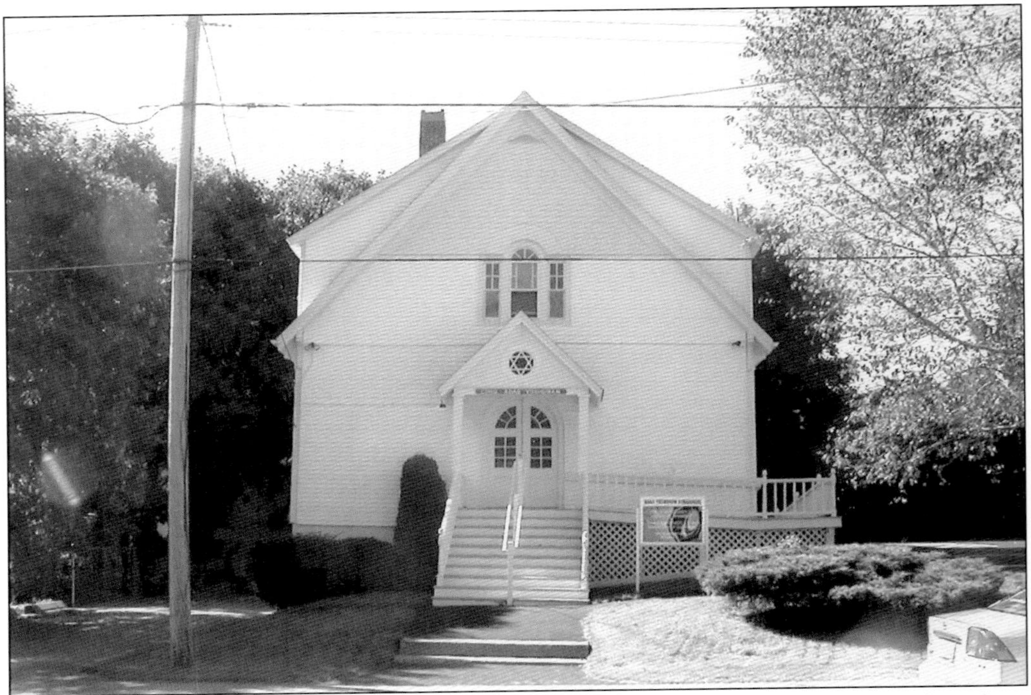

Congregation Adas Yoshuron was founded in Rockland in 1912. (Courtesy of Barbara Fishman, Rockland.)

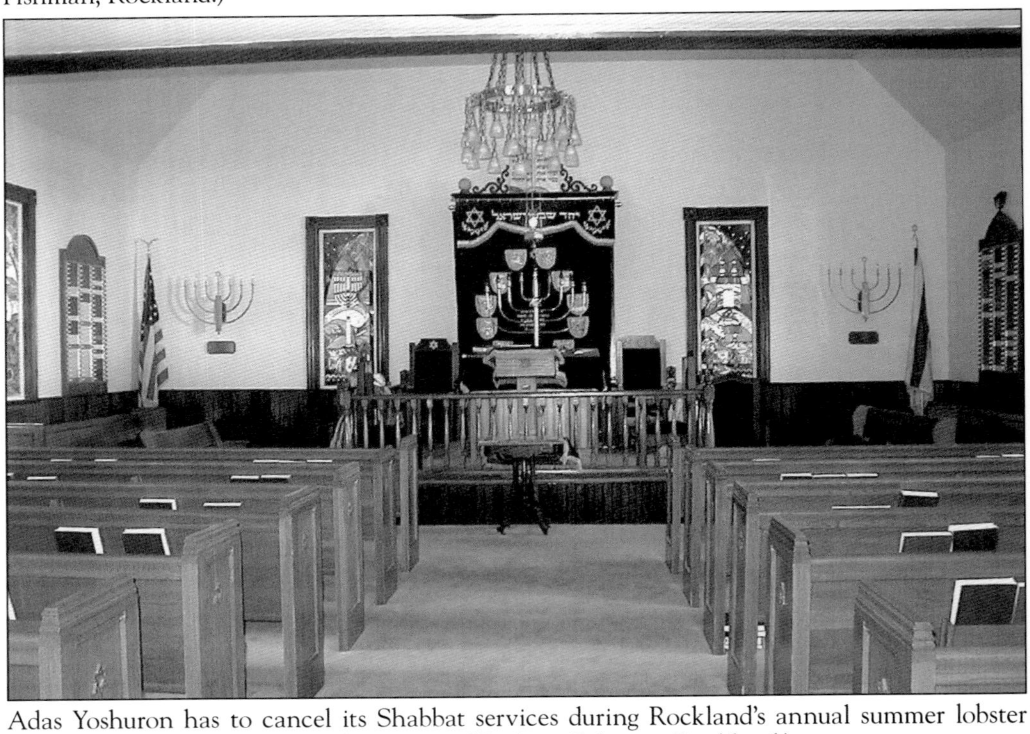

Adas Yoshuron has to cancel its Shabbat services during Rockland's annual summer lobster festival because of traffic jams. (Courtesy of Barbara Fishman, Rockland.)

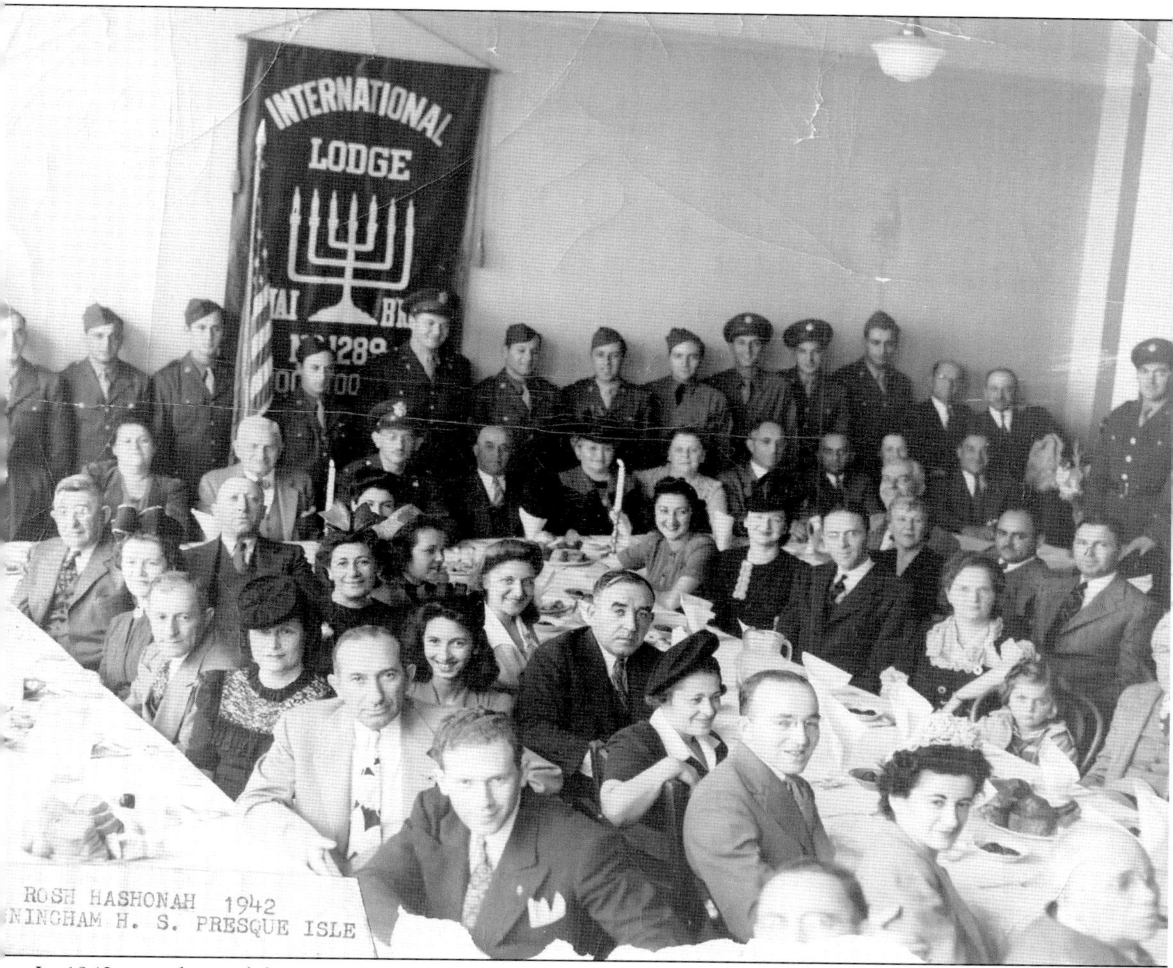

In 1942, members of the Presque Isle Jewish Community celebrated Rosh Hashanah with a meal at Cunningham High School. (Courtesy of Toby Adelman, San Francisco.)

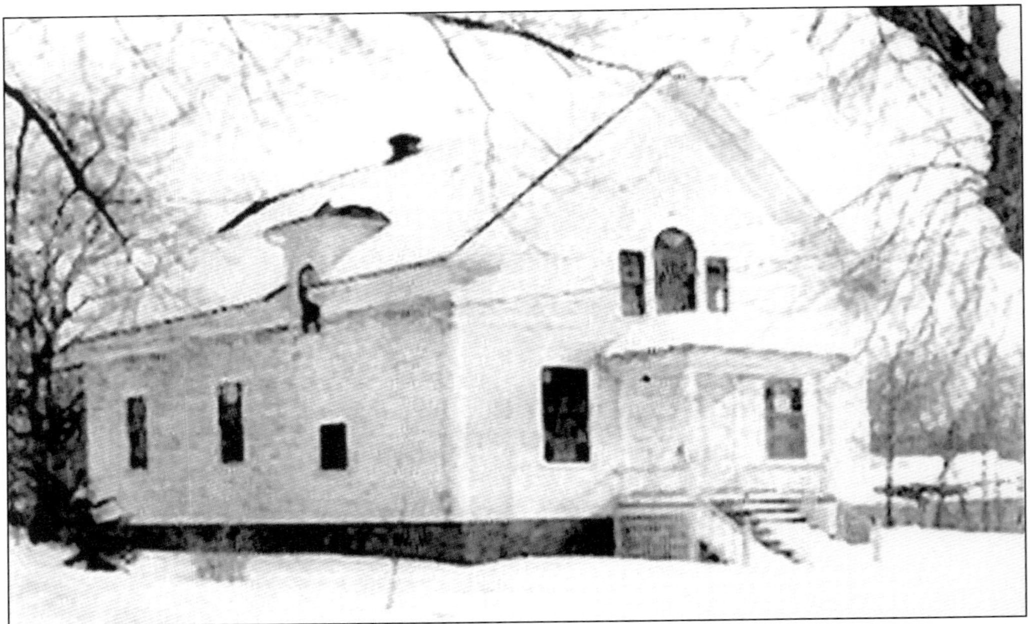

In 1905, the Jews of Waterville founded Congregation Beth Israel. According to city records, Waterville also had a Jewish burial ground. (Courtesy of Peter Beckerman, Waterville.)

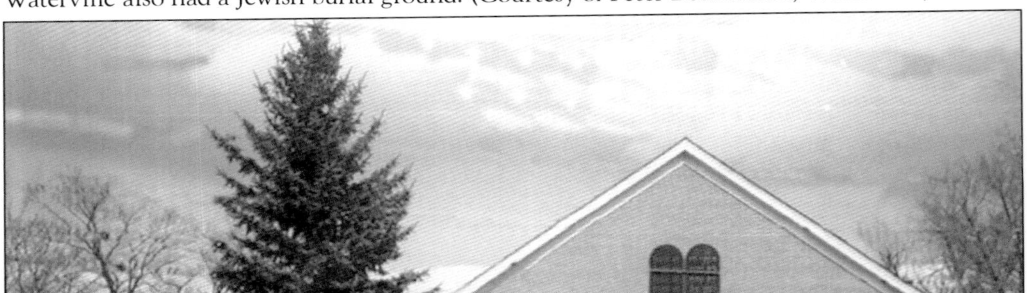

Currently members of Congregation Beth Israel in Waterville worship in this newer building. (Courtesy of Peter Beckerman, Waterville.)

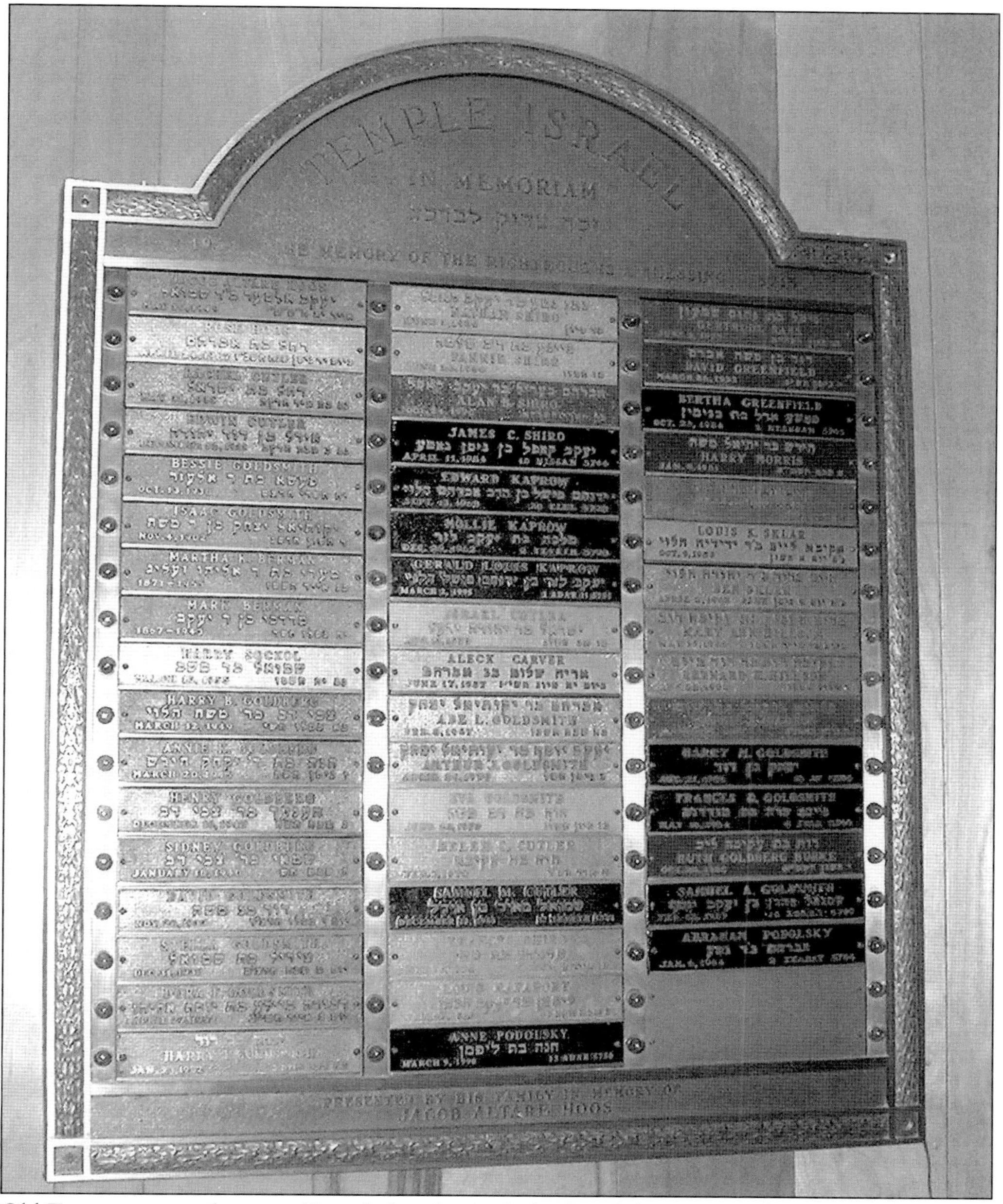

Old Town was once home to Temple Israel, which displayed this memorial plaque. It now hangs in Bangor's Congregation Beth Israel. (Courtesy of William Small, Bangor.)

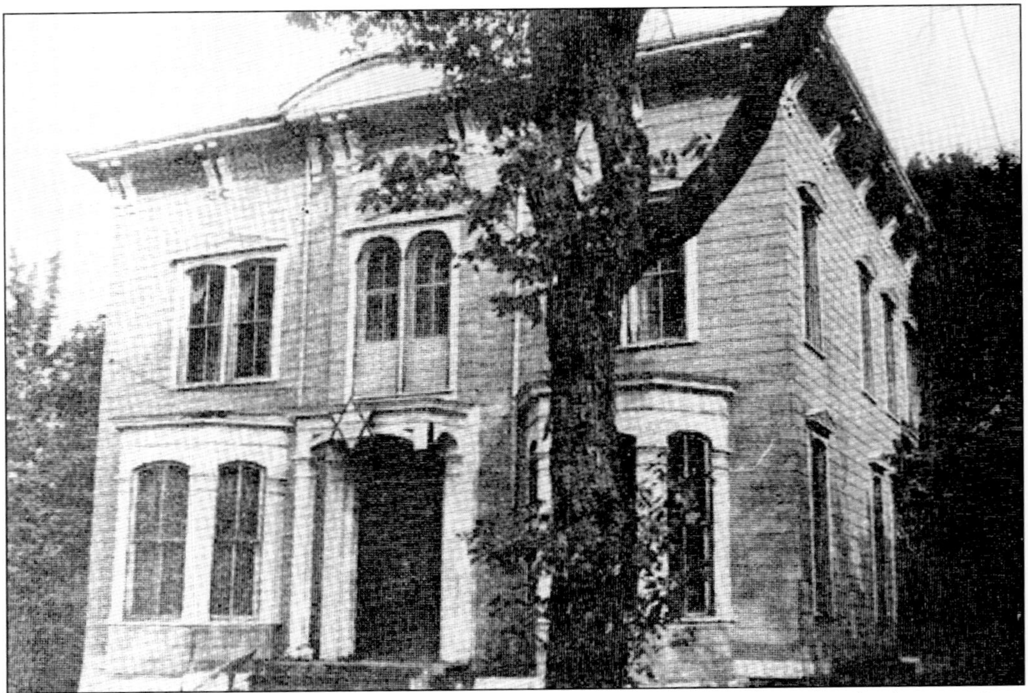

This building once housed Congregation Chaim Yosef of Calais. Unfortunately the temple is no longer active.

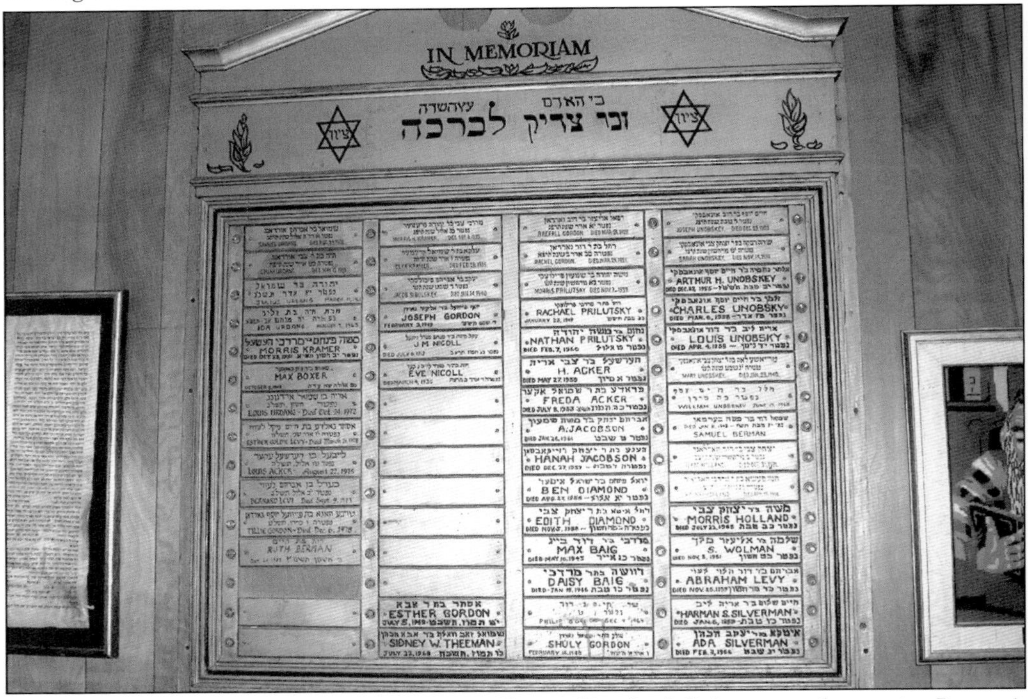

The memorial plaque from Congregation Chaim Yosef of Calais now hangs in Bangor's Congregation Beth Israel. (Courtesy of William Small, Bangor.)

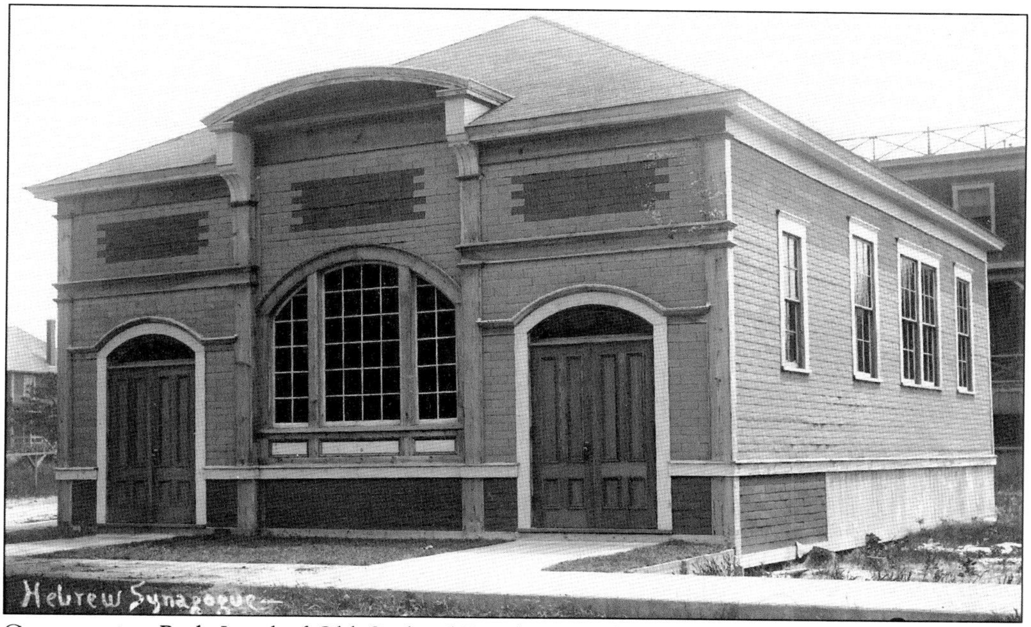

Congregation Beth Israel of Old Orchard Beach opened in 1912 to serve the needs of Jewish tourists and summer residents in this resort town. This was the original building. (Courtesy of Congregation Beth Israel, Old Orchard Beach.)

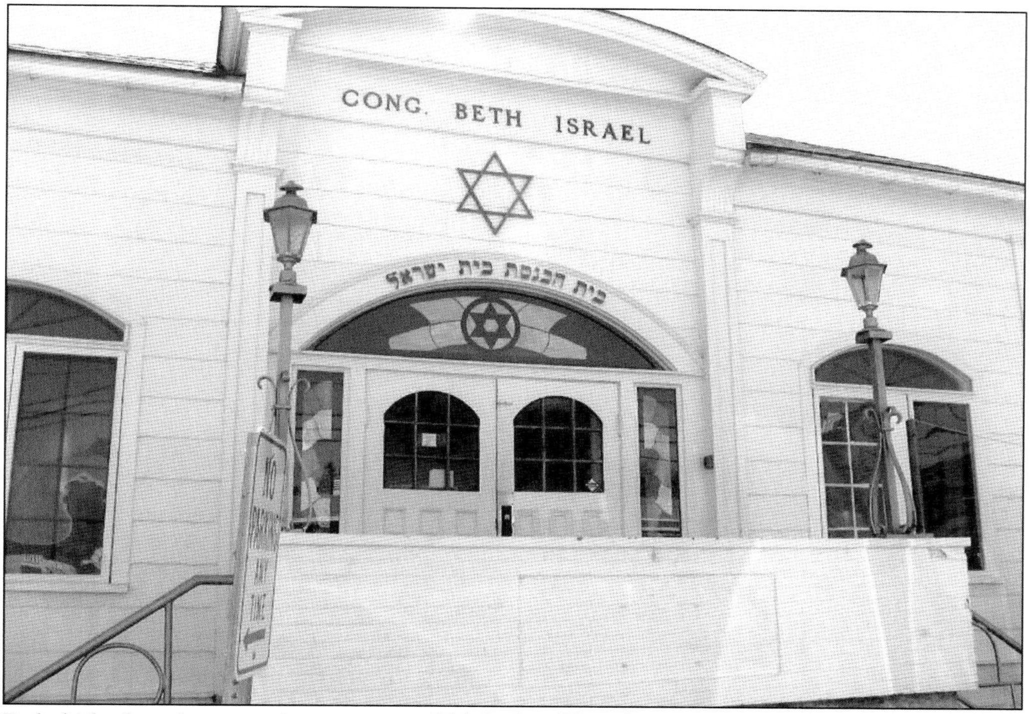

Refurbished on the same choice spot on Old Orchard Beach's East Grand Avenue, Congregation Beth Israel still holds services for Jewish summer visitors and year-round residents. (Courtesy of Congregation Beth Israel, Old Orchard Beach.)

Flag Dedication Ceremonies
of Congregation Beth Israel
OLD ORCHARD, MAINE
Sunday afternoon, September 4, 1949 at 3 o'clock

INVOCATION
RABBI MORRIS BEKRITSKY, Orthodox Synagogues of Portland

1. GREETINGS AND WELCOME
JULIUS MEYER, *President-elect*
2. PRESENTATION OF COLORS
JEWISH WAR VETERANS OF PORTLAND, MAINE
3. VOCAL SELECTIONS
CANTOR SAUL ZIMMERMAN of Portland
4. GREETINGS
RICHARD S. MORGRAGE,
Secretary to His Excellency, Frederick G. Paine, Governor of the State of Maine
5. ADDRESS
JUDGE MAX L. PINANSKI, Portland
6. ADDRESS
COLONEL IRWIN DAVID, *Commander*, American Legion of State of Maine
7. PRESENTATION OF FLAGS
JOSEPH WEINSTEIN of Boston and Old Orchard
8. ACCEPTANCE OF FLAGS
JULIUS MEYER, *President-elect* of Congregation Beth Israel
9. NATIONAL ANTHEM
10. ADDRESS
SAMUEL KALESKY, *President*, Hias of N. E., *Honorary President*, N. E. Division, American Jewish Congress
11. HATIKVAH

Committee of Arrangements
Hyman Buxstein — Saul Goodkowsky — Hyman Finkelman
Teva Glickman — Solomon Turetsky

When Congregation Beth Israel of Old Orchard Beach reopened in 1949, several dignitaries from Portland, including Rabbi Morris Bekritsky, Cantor Saul Zimmerman, and Judge Max Pinansky, were on the program. (Courtesy of Congregation Beth Israel, Old Orchard Beach.)

THE JEWISH THEOLOGICAL SEMINARY OF AMERICA.
531-535 WEST ONE HUNDRED AND TWENTY-THIRD STREET.
NEW YORK CITY.

August 28, 1912.

My dear Mr. Goodkowsky:

I just came from the hospital and am grateful to say that the boy is getting on very nicely, thank God.

I should like to ask of you the following favor: I took a small box of candy from Mr. Miller where we had service last Saturday. Of course, I did not pay him. Will you be so kind and call on him to pay him for me, and add this to my bill and send it to me. And give him my apologies for not seeing him before I left.

I take here the opportunity to thank you and Mrs. Goodkowsky most heartily for all the kindness you have shown to me. I wish only that the stay with you could have lasted longer.

With best regards and wishes of [illegible], and repeated thanks,

Yours sincerely,

[illegible]

J. H. Goodkowsky, Esq.,
Hotel Lafayette,
Old Orchard, Me.

A major figure in American Conservative Judaism, Rabbi Solomon Schechter, thanked J. H. Goodkowsky, owner of Old Orchard Beach's Lafayette Hotel, for his courtesy during his stay at the hotel in August 1912. (Courtesy of Harold "Babe" Goodkowsky, Old Orchard Beach.)

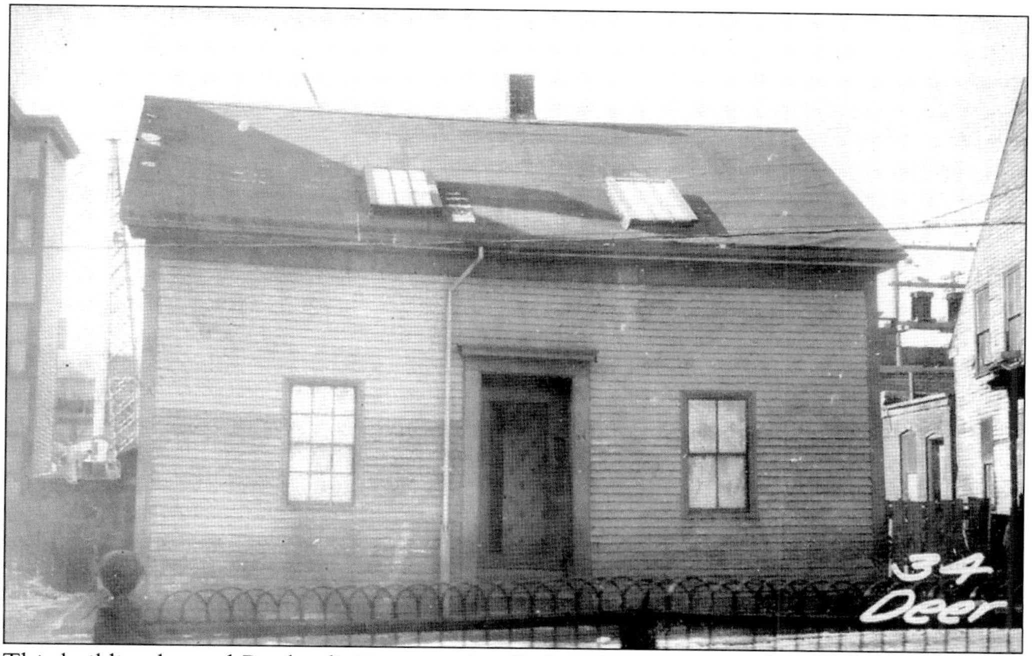

This building housed Portland's Congregation Beth Judah, Portland's first synagogue, founded in 1883. Also known as the Deer Street Shul, neither the congregation nor Deer Street exists anymore. (Courtesy of the Tax Assessor's Office, Portland.)

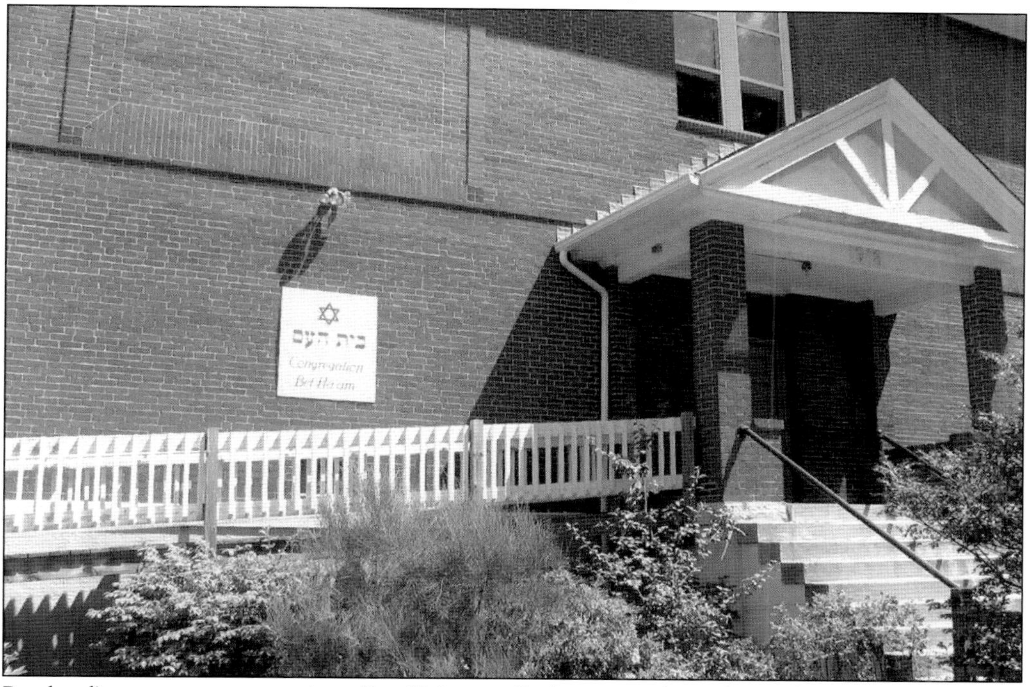

Portland's newest congregation, Bet Ha'am, a Reform temple, is located in South Portland. Bet Ha'am is currently planning to expand its building to accommodate its growing number of congregants.

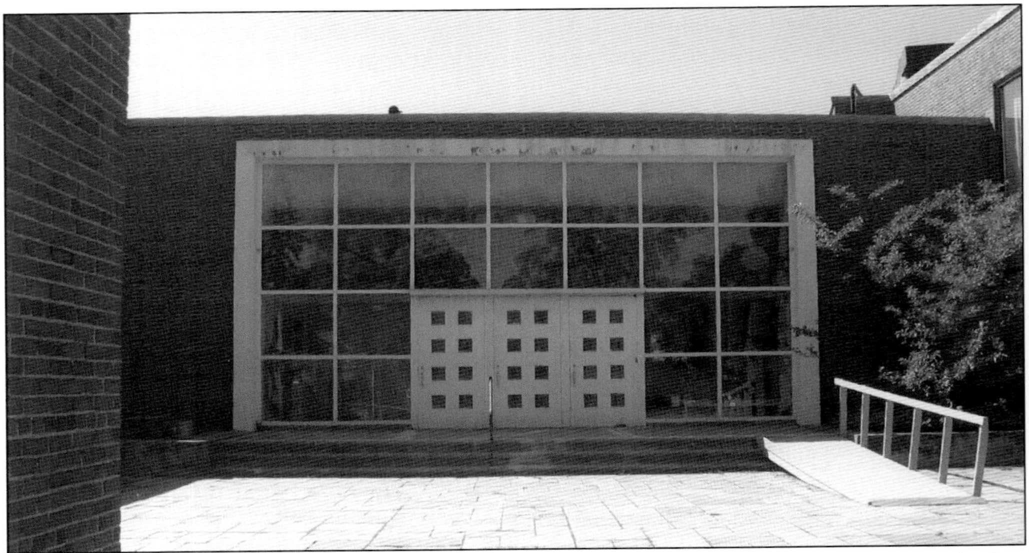

Temple Beth El, founded in 1948, opened its doors in 1949. The temple was Portland's first Conservative synagogue. This is a view from the entrance into the sanctuary.

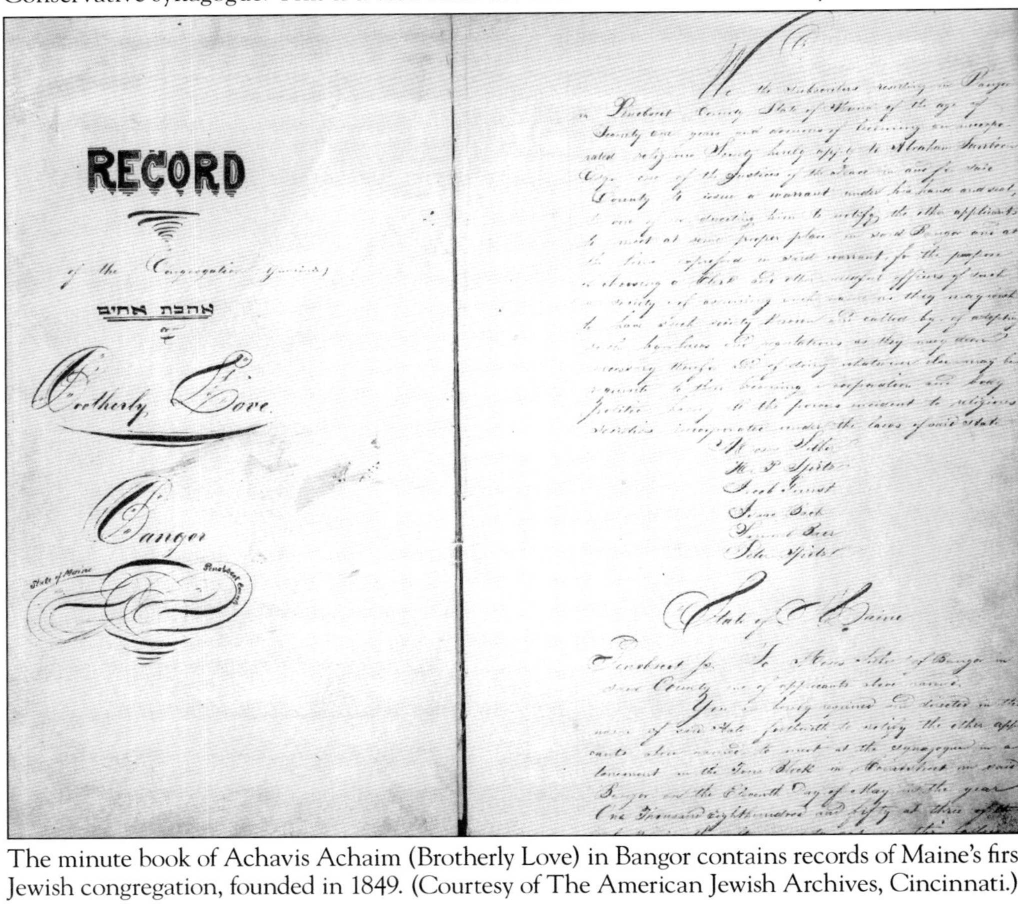

The minute book of Achavis Achaim (Brotherly Love) in Bangor contains records of Maine's first Jewish congregation, founded in 1849. (Courtesy of The American Jewish Archives, Cincinnati.)

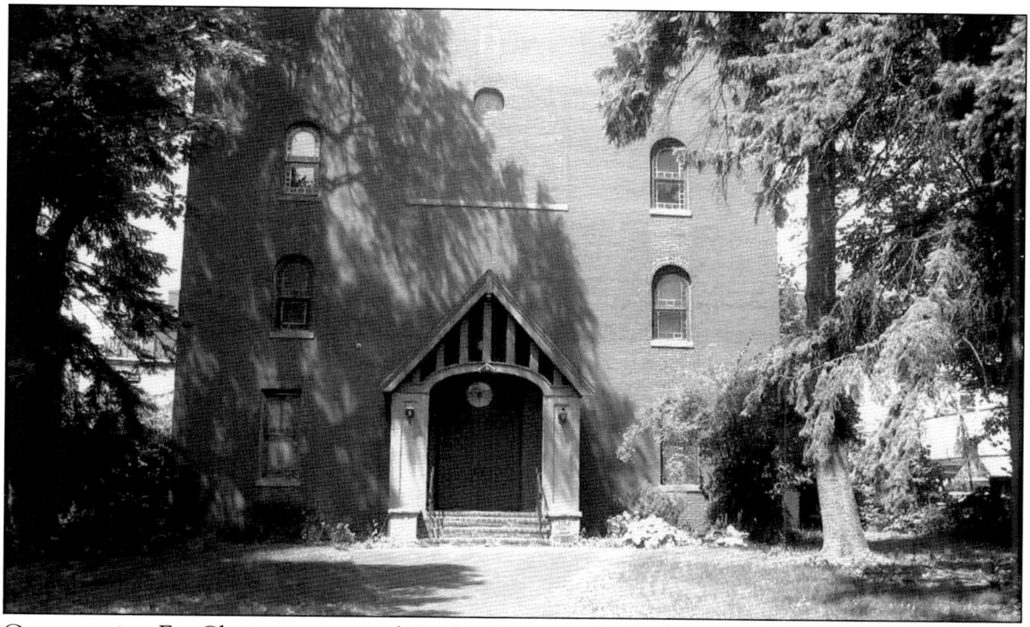

Congregation Etz Chaim was one of Portland's major Orthodox synagogues, founded in 1921. Membership dwindled during the last half of the 20th century, and the building was finally closed. Thanks to funds bequeathed for the purpose of refurbishing it, Etz Chaim is open again, the only synagogue still in existence in downtown Portland.

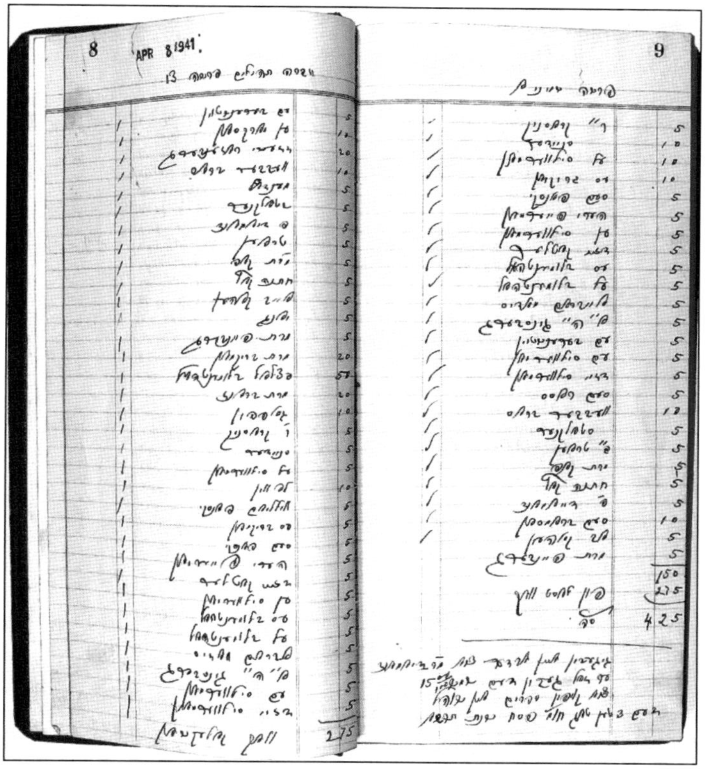

This 1941 document, written in Yiddish, is a list of those who contributed to—along with the amount of money given by each person—Etz Chaim's maintenance and expenses. (Courtesy of the Sampson Center for Diversity, University of Southern Maine.)

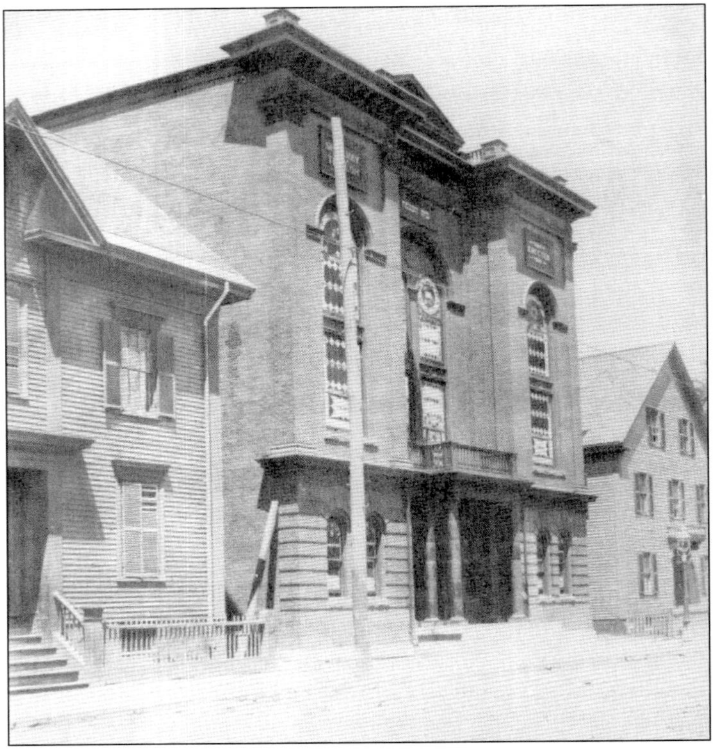

Congregation Shaarey Tphiloh, an Orthodox synagogue, began construction in 1901, was finished in 1905, and served Portland from its location on Newbury Street. The building still exists, but now houses offices and apartments. A plaque commemorates its years as a place of worship. (Courtesy of the Maine Historical Society, Portland.)

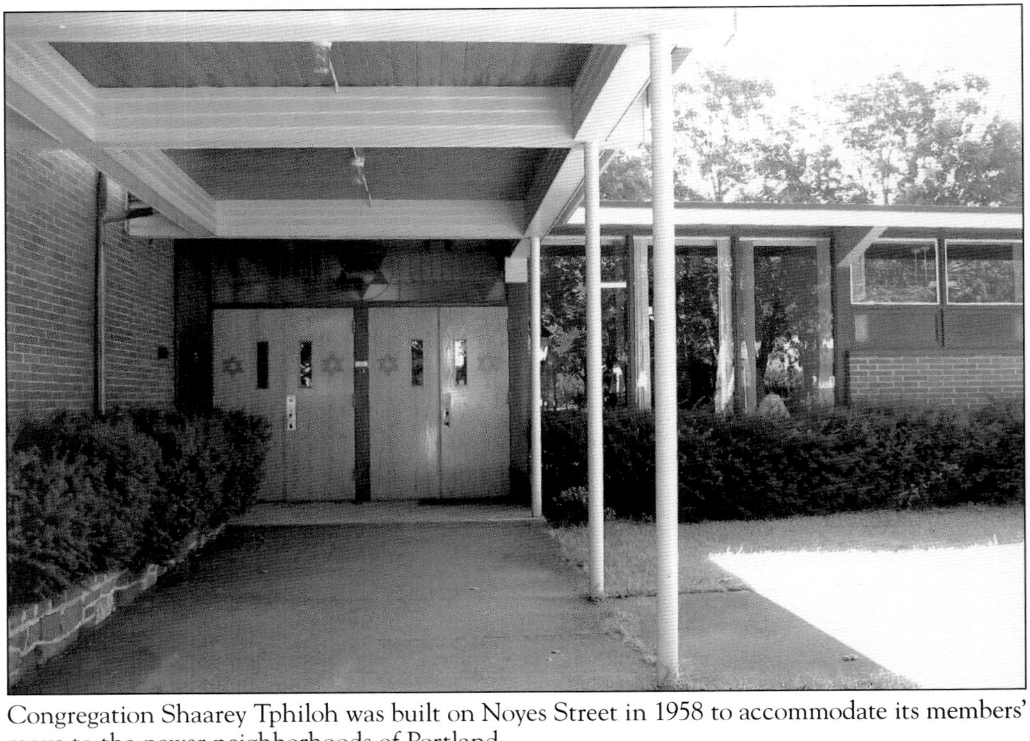

Congregation Shaarey Tphiloh was built on Noyes Street in 1958 to accommodate its members' move to the newer neighborhoods of Portland.

It may have been unusual for Maine to have three women rabbis, as this 1998 article in the *Maine Times* points out, but as of 2006, five of Maine's rabbis are women. They are Rabbi Carolyn Braun of Temple Beth El, Portland; Rabbi Alice Dubinsky of Congregation Bet Ha'am, South Portland; Rabbi Susan Bulba Carvutto of Temple Beth El, Augusta; Rabbi Amita Jarmon, of Adas Yoshuron, Rockland; and Rabbi Dara Lerner of Congregation Beth El of Bangor.

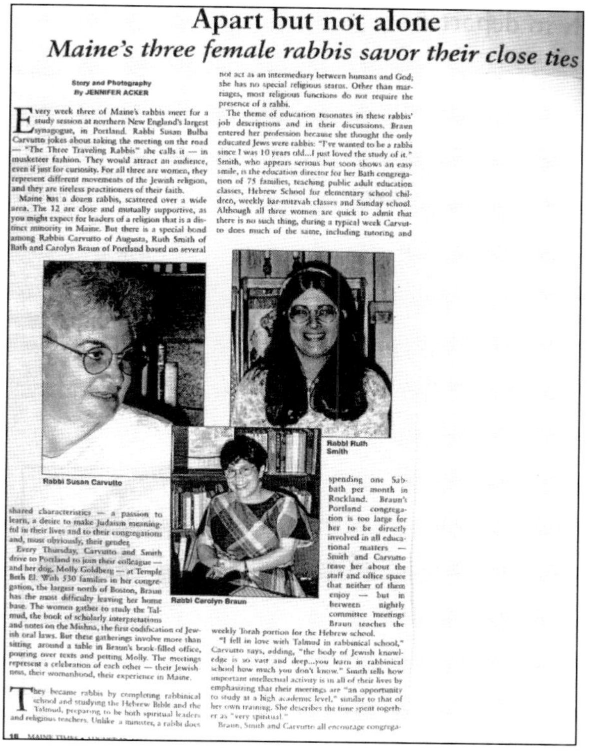

Apart but not alone

Maine's three female rabbis savor their close ties

Story and Photography
By JENNIFER ACKER

Every week three of Maine's rabbis meet for a study session at northern New England's largest synagogue, in Portland. Rabbi Susan Bulba Carvutto jokes about taking the meeting on the road — "The Three Traveling Rabbis" she calls it — in musketeer fashion. They would attract an audience, even if just for curiosity. For all three are women, they represent different movements of the Jewish religion, and they are tireless practitioners of their faith.

Maine has a dozen rabbis, scattered over a wide area. The 12 are close and mutually supportive, as you might expect for leaders of a religion that is a distinct minority in Maine. But there is a special bond among Rabbis Carvutto of Augusta, Ruth Smith of Bath and Carolyn Braun of Portland based on several shared characteristics — a passion to learn, a desire to make Judaism meaningful in their lives and to their congregations and, most obviously, their gender.

Every Thursday, Carvutto and Smith drive to Portland to join their colleague — and her dog, Molly Goldberg — at Temple Beth El. With 530 families in her congregation, the largest north of Boston, Braun has the most difficulty leaving her home base. The women gather to study the Talmud, the book of scholarly interpretations and notes on the Mishna, the first codification of Jewish oral laws. But these gatherings involve more than sitting around a table in Braun's book-filled office, pouring over texts and petting Molly. The meetings represent a celebration of each other — their Jewishness, their womanhood, their experience in Maine.

They became rabbis by completing rabbinical school and studying the Hebrew Bible and the Talmud, preparing to be both spiritual leaders and religious teachers. Unlike a minister, a rabbi does not act as an intermediary between humans and God; she has no special religious status. Other than marriages, most religious functions do not require the presence of a rabbi.

The theme of education resonates in these rabbis' job descriptions and in their discussions. Braun entered her profession because she thought the only educated Jews were rabbis: "I've wanted to be a rabbi since I was 10 years old...I just loved the study of it." Smith, who appears serious but soon shows an easy smile, is the education director for her Bath congregation of 75 families, teaching public adult education classes, Hebrew School for elementary school children, weekly bar-mitzvah classes and Sunday school. Although all three women are quick to admit that there is no such thing, during a typical week Carvutto does much of the same, including tutoring and spending one Sabbath per month in Rockland. Braun's Portland congregation is too large for her to be directly involved in all educational matters — Smith and Carvutto tease her about the staff and office space that neither of them enjoy — but in between nightly committee meetings Braun teaches the weekly Torah portion for the Hebrew school.

"I fell in love with Talmud in rabbinical school," Carvutto says, adding, "the body of Jewish knowledge is so vast and deep...you learn in rabbinical school how much you don't know." Smith tells how important intellectual activity is in all of their lives by emphasizing that their meetings are "an opportunity to study at a high academic level," similar to that of her own training. She describes the time spent together as "very spiritual."

Braun, Smith and Carvutto all encourage congrega-

Rabbi Susan Carvutto

Rabbi Ruth Smith

Rabbi Carolyn Braun

18 MAINE TIMES

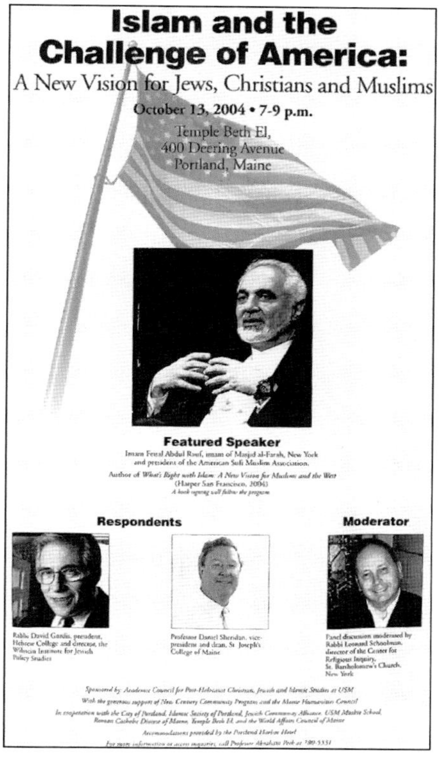

On October 13, 2004, a historic evening took place at Temple Beth El, Portland, when Jews, Christians, and Muslims met to discuss the influence of America on the three Abrahamic religions.

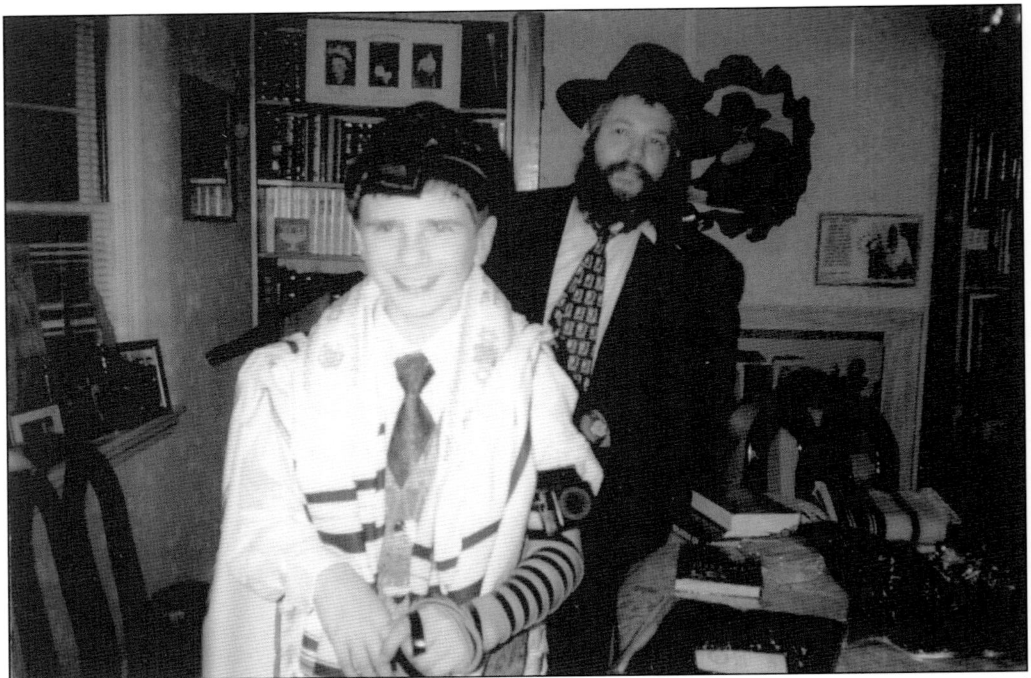

Kirill Shkolnick celebrated his bar mitzvah with the help of Rabbi Moshe Wilansky at Chabad of Maine, located in Portland. (Courtesy of the Shkolnick family, Portland.)

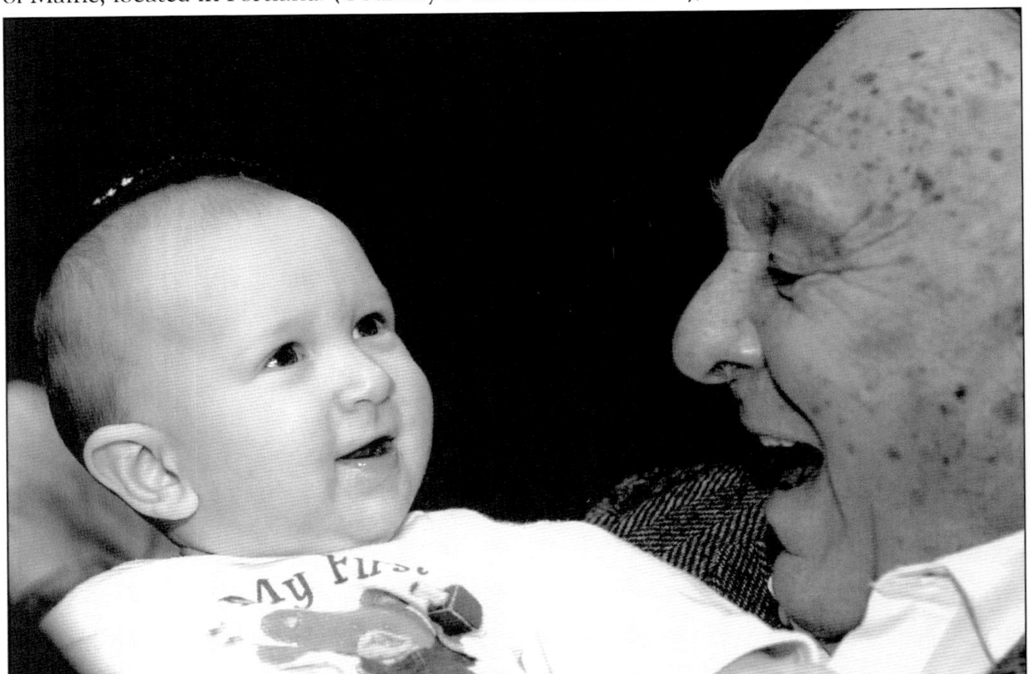

Noah Wahl-Rubin enjoyed his first Chanukah at the Auburn Synagogue Center with Temple Shalom member Milton Weiner. (Courtesy of Phyllis Graber Jensen, Lewiston.)

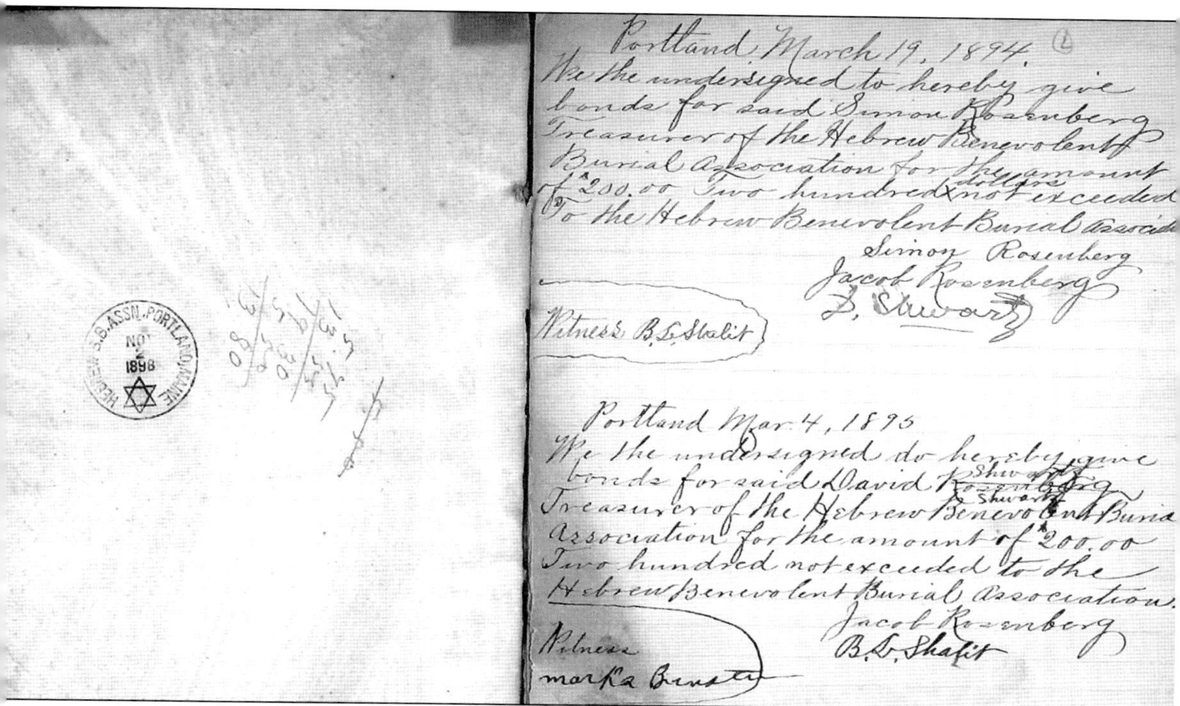
Portland March 19, 1894.
We the undersigned to hereby give bonds for said Simon Rosenberg Treasurer of the Hebrew Benevolent Burial Association for the amount of $200.00 Two hundred dollars not exceeded To the Hebrew Benevolent Burial Associa[tion]

Simon Rosenberg
Jacob Rosenberg
D. Shwartz

Witness B. L. Shalit

Portland Mar. 4, 1895
We the undersigned do hereby give bonds for said David Shwartz Treasurer of the Hebrew Benevolent Burial Association for the amount of $200.00 Two hundred not exceeded to the Hebrew Benevolent Burial Association.

Jacob Rosenberg
B. L. Shalit

Witness
marKa [illegible]

A page from a book with the names of members of the Portland Hebrew Burial Association reflects a community that gave generously to support Jewish charities and causes. (Courtesy of the Sampson Center for Diversity, University of Southern Maine.)

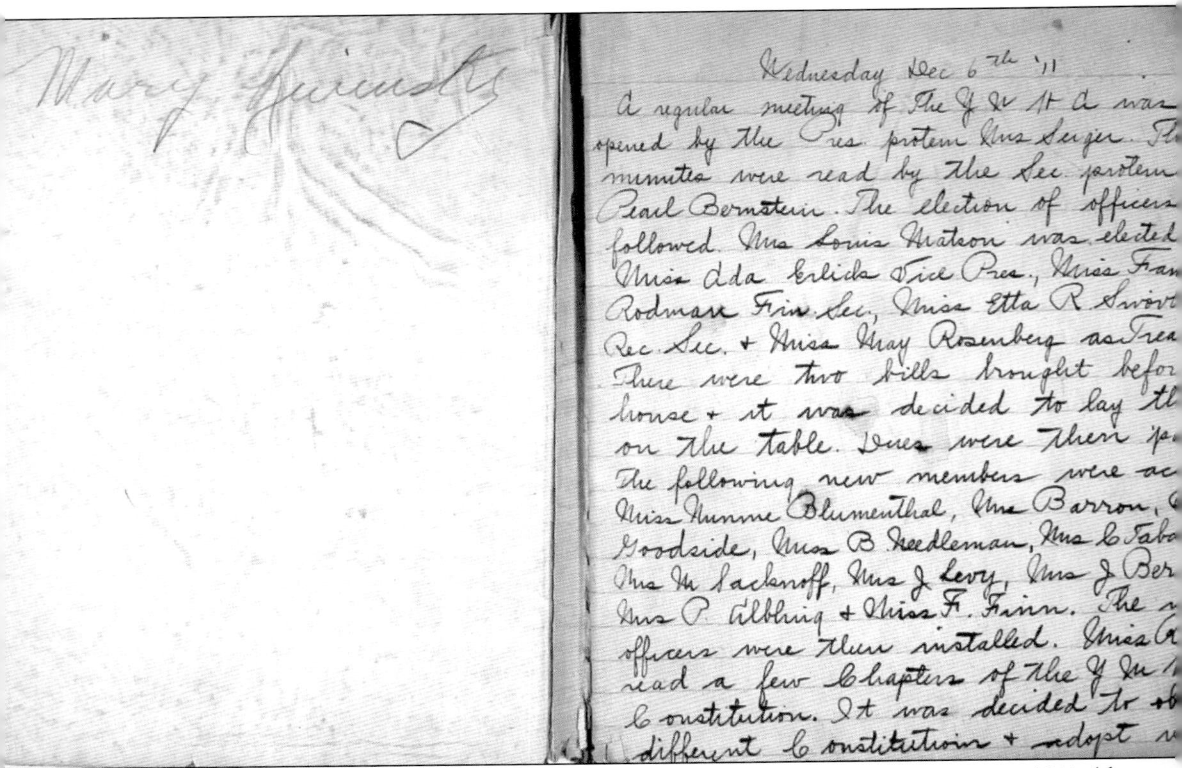

Wednesday Dec 6th '11
A regular meeting of the Y W H A was
opened by the Pres. protem Mrs Seiger. Th
minutes were read by the Sec. protem
Pearl Bernstein. The election of officers
followed. Mrs Louis Matson was elected
Miss Ada Erlick Vice Pres., Miss Fan
Rodman Fin. Sec., Miss Etta R Sworr
Rec. Sec. + Miss May Rosenberg as Trea
There were two bills brought befor
house + it was decided to lay th
on the table. Dues were then pa
The following new members were ac
Miss Minnie Blumenthal, Mrs Barron,
Goodside, Miss B Needleman, Mrs C Taba
Mrs M Sackroff, Mrs J Levy, Mrs J Ber
Mrs P. Albling + Miss F. Finn. The
officers were then installed. Miss A
read a few chapters of the Y W
Constitution. It was decided to ob
different Constitution + adopt

The minutes page from a meeting of the Young Women's Hebrew Association in 1911 (the organization was founded in 1907) reported the election of new offices for the coming year. Mrs. Louis Matson was elected president and Ada Erlick as vice president. (Courtesy of the Sampson Center for Diversity, University of Southern Maine.)

Two

MAKING A LIVING

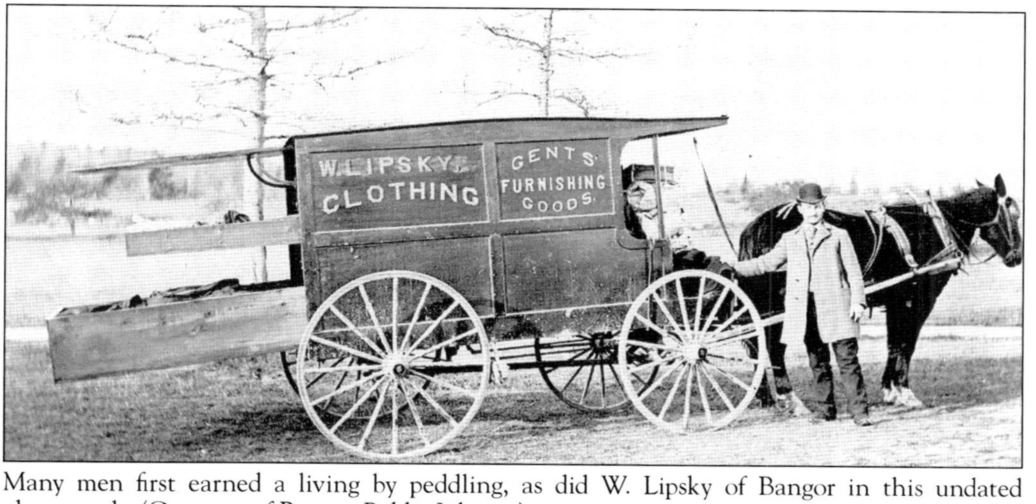

Many men first earned a living by peddling, as did W. Lipsky of Bangor in this undated photograph. (Courtesy of Bangor Public Library.)

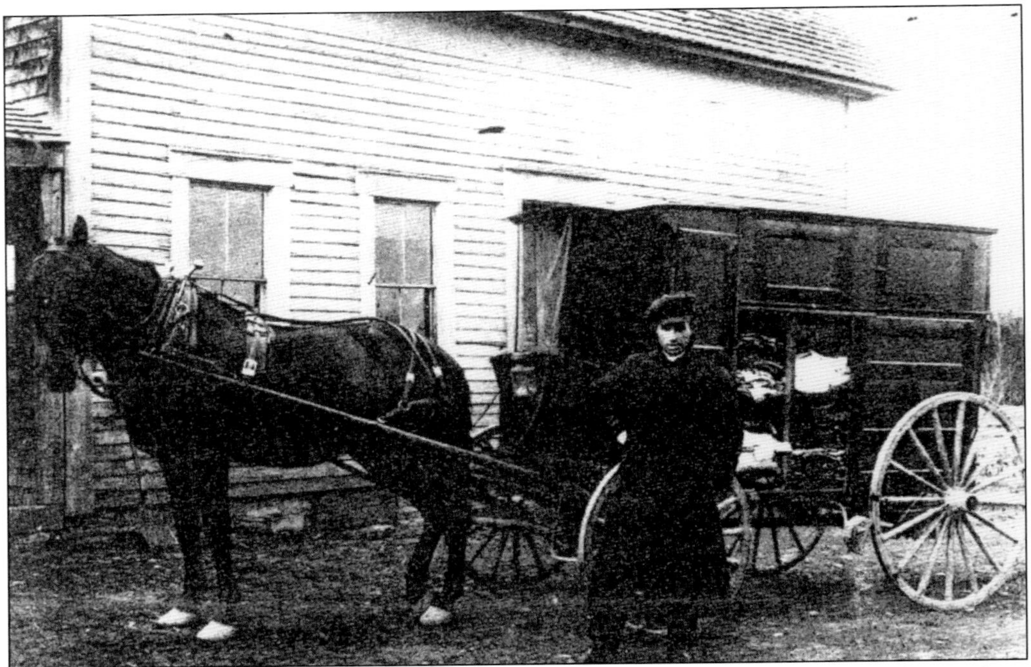

Israel Goodman of Old Town sold dry goods from the Old Town-Bangor area as far north as Fort Kent. Later Goodman had stores in Old Town and Danforth. (Courtesy of the Bangor Public Library.)

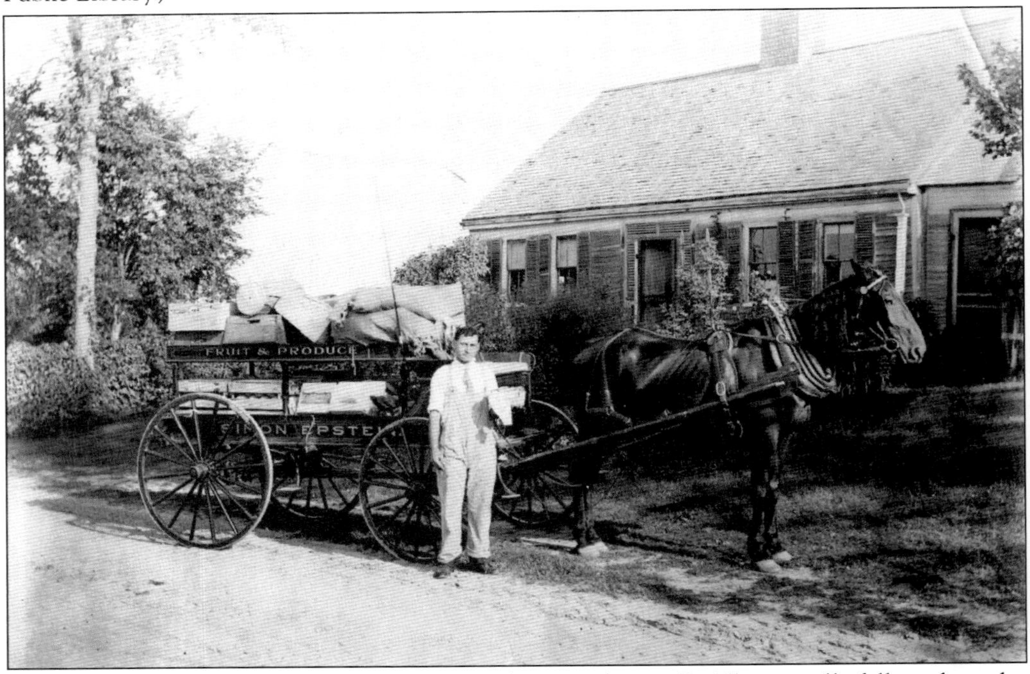

Simon Epstein of Biddeford peddled fruit from house to house. Peddlers usually followed regular weekly, monthly, or twice-a-year cycles as they traveled from neighborhood to neighborhood. (Courtesy of McArthur Library, Biddeford.)

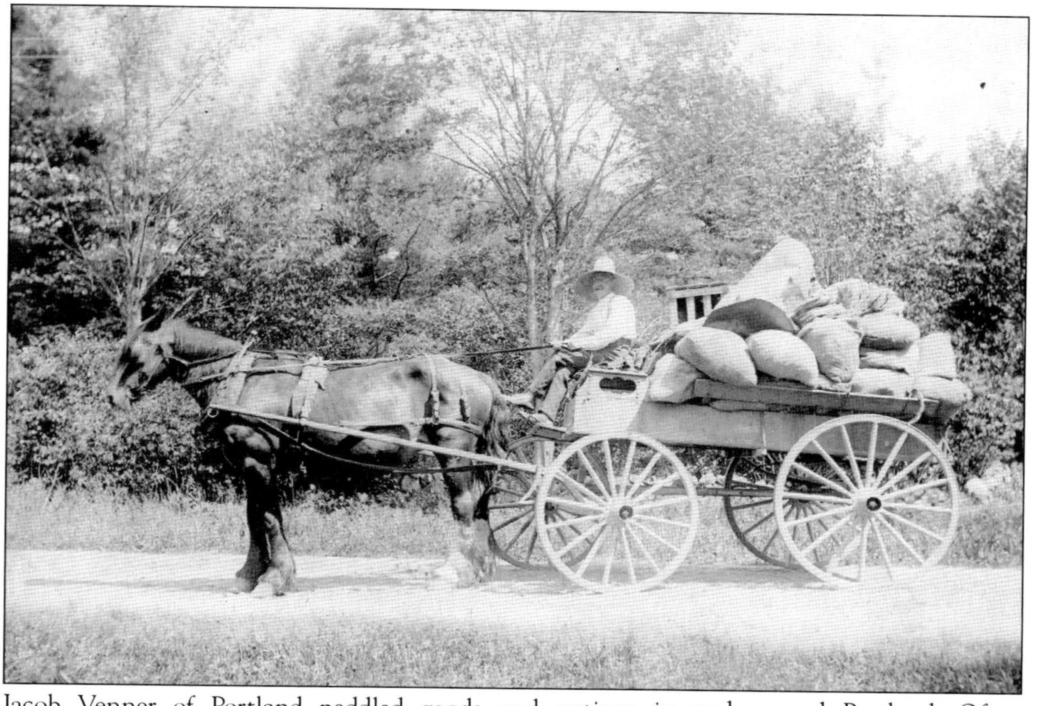

Jacob Venner of Portland peddled goods and notions in and around Portland. Often peddlers traveled to distant neighborhoods to sell their wares. (Courtesy of Judy Venner Halpert, Portland.)

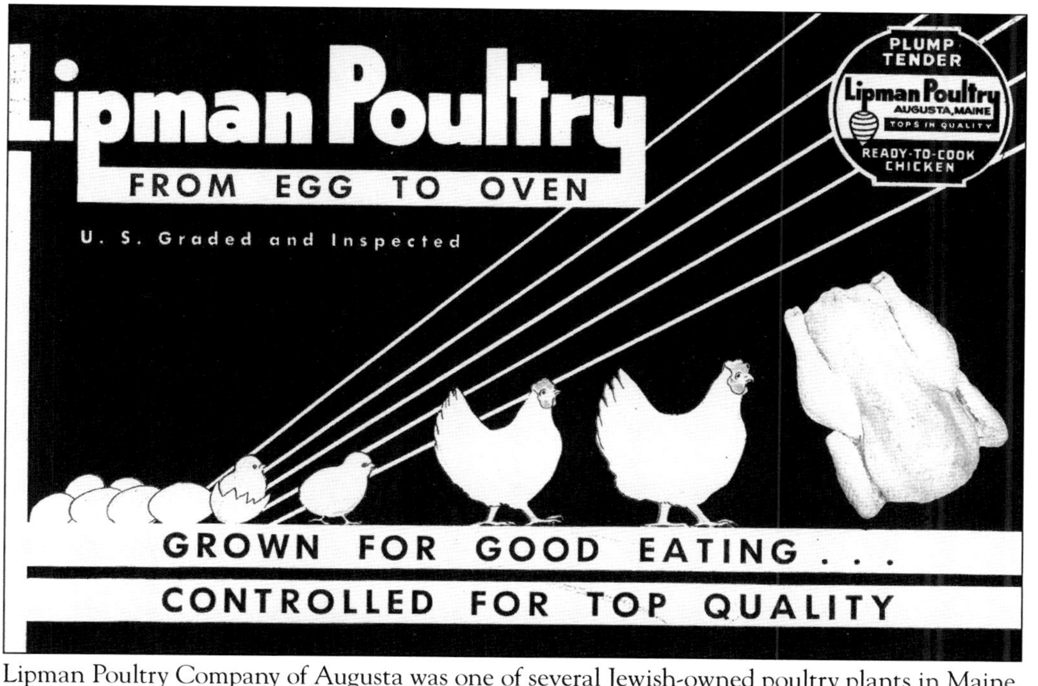

Lipman Poultry Company of Augusta was one of several Jewish-owned poultry plants in Maine. (Courtesy of Temple Beth El, Augusta.)

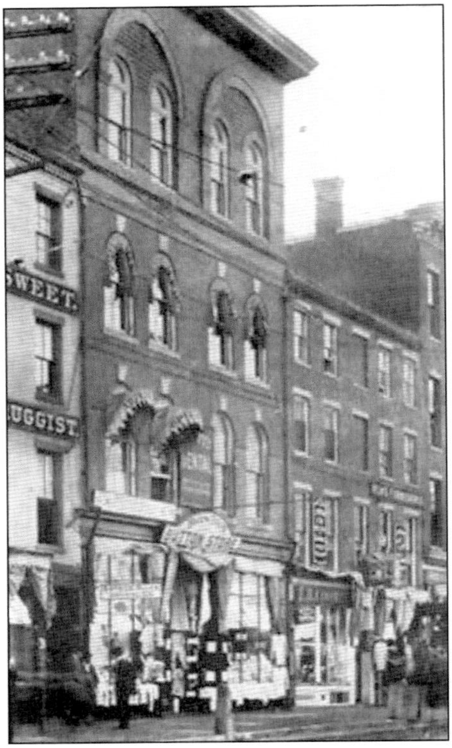

The Boston Button Store, owned by Irving Broder, was located in Bangor. (Courtesy of the Broder Family.)

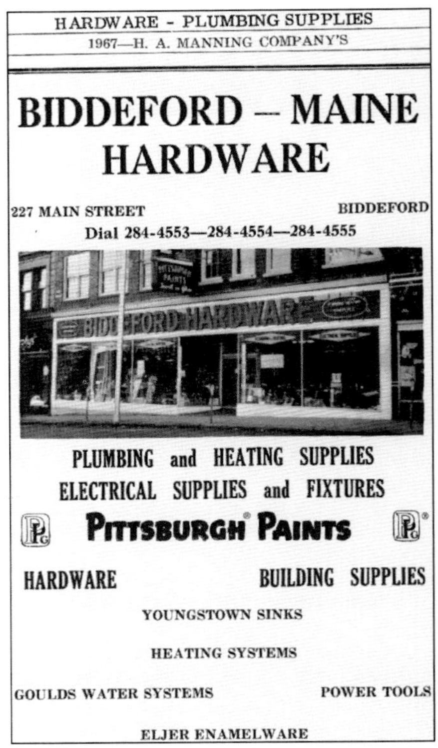

This is just one of many Jewish-owned stores in Biddeford.

12

A. H. BENOIT & CO.,

Mens' and Boys' Cash Outfitters,

MASONIC BUILDING,

BIDDEFORD, MAINE.

F. X. COTE & CO.,

DEALERS IN

...FURNITURE...

Stoves, Bedding, Etc.

178 MAIN STREET, BIDDEFORD, ME.

S. E. BEAN,

DEALER IN

Hardware, Dynamite, Powder and Fuse.

GUN AND LOCKSMITH.

A LARGE SUPPLY OF CUT SOLES.

10 ALFRED STREET, BIDDEFORD, MAINE.

POLAKEWICH BROS. & CO.,

Dry Goods, Clothing and Shoes,

69 MAIN STREET,

Jos. Polakewich.
L. Polakewich.
M. Silverman.

BIDDEFORD, MAINE.

Biddeford businesses owned by Jews advertised in the local Biddeford/Saco business directory. The Polakewich family owned Polakewich Brothers and Company, and the Cohen brothers owned York Bottling Works. (Courtesy of the McArthur Library, Biddeford.)

14 BIDDEFORD AND SACO DIRECTORY

THROUMOULOS BROS.

. . . Fancy Fruit . . .

The Largest and Finest Fruit Store in the Two Cities

77-79 Main Street, Corner Foss

Tels. 8425, 831-M Biddeford, Maine

LOUIS TROUGAKOS

Confectionery, Soda, College Ices of all kinds, Fruit

We have the coolest place in the hot weather

163 MAIN STREET, SACO, MAINE

MAPLE FARM

ARTHUR GUERTIN

MILK DEALER

LOUDON ROAD, SACO, MAINE

Telephone Connection

York Bottling Works

Manufacturers and Bottlers of

HIGH GRADE GINGER ALE, SODA AND MINERAL WATERS

KOVAR AND MOXIE DISTRIBUTORS

Special Agents For All Kinds of

NON-INTOXICATING BEERS

J. COHEN, Prop. Telephone 463

60-62 ELM STREET, BIDDEFORD, ME.

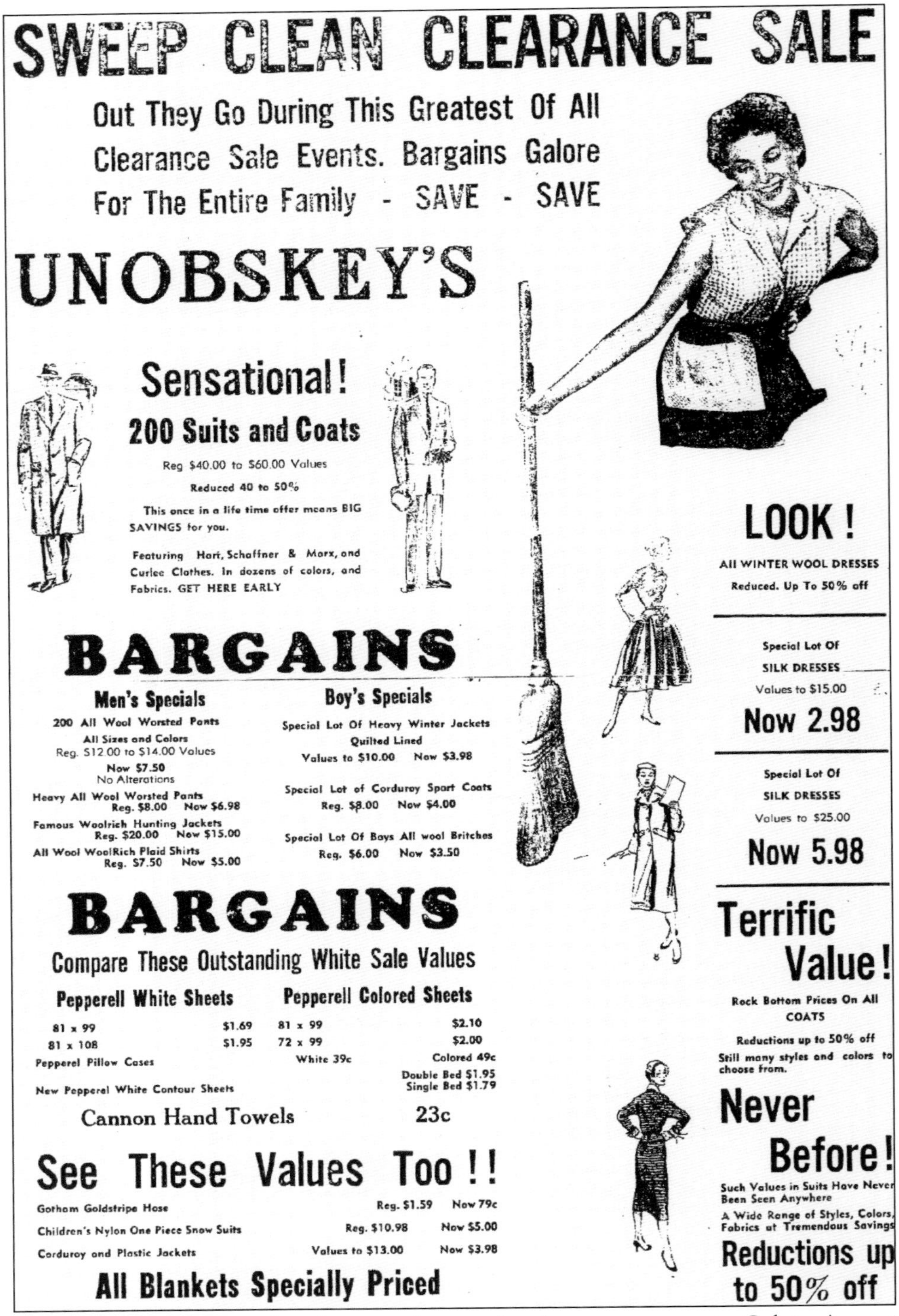

The Unobskey family owned and operated a popular department store in Calais. An article written about them said the Unobskeys, as well as other Jewish families, came to Calais because of the city's reputation for tolerance.

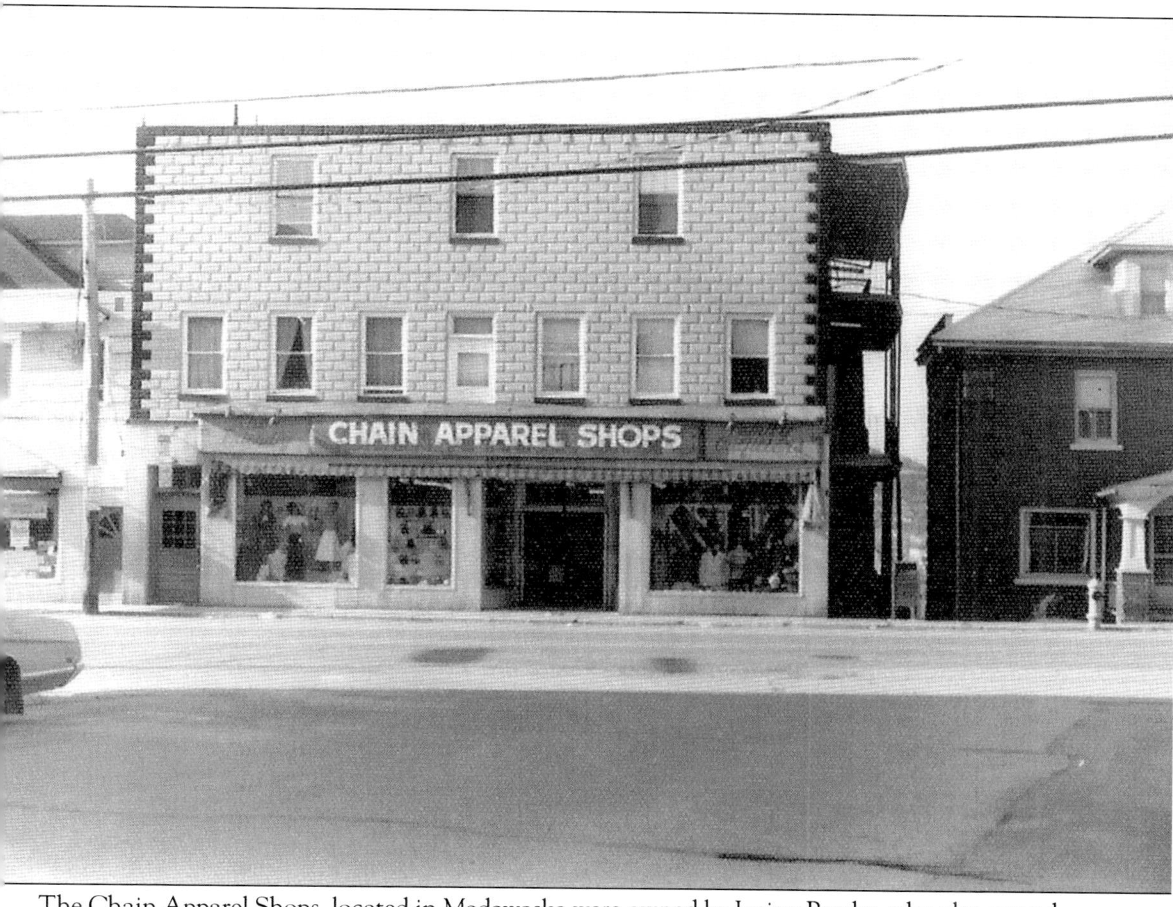

The Chain Apparel Shops, located in Madawaska were owned by Irving Broder, who also owned several stores in Bangor. (Courtesy of the Broder family.)

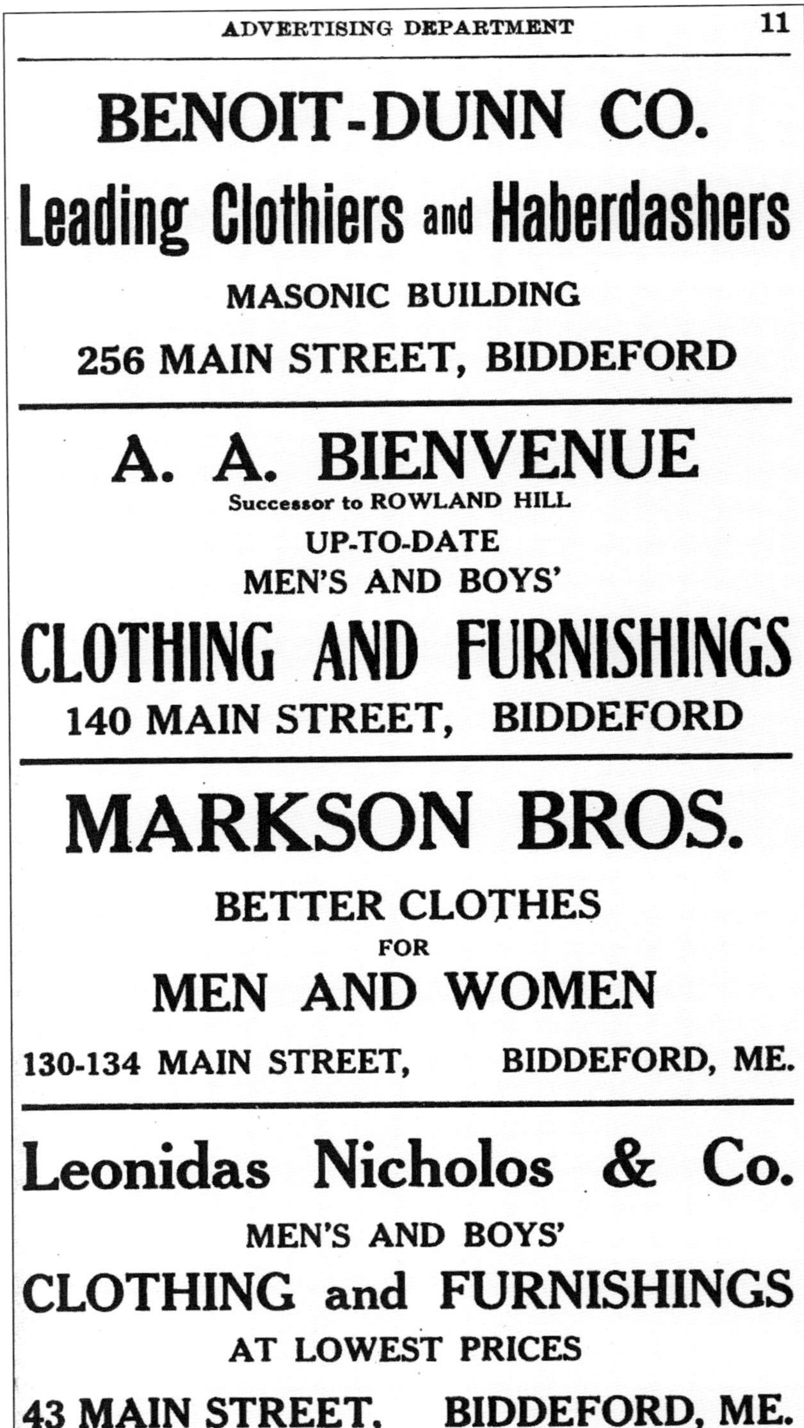

ADVERTISING DEPARTMENT 11

BENOIT-DUNN CO.

Leading Clothiers and Haberdashers

MASONIC BUILDING

256 MAIN STREET, BIDDEFORD

A. A. BIENVENUE

Successor to ROWLAND HILL

UP-TO-DATE

MEN'S AND BOYS'

CLOTHING AND FURNISHINGS

140 MAIN STREET, BIDDEFORD

MARKSON BROS.

BETTER CLOTHES

FOR

MEN AND WOMEN

130-134 MAIN STREET, BIDDEFORD, ME.

Leonidas Nicholos & Co.

MEN'S AND BOYS'

CLOTHING and FURNISHINGS

AT LOWEST PRICES

43 MAIN STREET, BIDDEFORD, ME.

A page from a Biddeford business directory showed the Markson Brothers store, advertising "Better Clothes for Men and Women." (Courtesy of the McArthur Library, Biddeford.)

CHAMBER OF COMMERCE

74 1950—MANNING'S BIDDEFORD DIRECTORY—1950

BIDDEFORD - SACO CHAMBER OF COMMERCE

13 Adams Street
Biddeford, Maine

Established 1927
Tel. 3-3251

OFFICERS

MAURICE L. SANDLER, President
MAURICE C. E. ROUX, 1st Vice-President
WILBUR H. DEWEY, 2nd Vice-President
C. RAYMOND MEANS, Treasurer
MELBOURNE F. MEANS, Clerk
CLAYTON W. CARTMILL, Secretary

Alfred S. Bradford
George R. Bridge
Harold D. Carroll
Albert F. Deshaies
John R. Gibson
Roy MacNaughton
J. Paul Marcous
Armand J. Paulhus
Edward H. Reny
Walter M. Whitney

The Chamber of Commerce is an organization through which the business people and industries work cooperatively for the betterment of the community by encouraging new industries to locate here.

YOU ARE INVITED:

To read carefully the detailed facts about Biddeford and Saco contained in the sketch of the community, which will be found at the beginning of this volume.

Residents and Visitors are cordially invited to use the facilities of the Chamber of Commerce Office.

(SEE PAGE FOURTEEN)

The 1950 business directory listed the members of the Biddeford-Saco Chamber of Commerce. The president, Maurice Sandler, owner of a fruit wholesale company, was Jewish. (Courtesy of the McArthur Library, Biddeford.)

N. GOODKOWSKY,

PAWN BROKER,

Money Loaned on Watches, Jewelry, Diamonds and other Personal Property.

Musical Instruments of all kinds, and Unredeemed Pledges for sale at half their value.

78 Main Street, BIDDEFORD, MAINE.

RESIDENCE, 50 FOSS STREET.

"La Justice"

PUBLISHING AND PRINTING OFFICE . .

13 ALFRED STREET. A. BONNEAU, Prop.

French and English Printing a Specialty, at Reasonable Prices.

YES, there are some people who don't read

WATSON'S -- ILLUMINATOR.

We are contemplating getting out an edition for the blind, however.

Circulates from Maine to the Philippines.
ONLY 50 CENTS A YEAR.

Address, WILL H. WATSON, Biddeford, Maine.

THE RECORD.

DAILY. WEEKLY.

Only Democratic Paper in York County.

RECORD PUBLISHING CO.,

200 Main Street, Biddeford, Maine.

N. Goodkowsky, a pawnbroker, listed his home address as well as his business address on the off chance that a customer might need to pawn jewelry or a musical instrument in an emergency when the shop was closed. (Courtesy of the McArthur Library, Biddeford.)

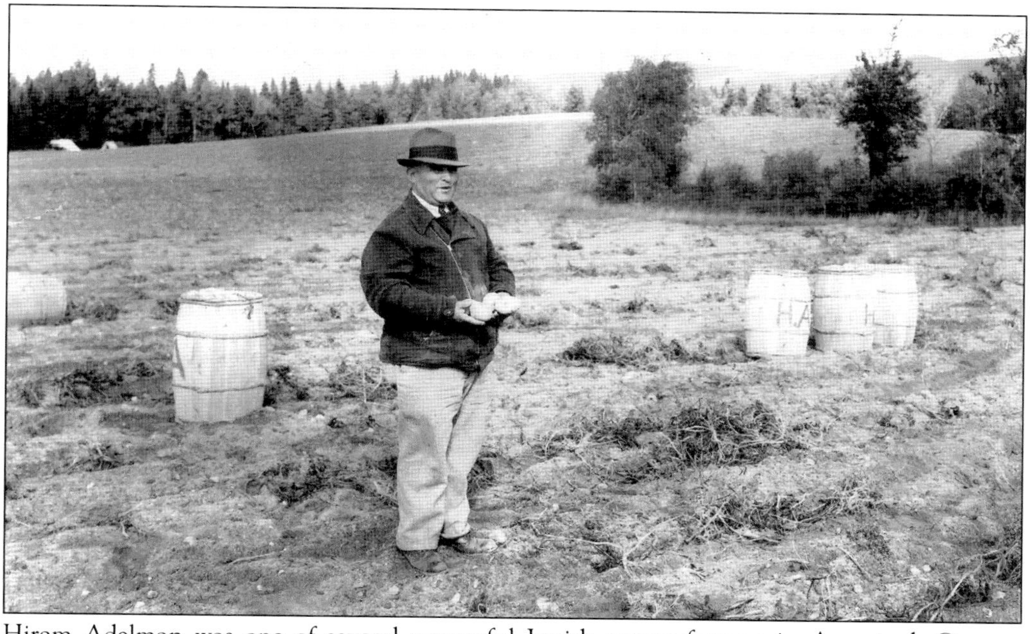

Hiram Adelman was one of several successful Jewish potato farmers in Aroostook County. (Courtesy of Milton Adelman, Mars Hill.)

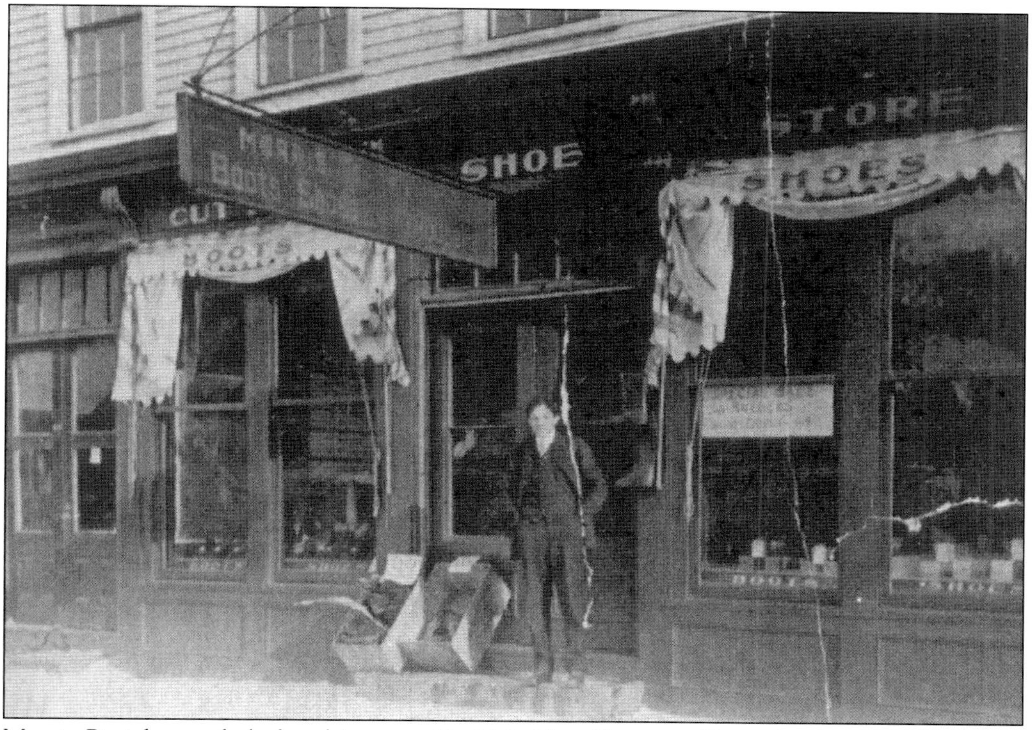

Morris Povich stands before his store, Povich's Men Shop, on Front Street in Bath. Povich opened the store in 1916. His son, Don, took over the store and ran it until it closed in 1994.

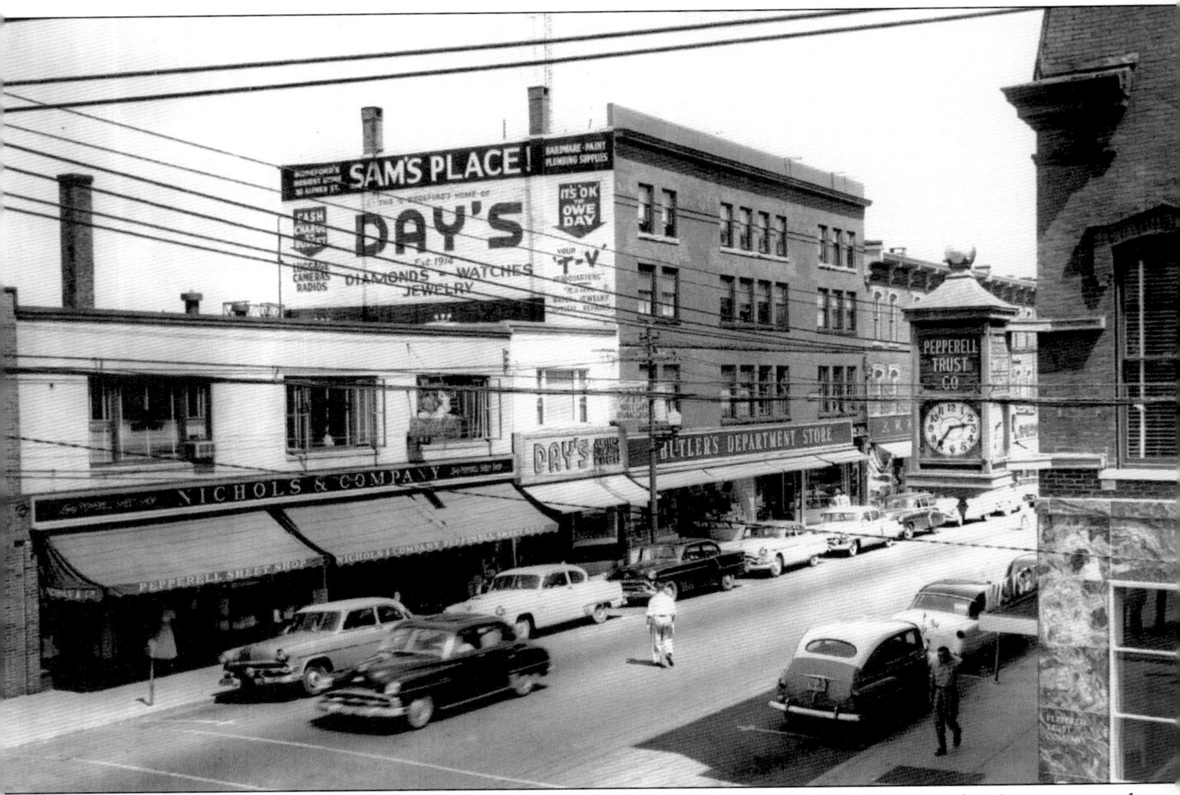

Sam's Place, a hardware store in Biddeford, was owned by Sam Osher. Day's Jewelry Store, owned by the Davidson brothers, is advertised just below the Sam's Place advertisement. (Courtesy of the McArthur Library, Biddeford.)

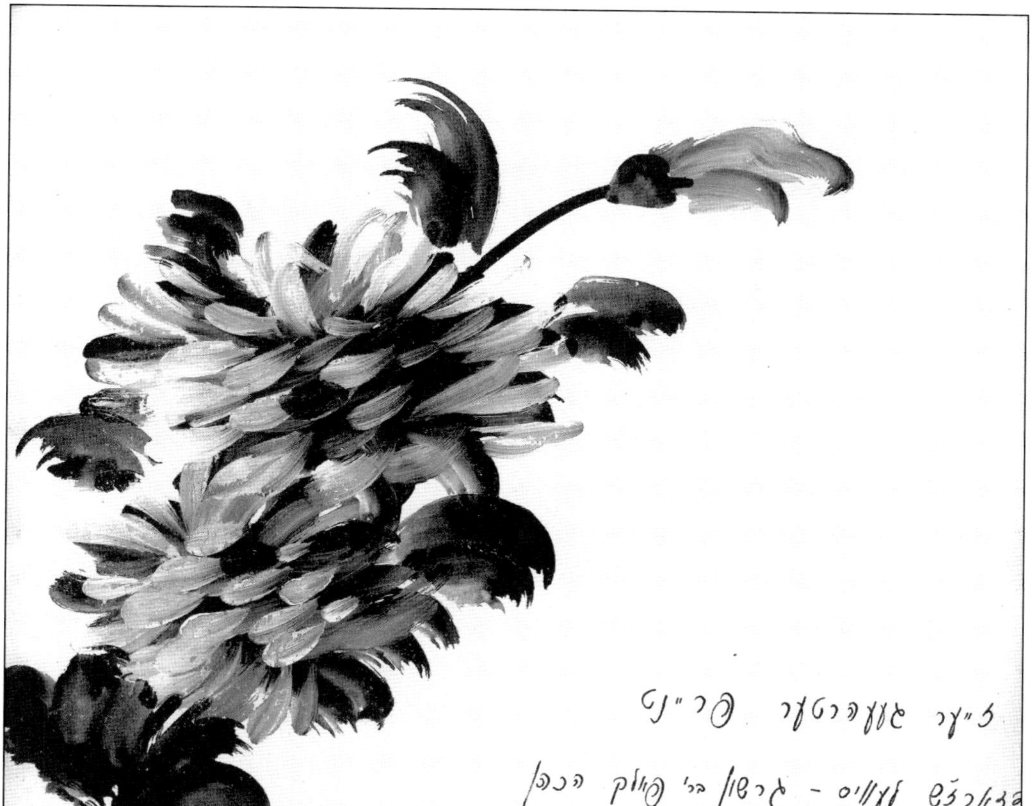

In 1938, Falk Ilowitski visited his son, Portland businessman George Lewis. He presented his son with a Yiddish language honorary membership in the Tarbut (culture) school in Lewis's native town of Kossovo, Poland. Ilowitski returned to Kossovo a short time later, where he and his family were murdered during the Holocaust. (Courtesy of David Lewis and Peter Lewis, Portland.)

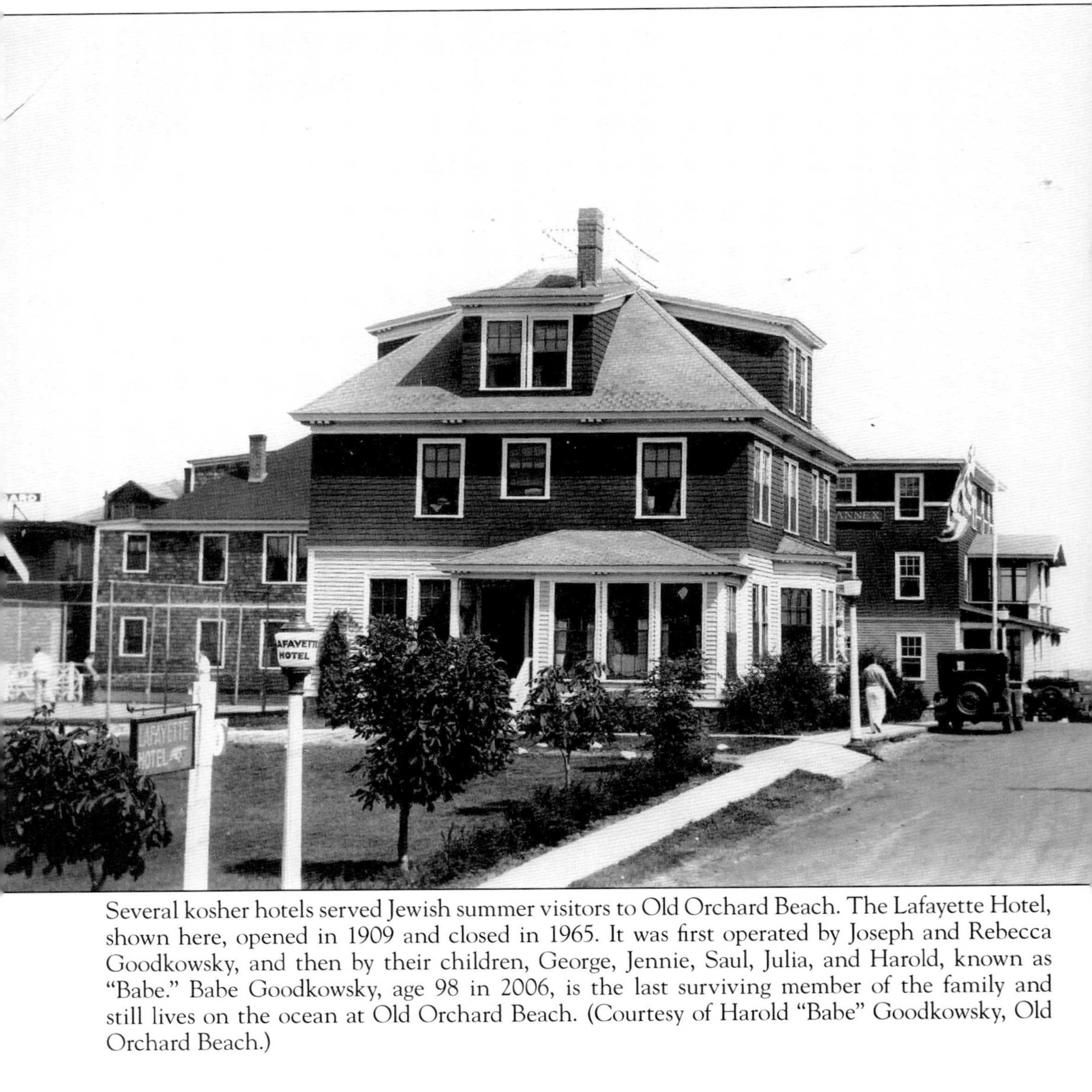

Several kosher hotels served Jewish summer visitors to Old Orchard Beach. The Lafayette Hotel, shown here, opened in 1909 and closed in 1965. It was first operated by Joseph and Rebecca Goodkowsky, and then by their children, George, Jennie, Saul, Julia, and Harold, known as "Babe." Babe Goodkowsky, age 98 in 2006, is the last surviving member of the family and still lives on the ocean at Old Orchard Beach. (Courtesy of Harold "Babe" Goodkowsky, Old Orchard Beach.)

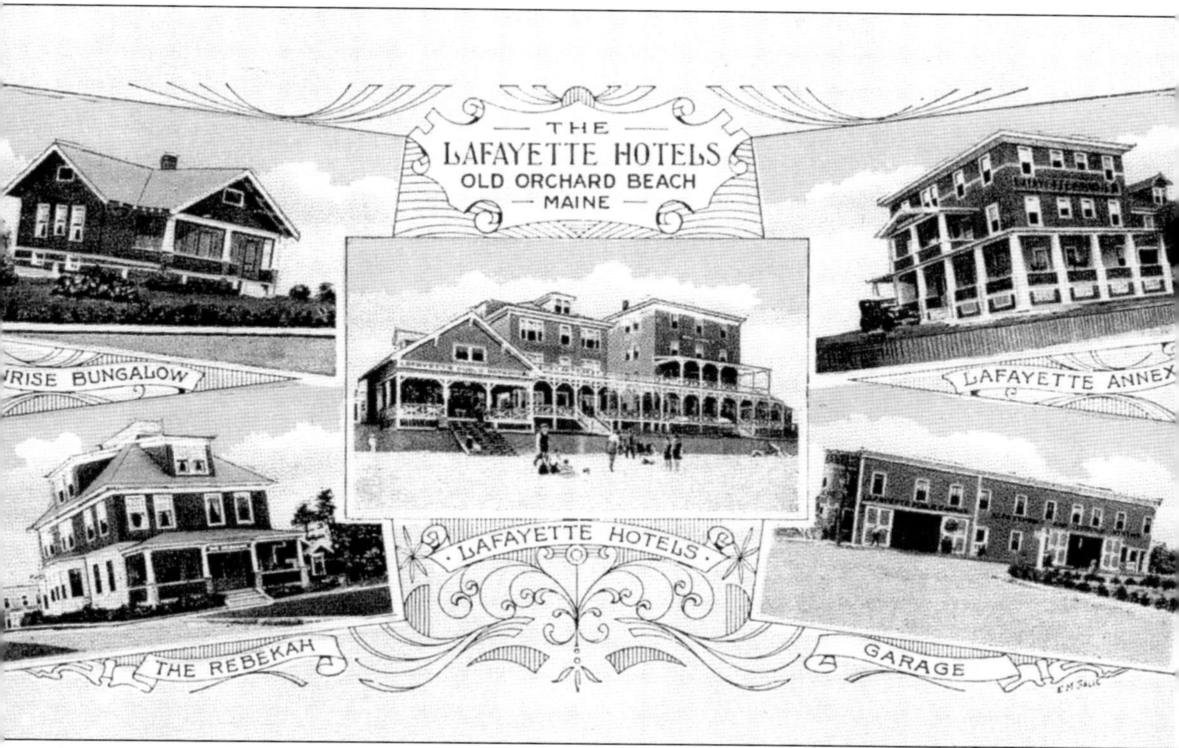

This postcard was for sale at the Lafayette Hotel, which comprised several buildings with many modern amenities for the time. Among the guests were members of the Bronfman family from Canada; Rabbi Solomon Schechter, president of the Jewish Theological Seminary; and families from across the country, who stayed for many weeks. (Courtesy of Harold "Babe" Goodkowsky, Old Orchard Beach.)

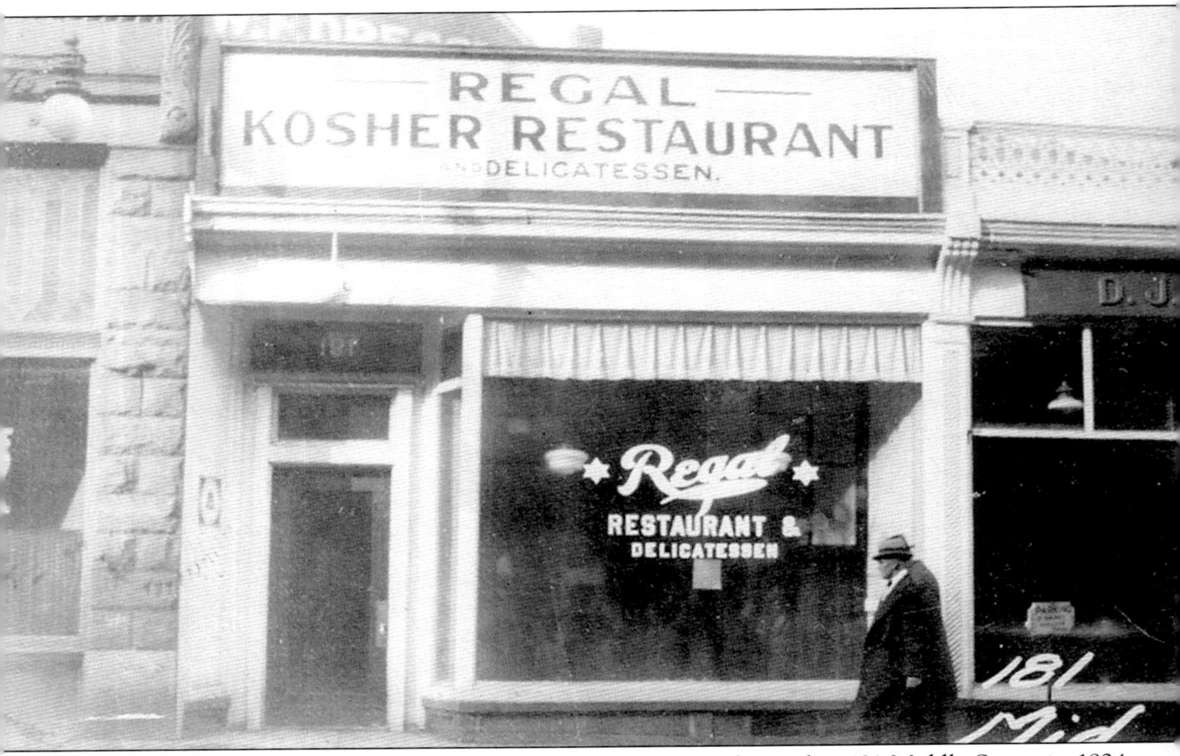

Portland's Regal Kosher Restaurant and Delicatessen was located at 181 Middle Street in 1924. (Courtesy of the Tax Assessor's Office, Portland.)

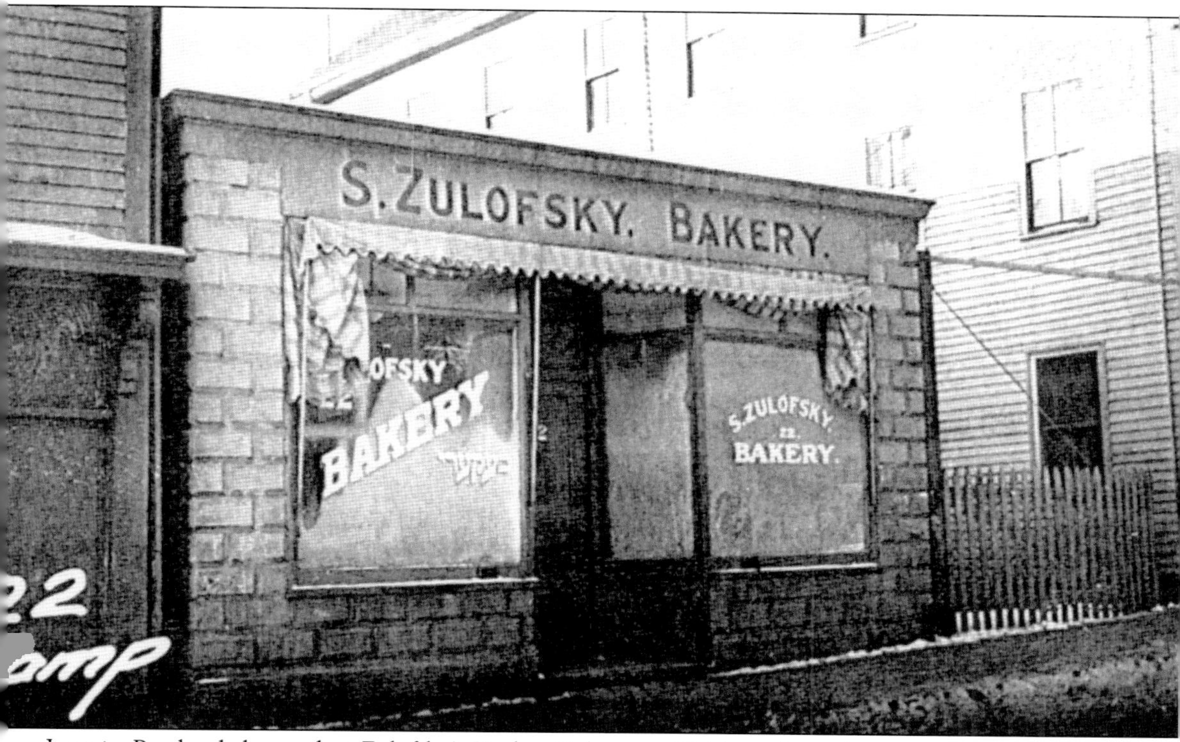

Jews in Portland shopped at Zulofsky's Kosher Bakery at 22 Hampshire Street, one of several kosher bakeries. (Courtesy of the Tax Assessor's Office, Portland.)

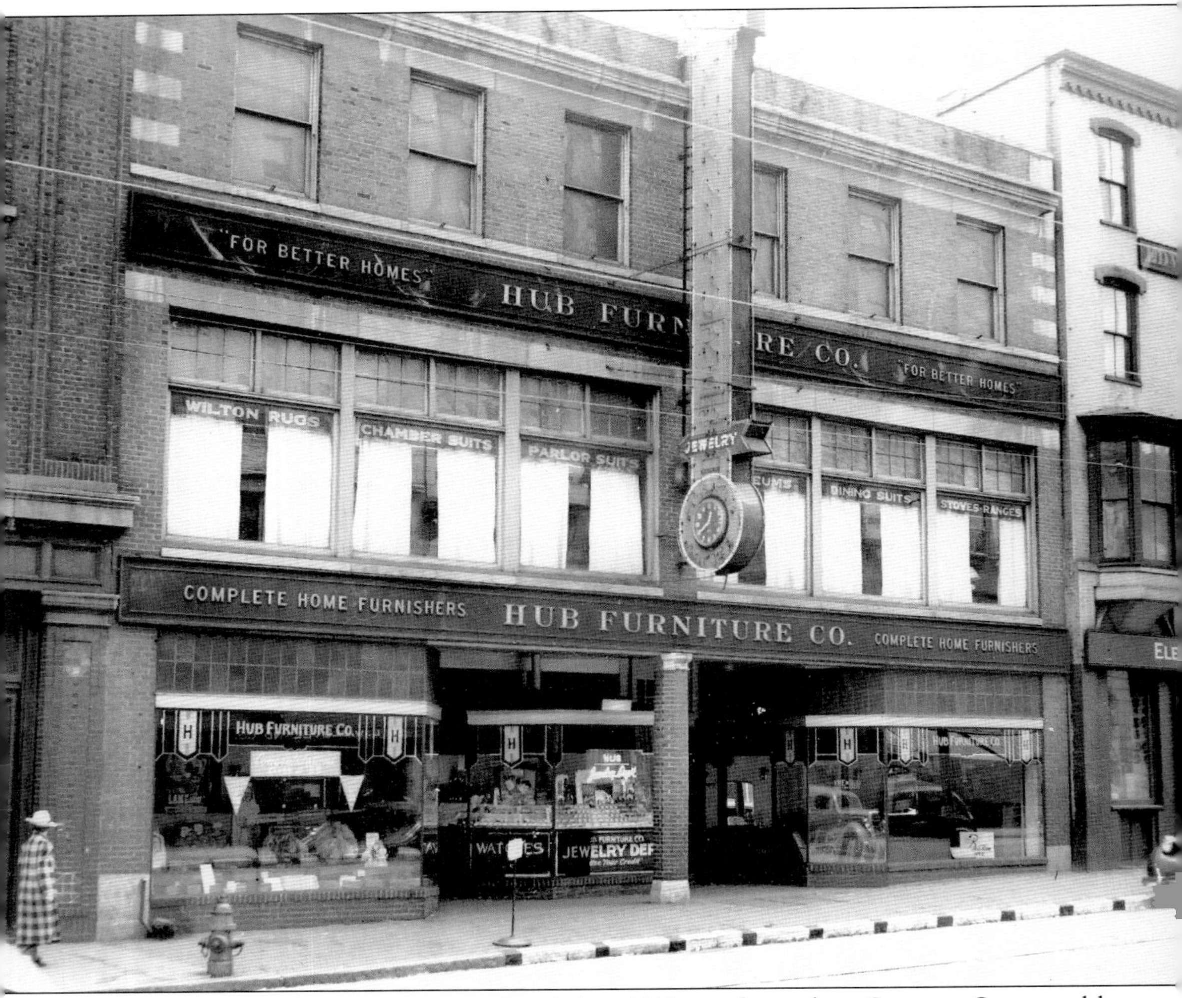

The original Hub Furniture store, founded in 1913, was located on Congress Street and has always been in the Novick family. (Courtesy of Sam Novick, Portland.)

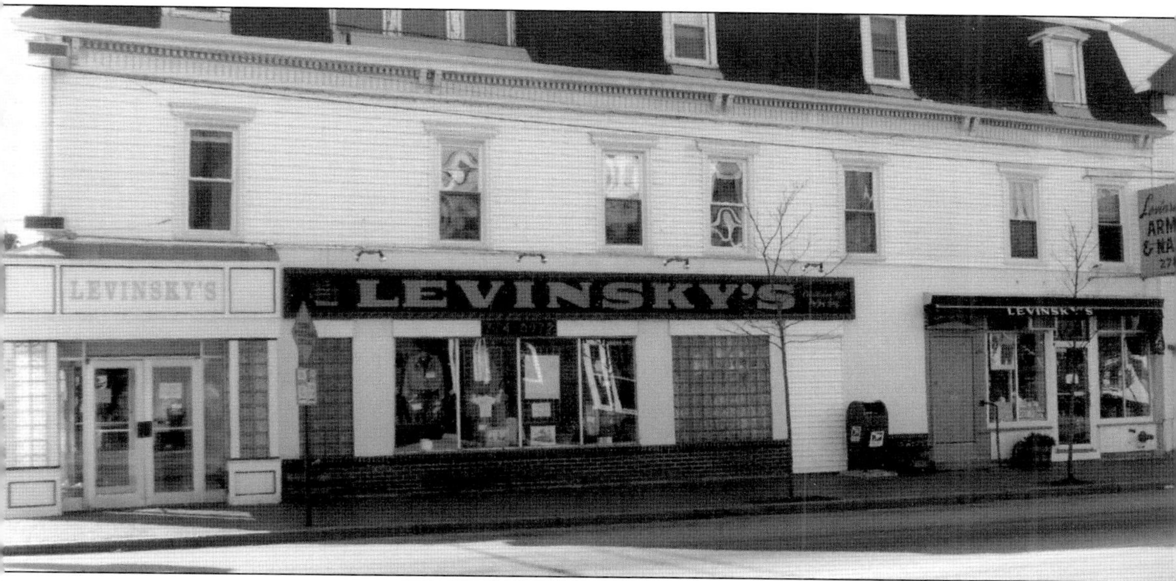

The original Levinsky's Army-Navy store was located on Congress Street across from the Etz Chaim synagogue. (Courtesy of Jerry Robinov, photographer, Portland.)

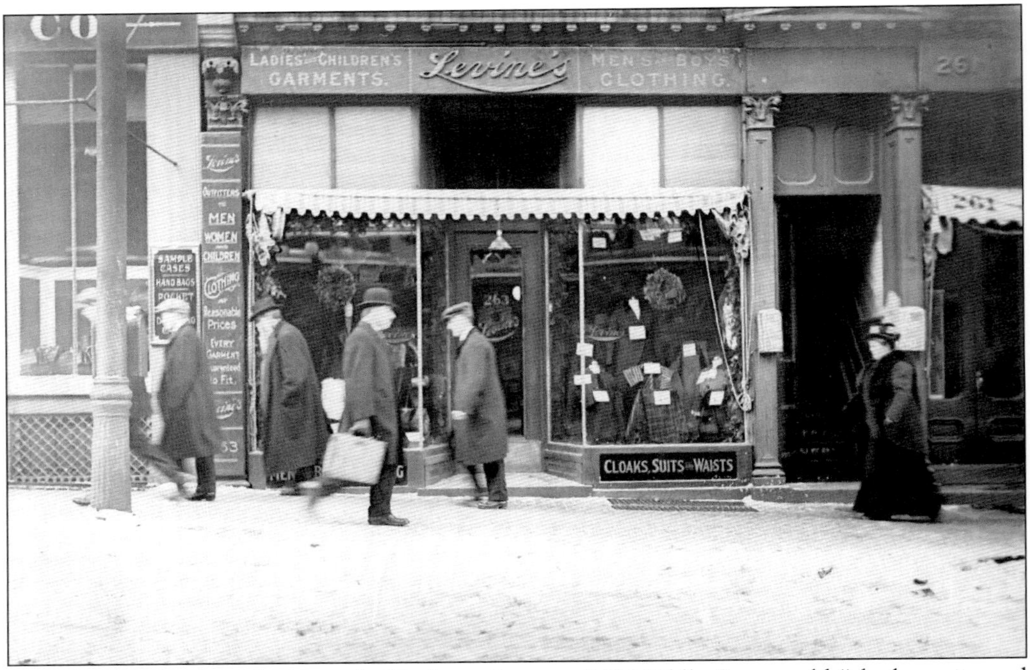

In this 1912 photograph, Levine's Clothing Store at 263 Middle Street sold "cloaks, suits and waists." The building was later bought by Saul Marcus, the author's grandfather, who opened the United Clothing Company. (Courtesy of the Maine Historical Society, Portland.)

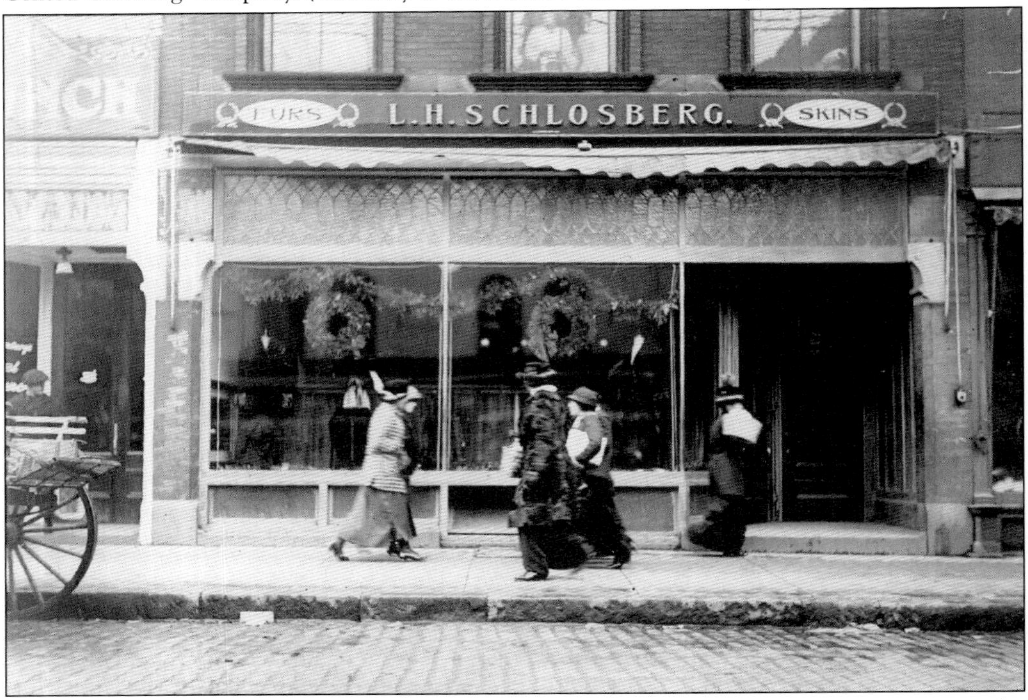

The L. H. Shlosberg Fur Store, on Portland's Congress Street, kept Maine women warm for many years. (Courtesy of the Tax Assessor's Office, Portland.)

Finks Clothing Company was where the well-dressed man could buy a suit or an overcoat "at almost your own price." (Courtesy of the Tax Assessor's Office, Portland.)

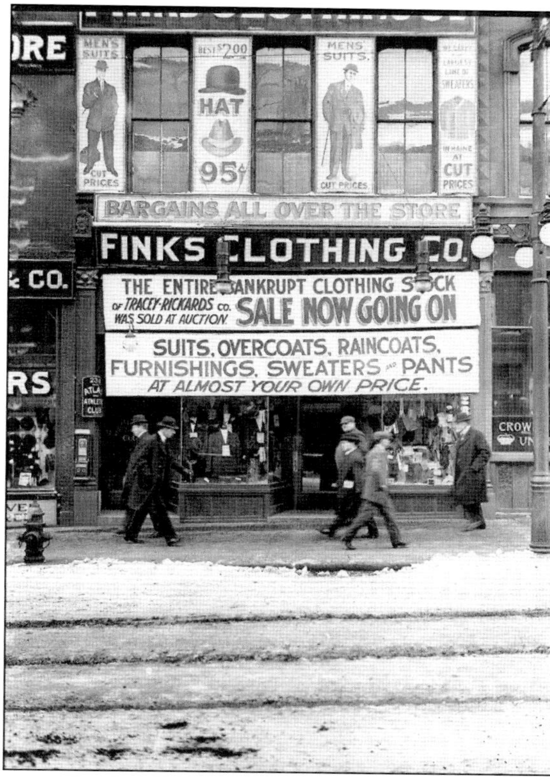

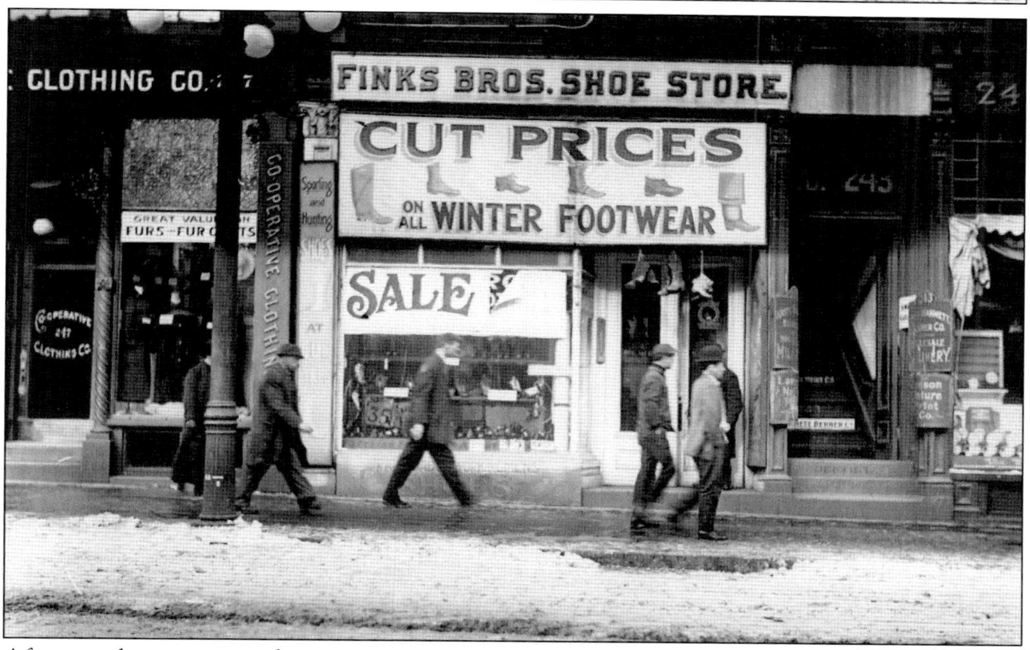

After purchasing a suit for a song, a man could complete his outfit with a pair of shoes at the nearby Finks Brothers Shoe Store on Middle Street. (Courtesy of the Maine Historical Society, Portland.)

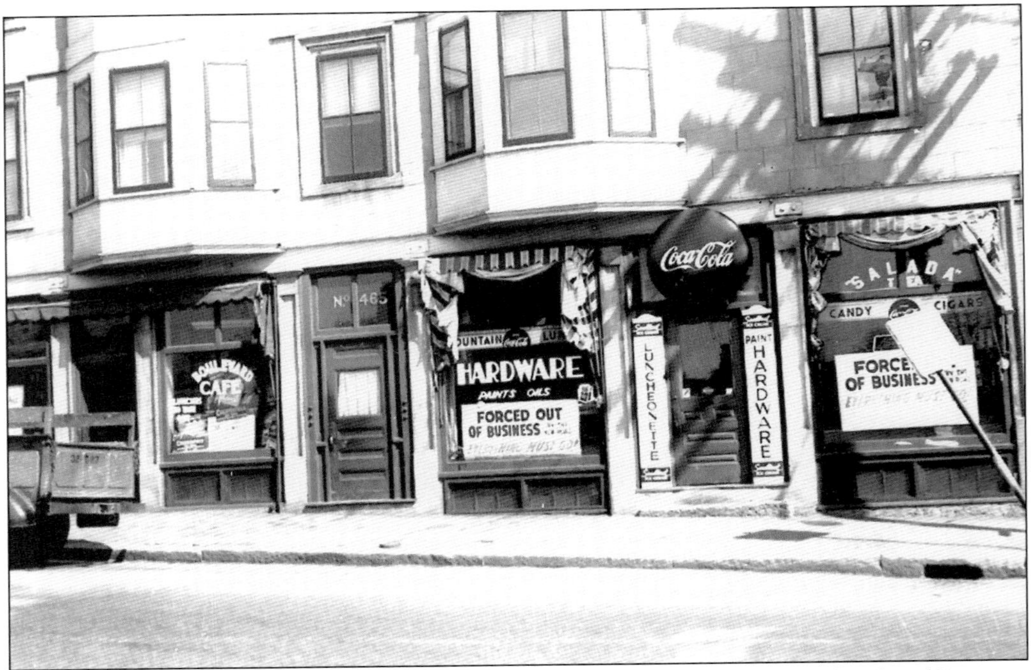

The block of stores on Portland's Washington Avenue was owned by Samuel Zolov. (Courtesy of Mark Stern, Portland.)

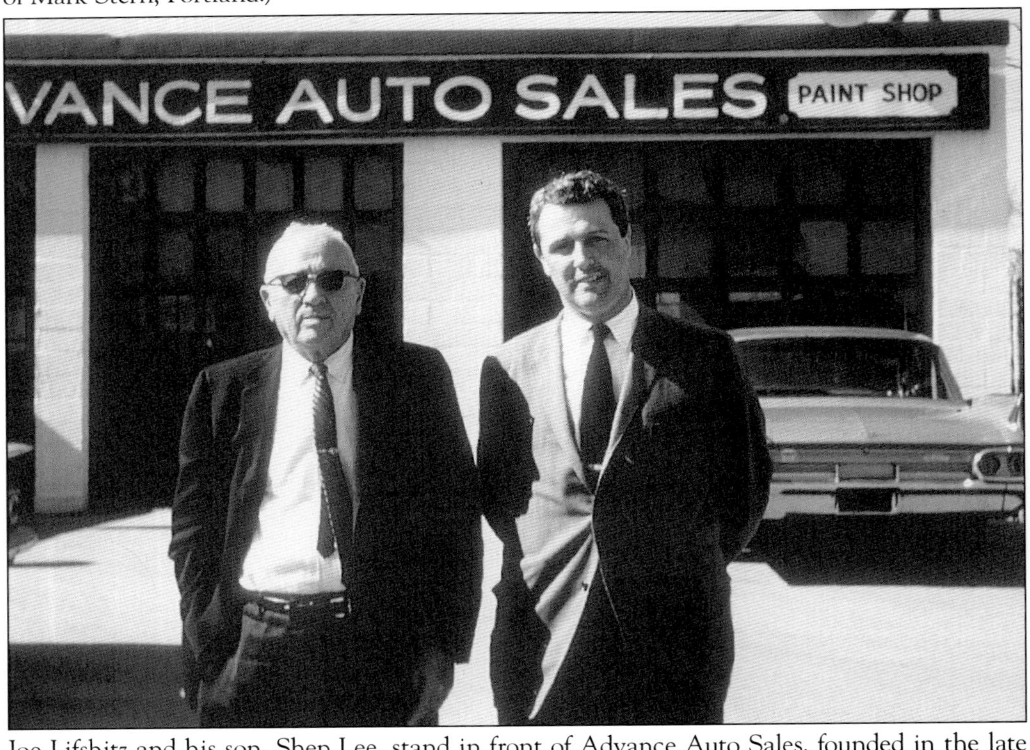

Joe Lifshitz and his son, Shep Lee, stand in front of Advance Auto Sales, founded in the late 1930s in Lewiston. (Courtesy of Shep and Don Lee, Cape Elizabeth and Portland.)

Three

Breaking Down Barriers

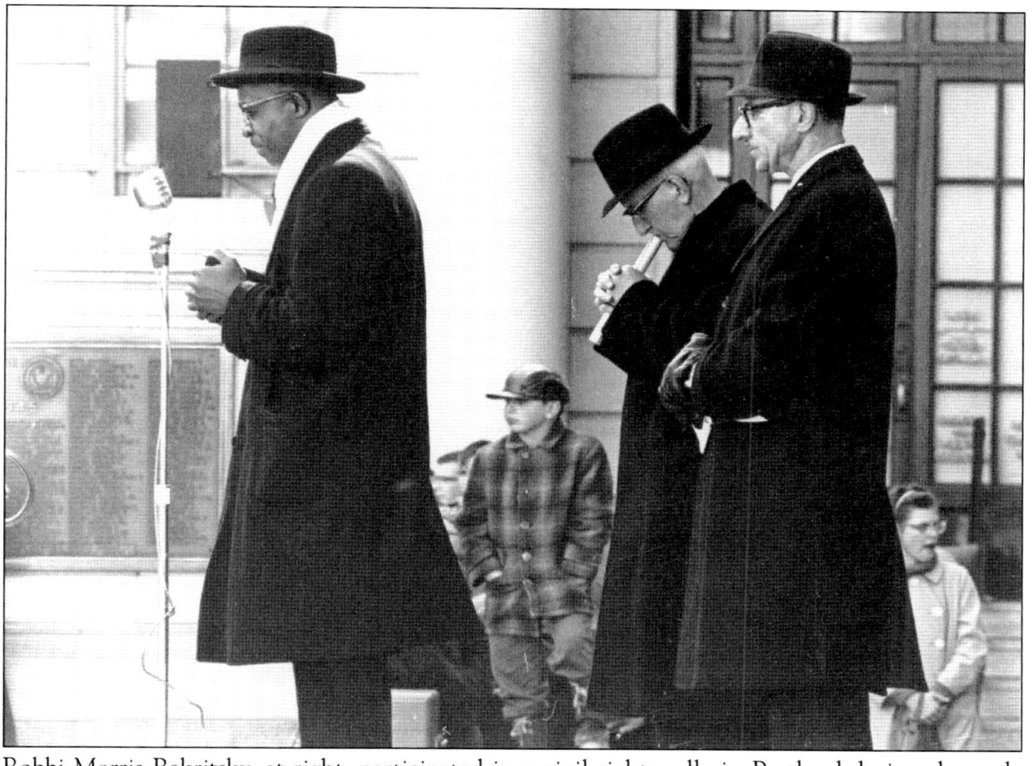

Rabbi Morris Bekritsky, at right, participated in a civil rights rally in Portland during the early 1960s. The other clergy in the photograph are Rev. Clarence Tyson at the microphone and Rev. W. Coneen. (Courtesy of the Sampson Center for Diversity at the University of Southern Maine.)

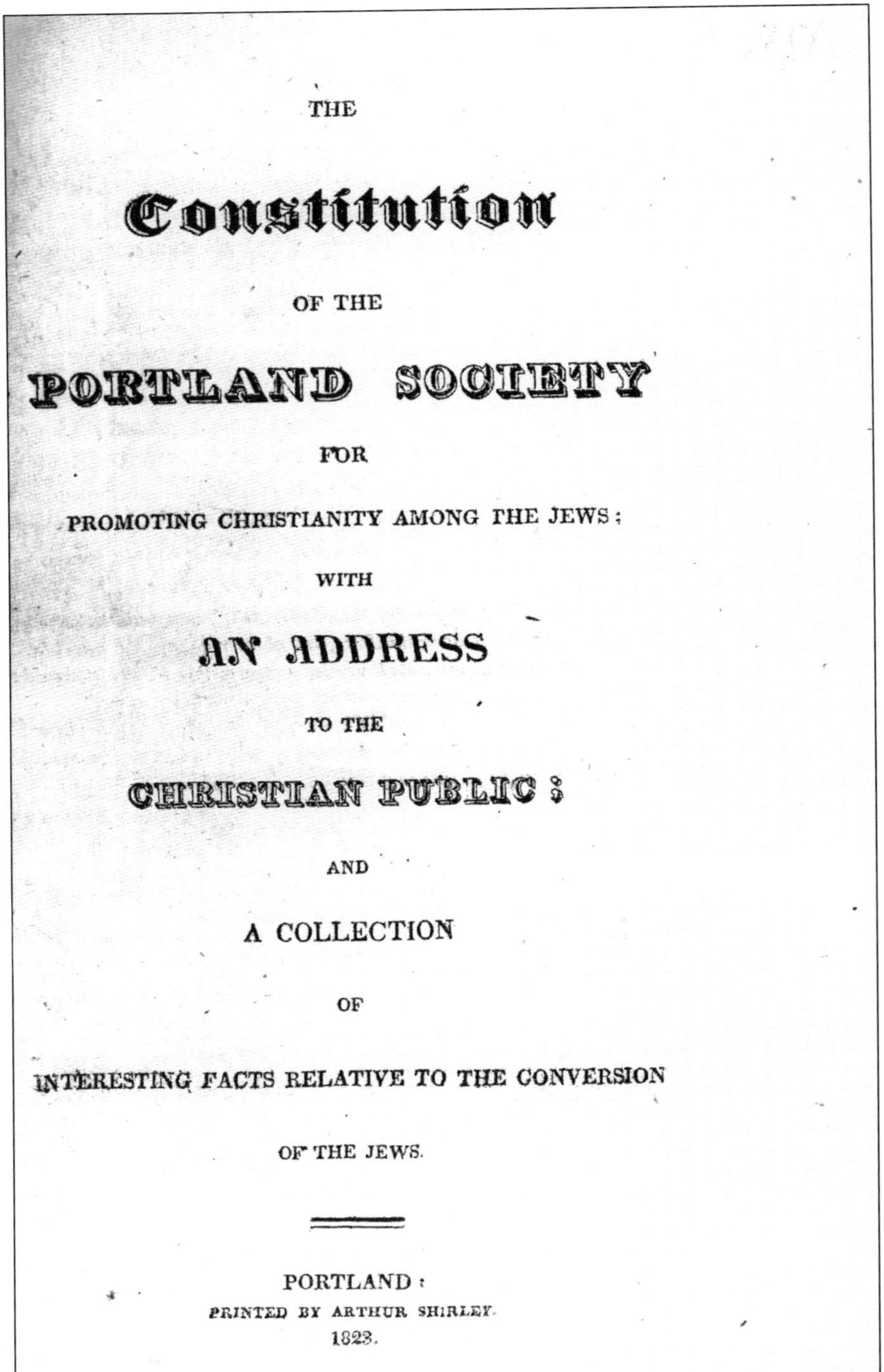

THE

Constitution

OF THE

PORTLAND SOCIETY

FOR

PROMOTING CHRISTIANITY AMONG THE JEWS;

WITH

AN ADDRESS

TO THE

CHRISTIAN PUBLIC;

AND

A COLLECTION

OF

INTERESTING FACTS RELATIVE TO THE CONVERSION

OF THE JEWS.

PORTLAND:

PRINTED BY ARTHUR SHIRLEY.

1823.

The title page from an 1823 pamphlet distributed by a Portland organization urged the proselytizing of Jews in Portland, although few, if any, Jews could be found in the city. (Courtesy of the Maine Historical Society.)

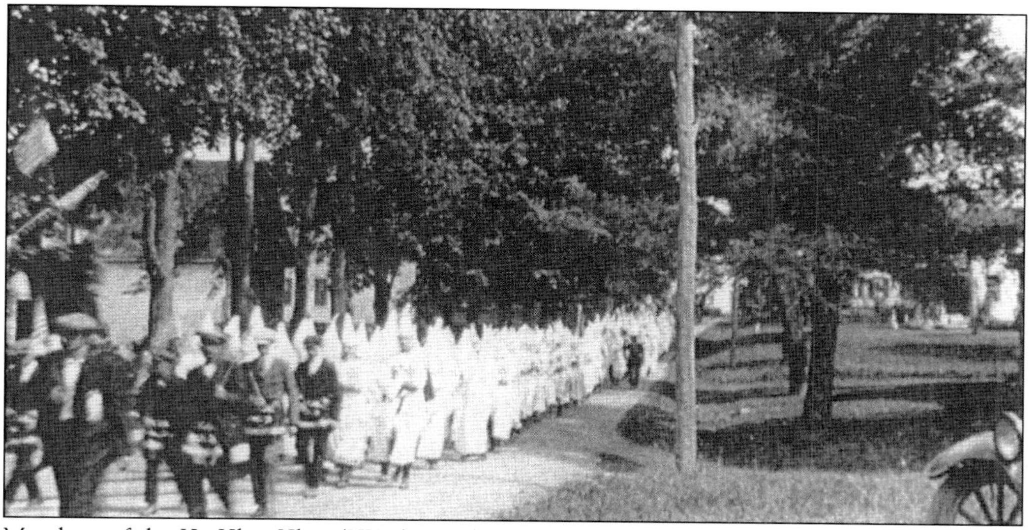

Members of the Ku Klux Klan (KKK) marched through Brewer in the 1920s. The KKK's focus was on scaring Maine's Catholics, although one attack on a Jewish person was reported. The small population of African Americans and Jews in Maine kept KKK activity at bay. (Courtesy of the Bangor Public Library.)

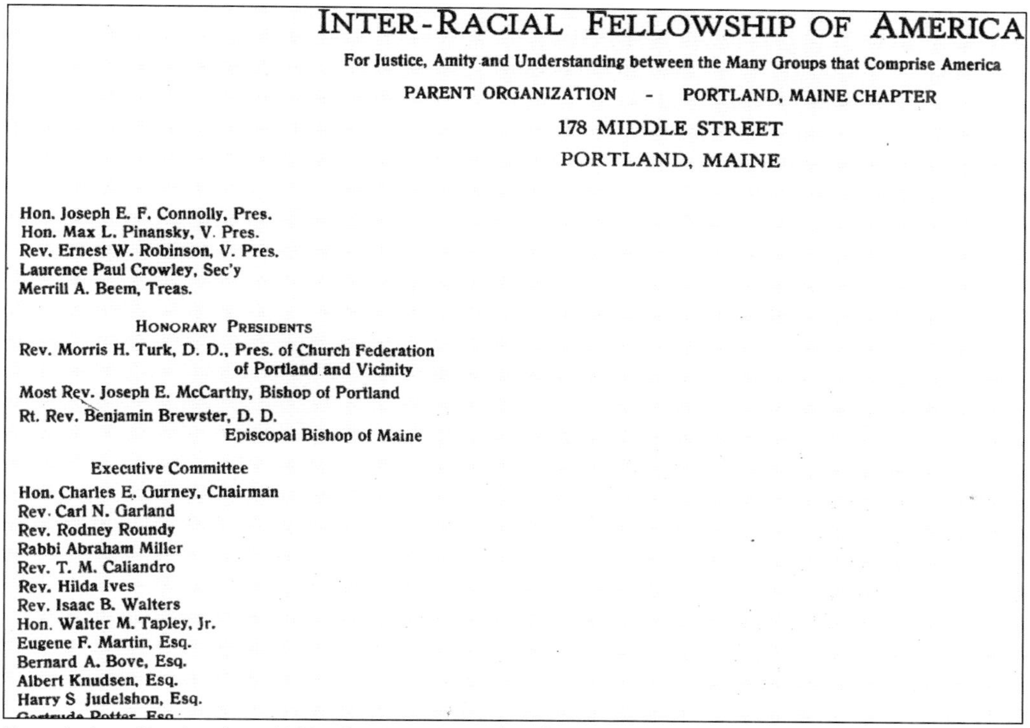

INTER-RACIAL FELLOWSHIP OF AMERICA

For Justice, Amity and Understanding between the Many Groups that Comprise America

PARENT ORGANIZATION - PORTLAND, MAINE CHAPTER

178 MIDDLE STREET

PORTLAND, MAINE

Hon. Joseph E. F. Connolly, Pres.
Hon. Max L. Pinansky, V. Pres.
Rev. Ernest W. Robinson, V. Pres.
Laurence Paul Crowley, Sec'y
Merrill A. Beem, Treas.

HONORARY PRESIDENTS

Rev. Morris H. Turk, D. D., Pres. of Church Federation of Portland and Vicinity
Most Rev. Joseph E. McCarthy, Bishop of Portland
Rt. Rev. Benjamin Brewster, D. D. Episcopal Bishop of Maine

Executive Committee

Hon. Charles E. Gurney, Chairman
Rev. Carl N. Garland
Rev. Rodney Roundy
Rabbi Abraham Miller
Rev. T. M. Caliandro
Rev. Hilda Ives
Rev. Isaac B. Walters
Hon. Walter M. Tapley, Jr.
Eugene F. Martin, Esq.
Bernard A. Bove, Esq.
Albert Knudsen, Esq.
Harry S Judelshon, Esq.

Founded in Portland in 1930, the Inter-Racial Fellowship of America, established to promote "justice, amity, and understanding" among races and religions, featured many prominent Portland Jewish names on its masthead. The Honorable Max Pinansky, Rabbi Abraham Miller, Harry Judelshon, and Gertrude Potter were among them. (Courtesy of the Maine Historical Society, Portland.)

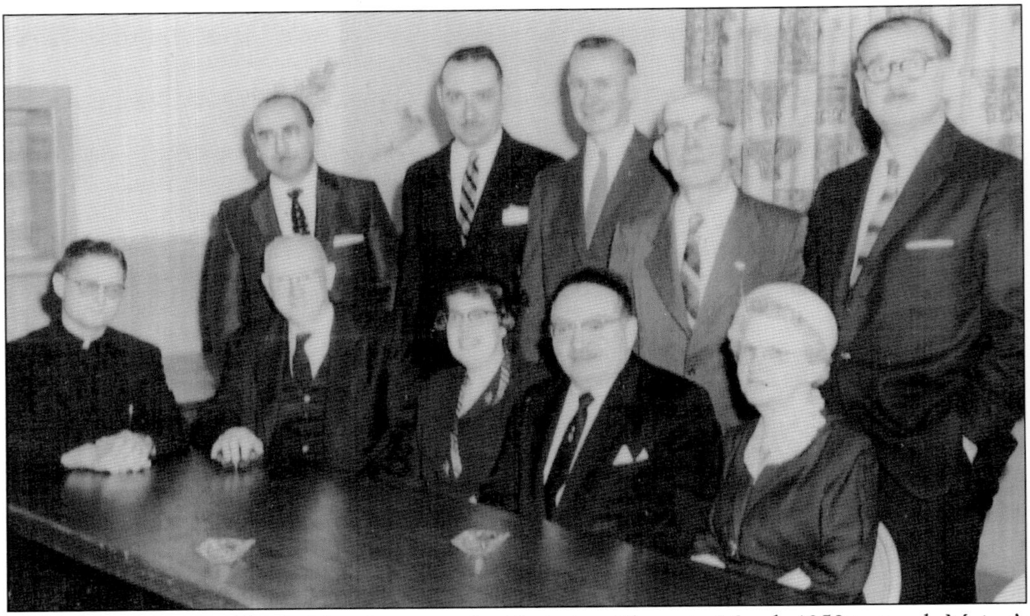

Several prominent rabbis held an Institute for Christian Clergy in March 1958 to teach Maine's Christian leaders about Judaism. Seen here are, from left to right, (first row) Rev. Armand Cyr, school superintendent for the Catholic diocese; Rev. Alfred Hempstead, superintendent of the Augusta District of Methodist Churches; Marion Ulmer, executive secretary of the Maine Council of Churches; Rabbi David Berent, Lewiston; and Rev. Mildred Hoffman, Maine Council of Churches; (second row) Rabbi Norman Zdanowitz, Auburn; Rabbi Morris Bekritsky, Portland; Rev. Elliot Bodwell, Androscoggin Pastors Union; Arthur Jones, Winthrop; and Rabbi Avraham Friedman, Bangor. (Courtesy of Phyllis Graber Jensen and Tim McCall, Lewiston.)

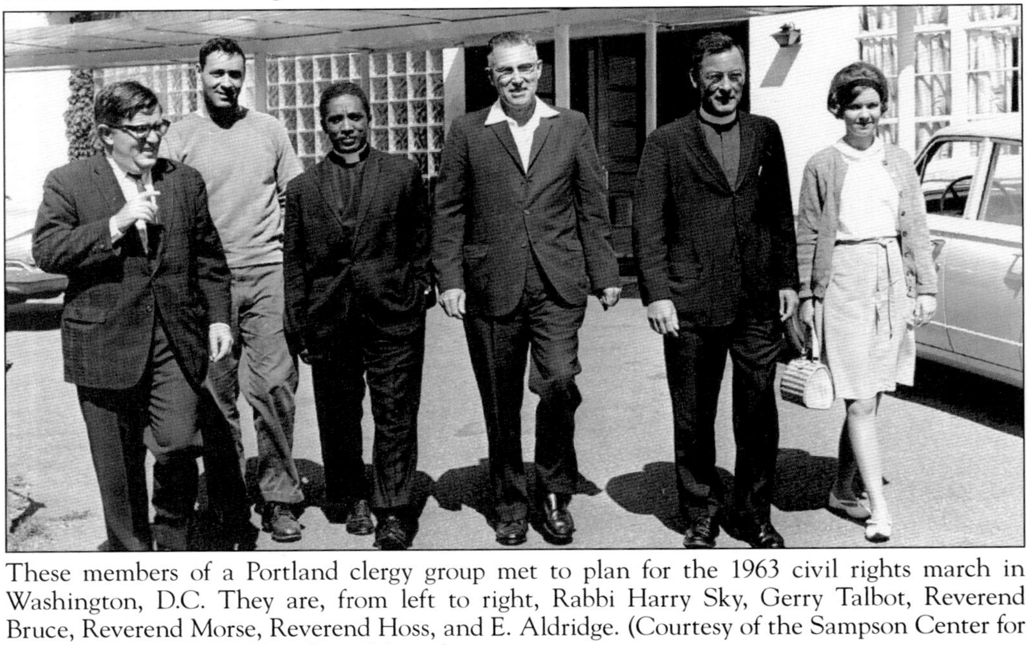

These members of a Portland clergy group met to plan for the 1963 civil rights march in Washington, D.C. They are, from left to right, Rabbi Harry Sky, Gerry Talbot, Reverend Bruce, Reverend Morse, Reverend Hoss, and E. Aldridge. (Courtesy of the Sampson Center for Diversity, University of Southern Maine.)

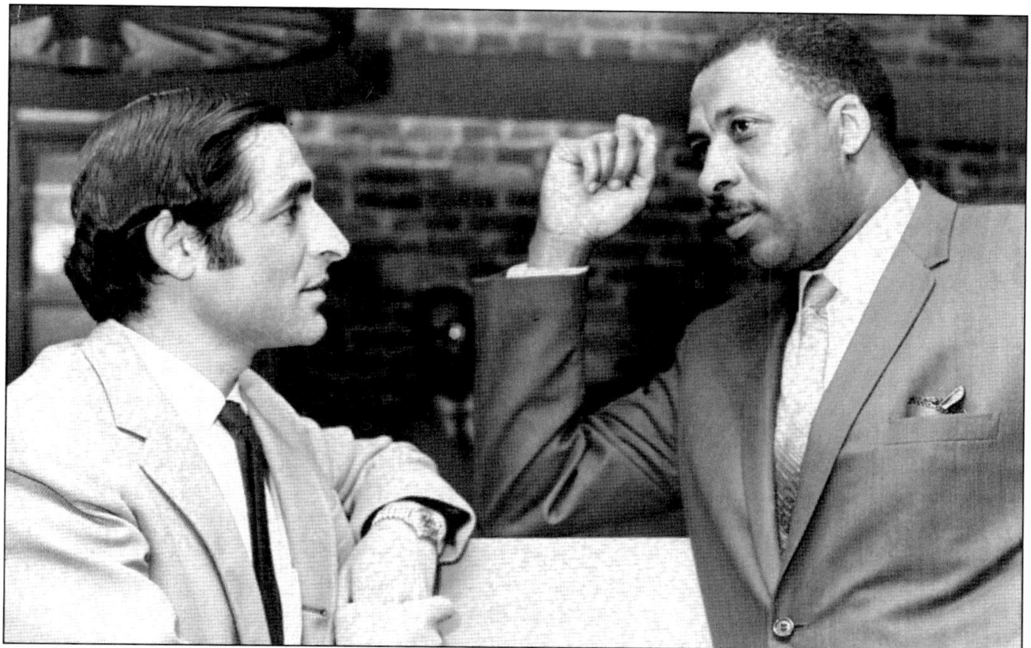

Stephen Halpert (left), the first Jew to serve as president of the Portland chapter of the NAACP, discusses strategy with Robert Teague, his predecessor. (Courtesy of the Sampson Center for Diversity, University of Southern Maine.)

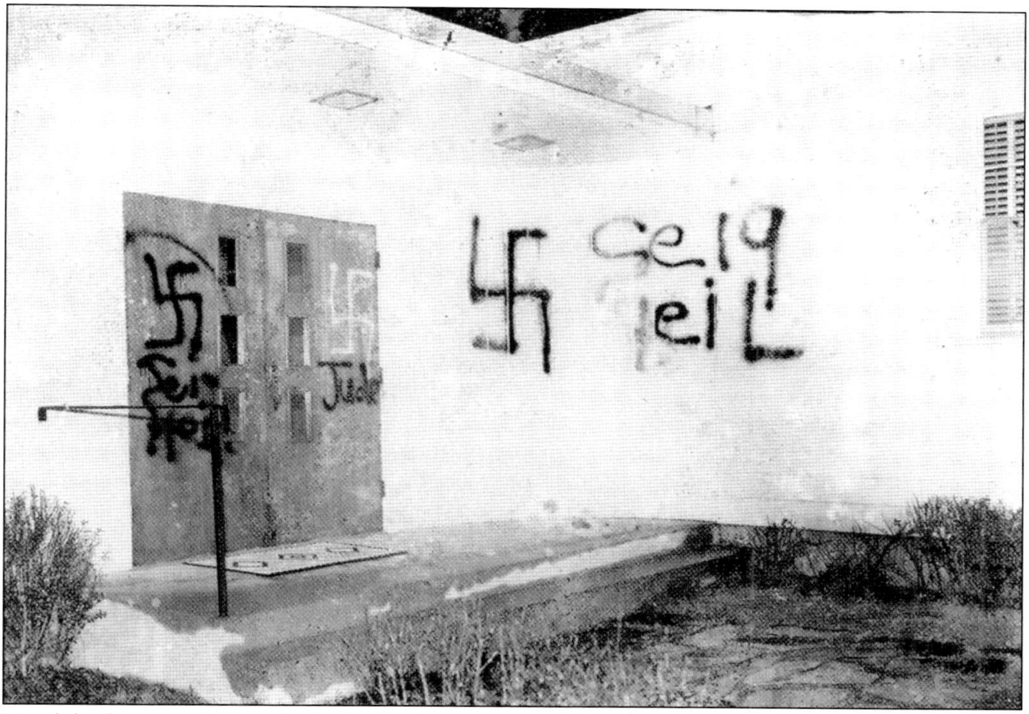

Vandals desecrated Temple Beth El, Augusta, in the early 1960s. (Courtesy of Temple Beth El, Augusta.)

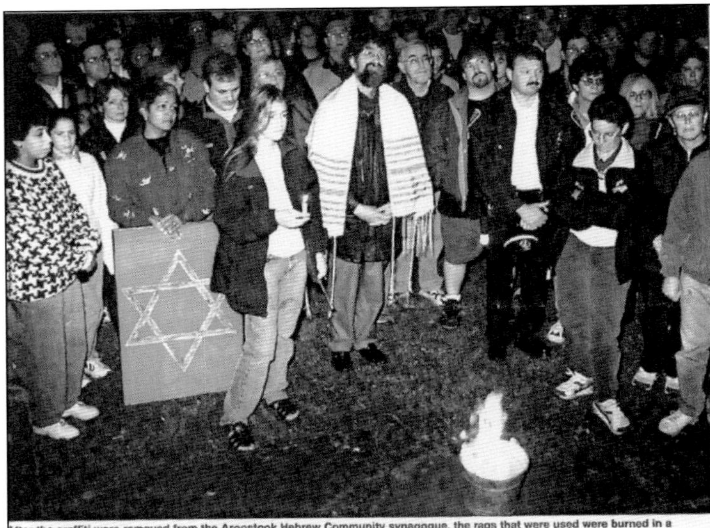

After the graffiti were removed from the Aroostook Hebrew Community synagogue, the rags that were used were burned in a "cleansing" fire. About 400 people attended. (NEWS Photo by Wayne Brown)

Presque Isle rallies against hate crime

By Debra Sund
Of the NEWS Staff

PRESQUE ISLE — The symbols of hate scrawled on the Aroostook Hebrew Community synagogue were washed away Thursday night during a demonstration of support for the County's Jewish community.

Rags used to scrub off the two swastikas and an anti-Semitic threat, found last weekend on the Maple Street temple, were burned as a sign of hope for the future.

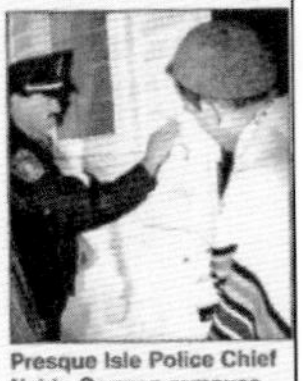

Presque Isle Police Chief Naldo Gagnon removes graffiti from a synagogue wall as Ray Gribetz, spiritual leader of the synagogue, looks on.

Nearly 400 people marched from the University of Maine at Presque Isle to the temple, according to police estimates.

"We gather here to confront the ignorance and hate shown by these vandals," said David Rolloff, a speaker at the vigil and a UMPI instructor. "In Presque Isle, this will not happen without our forged response of solidarity as a community of hearts.

See Hate Crime, A6, Col. 3

In Presque Isle, a rally was held in support of the small Jewish community there, after vandals wrote hate messages on the outside of the Aroostook County Hebrew Community building.

PAGE TWO

PPH MAY 7, 2001

Police investigate hateful graffiti

• Vandals soil Portland with menacing messages, including swastikas on gravestones.

By JOSHUA L. WEINSTEIN
Staff Writer

> *"It strikes at the heart of any sense of decency."*
> **The Very Rev. Stephen Foote, dean of St. Luke's Episcopal Cathedral**

Portland police want to find out who painted racist and anti-semitic graffiti – including at least four swastikas on gravestones in a Jewish cemetery.

Police Chief Michael Chitwood has assigned two detectives to work on the case full time.

"It is a very, very important priority," he said Sunday. "This is unacceptable . . . We cannot tolerate it as a community. I feel very, very strong about this, and that it has to be solved and the parties have to be held responsible."

Chitwood said that about 3 a.m. Sunday, an officer on her rounds noticed a car with four men in it parked behind the Country Kitchen at 276 Warren Ave. They told her that they were waiting for friends who were in the woods.

As she investigated, she found that someone had painted something about killing Jews and African Americans on streets and buildings in the area.

The more police looked, the more they found. By Sunday afternoon, they had found graffiti at 17 different locations, including Mt. Sinai cemetery. Of that number, at least seven messages were racist.

Chitwood said his department is investigating the swastikas and threats as hate crimes and the other graffiti as aggravated criminal mischief.

David Unger, executive director of Southern Maine's Jewish Community Alliance, called the graffiti "a very, very tragic, disappointing statement regarding our times. Just when you think that things are moving along nicely and people are beginning to understand and accept one another for who we are, something like this happens."

And he said it should not be minimized.

"This is not a prank," Unger said. "It is a malicious statement against a certain group of people."

Unger said he is heartened that Chitwood is taking the matter seriously. "It is a statement on the city level that this is intolerable and that they have made a full commitment to resolving this."

The Very Rev. Stephen Foote, dean o St. Luke's Episcopal Cathedral in Port land, was appalled by the graffiti.

"It strikes at the heart of any sense o decency," he said. "I join in a sense o outrage and fright that such action exist right here in Portland."

Foote said that people of good fait everywhere are naturally aghast by th action and he offered solidarity from th Christian community. "A sense of human ity joins us, regardless of our faith," h said. "We are joined by a sense o outrage."

Ironically, Chitwood spoke Sunda morning at the YWCA Race Against Rac ism. "I got up and talked about what great community we live in, and that a people should be allowed to worship an live in peace and freedom," Chitwoo said. "And now this."

Staff Writer Joshua L. Weinstein ca be contacted at 791-6368 or at:
jweinstein@pressherald.com

In May 2001, Portland police found racial and religious hate messages at 17 separate locations including four swastikas on gravestones at the Mount Sinai cemetery.

Raphael Gribetz, the spiritual leader of the Aroostook County Hebrew Community, is also a sculptor who was commissioned by the St. Mary's Roman Catholic Church in Presque Isle to sculpt a crucifix in 2002. (Courtesy of Raphael Gribetz, Presque Isle.)

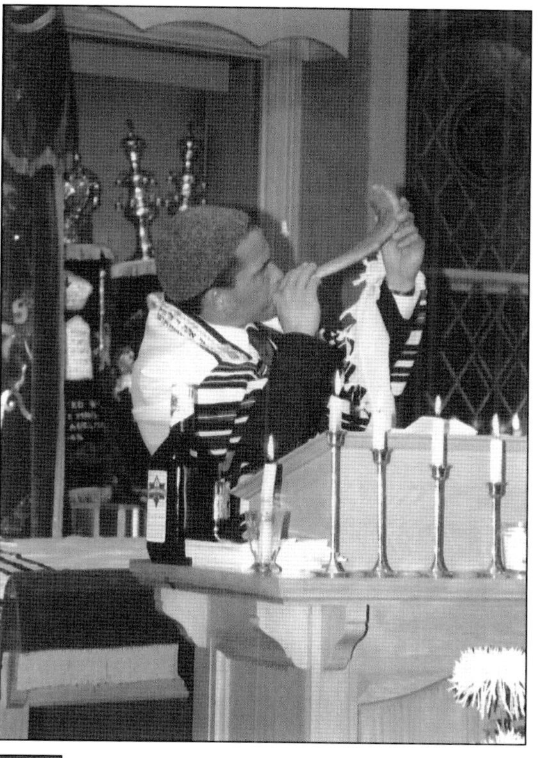

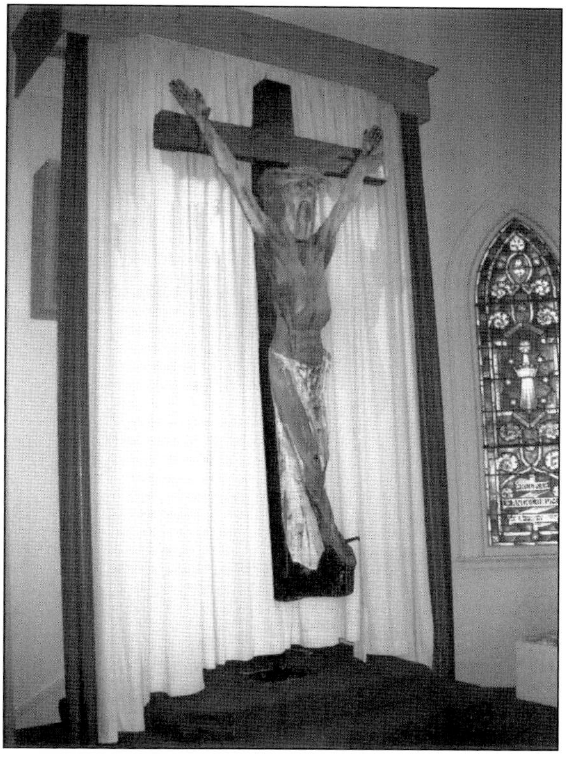

The crucifix sculpted by Raphael Gribetz hangs in the sanctuary of St. Mary's Roman Catholic Church. (Courtesy of Raphael Gribetz, Presque Isle.)

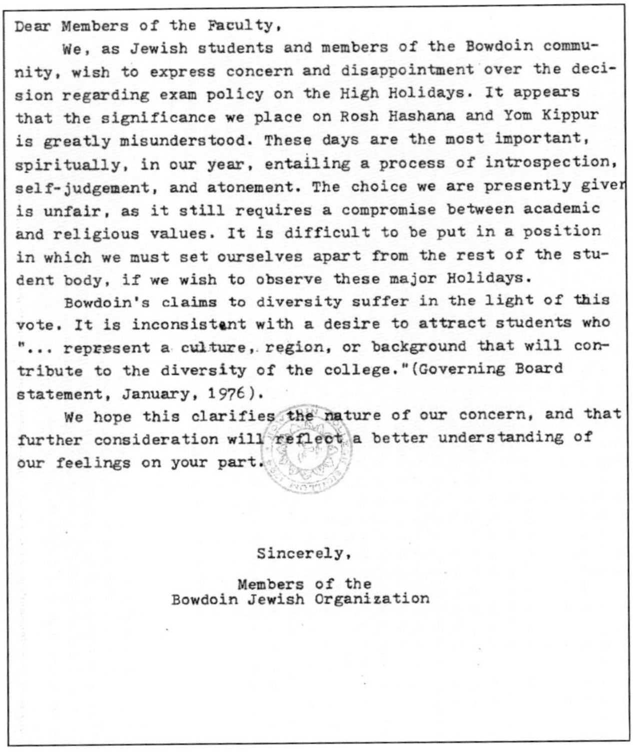

Dear Members of the Faculty,

We, as Jewish students and members of the Bowdoin community, wish to express concern and disappointment over the decision regarding exam policy on the High Holidays. It appears that the significance we place on Rosh Hashana and Yom Kippur is greatly misunderstood. These days are the most important, spiritually, in our year, entailing a process of introspection, self-judgement, and atonement. The choice we are presently given is unfair, as it still requires a compromise between academic and religious values. It is difficult to be put in a position in which we must set ourselves apart from the rest of the student body, if we wish to observe these major Holidays.

Bowdoin's claims to diversity suffer in the light of this vote. It is inconsistent with a desire to attract students who "... represent a culture, region, or background that will contribute to the diversity of the college."(Governing Board statement, January, 1976).

We hope this clarifies the nature of our concern, and that further consideration will reflect a better understanding of our feelings on your part.

Sincerely,

Members of the
Bowdoin Jewish Organization

Despite Bowdoin College's greater sensitivity to the needs of its Jewish students, the members of the Bowdoin Jewish Organization felt compelled to write this letter when Bowdoin professors continued to give exams on the Jewish High Holidays. The letter is undated, but was obviously written in the pre-computer era. (Courtesy of the George J. Mitchell Department of Special Collections and Archives, Bowdoin College Library, Brunswick.)

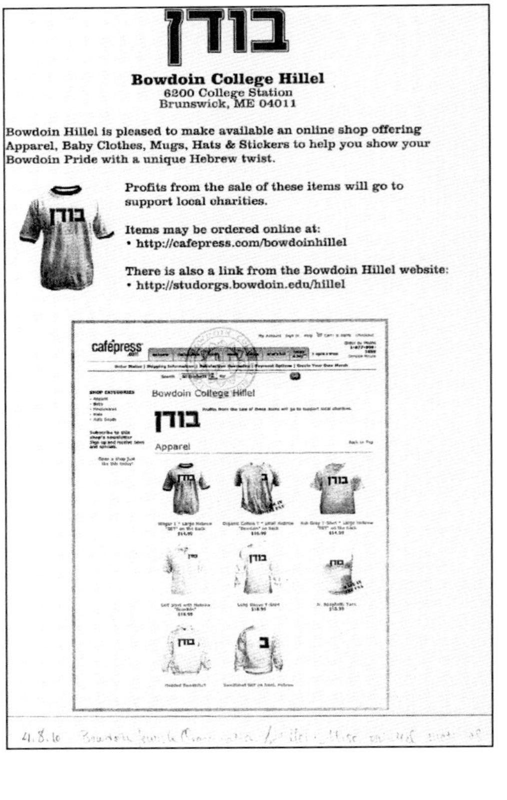

בודן

Bowdoin College Hillel
6200 College Station
Brunswick, ME 04011

Bowdoin Hillel is pleased to make available an online shop offering Apparel, Baby Clothes, Mugs, Hats & Stickers to help you show your Bowdoin Pride with a unique Hebrew twist.

Profits from the sale of these items will go to support local charities.

Items may be ordered online at:
- http://cafepress.com/bowdoinhillel

There is also a link from the Bowdoin Hillel website:
- http://studorgs.bowdoin.edu/hillel

In 2005, the Bowdoin College Hillel organization gave its pride in the college a Hebrew twist. (Courtesy of the George J. Mitchell Department of Special Collections and Archives, Bowdoin College Library, Brunswick.)

Four

Jewish Organizations

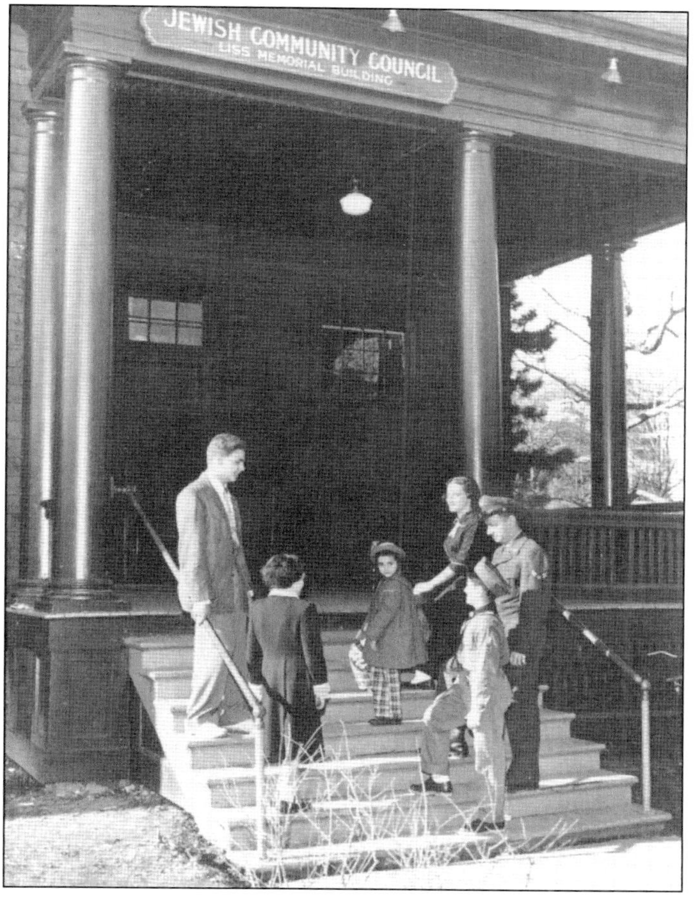

During the 1940s, many events were held to honor soldiers at the Jewish Community Council's Liss Memorial Building in Bangor. (Courtesy of the Bangor Public Library.)

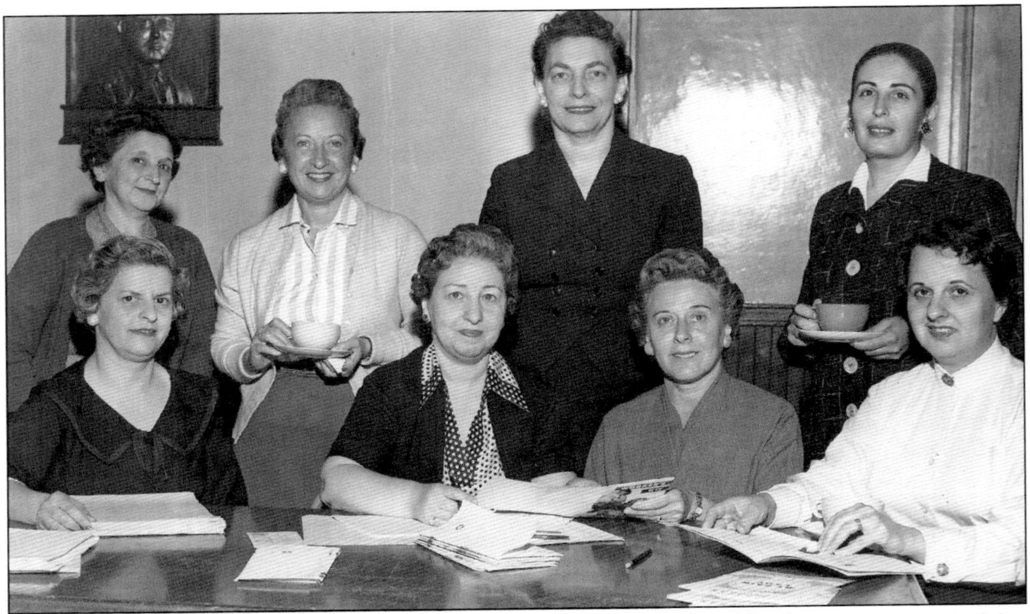

The Women's Division of the Bangor Jewish Community Center held a dinner meeting in May 1957. Among those pictured (not all could be identified) are Ida Rosen Fogelmann Gass, Pauline Rappaport, Betty Cooper Colton Kutov, Edna Rappaport, Bela Katz Gooden. (Courtesy of the Bangor Public Library.)

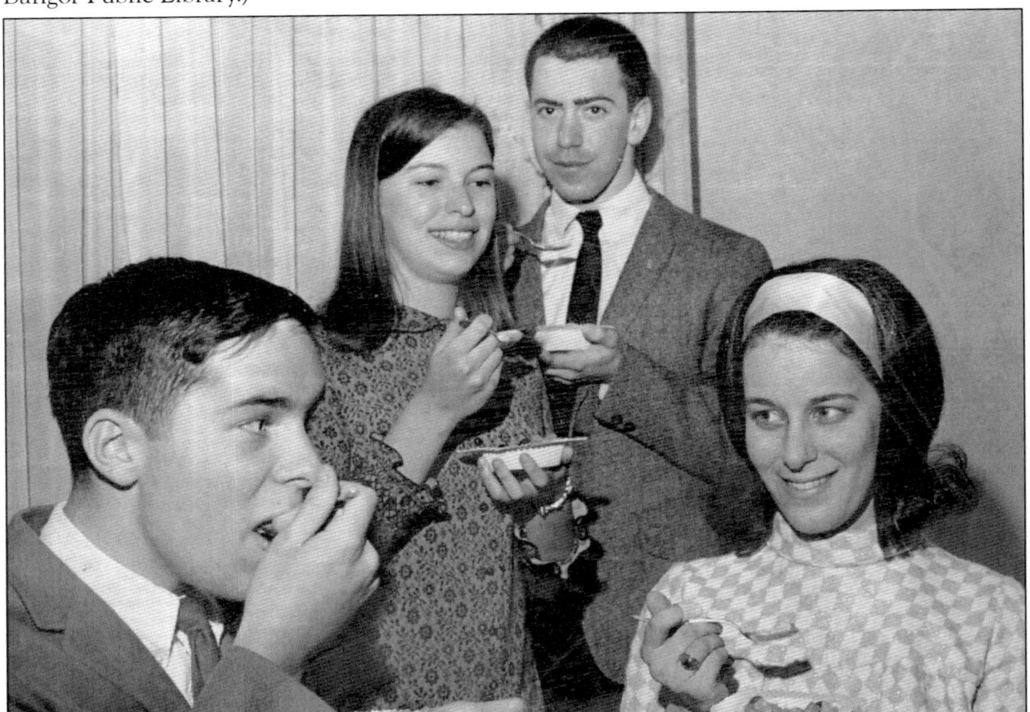

Here Bangor teenagers enjoy dessert at a Jewish Community event. (Courtesy of the Bangor Public Library.)

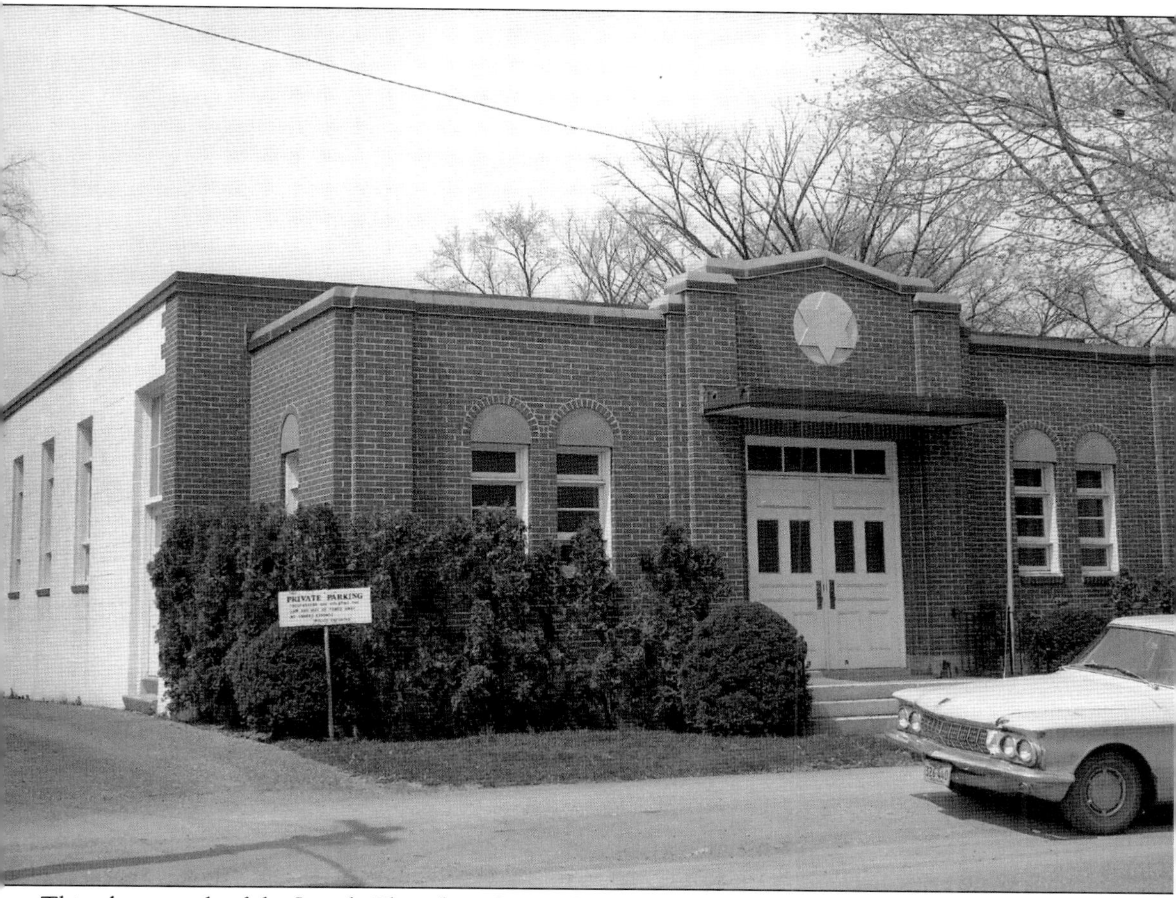

This photograph of the Jewish Chapel on Center Street in Bangor was taken in 1965. (Courtesy of the Bangor Public Library.)

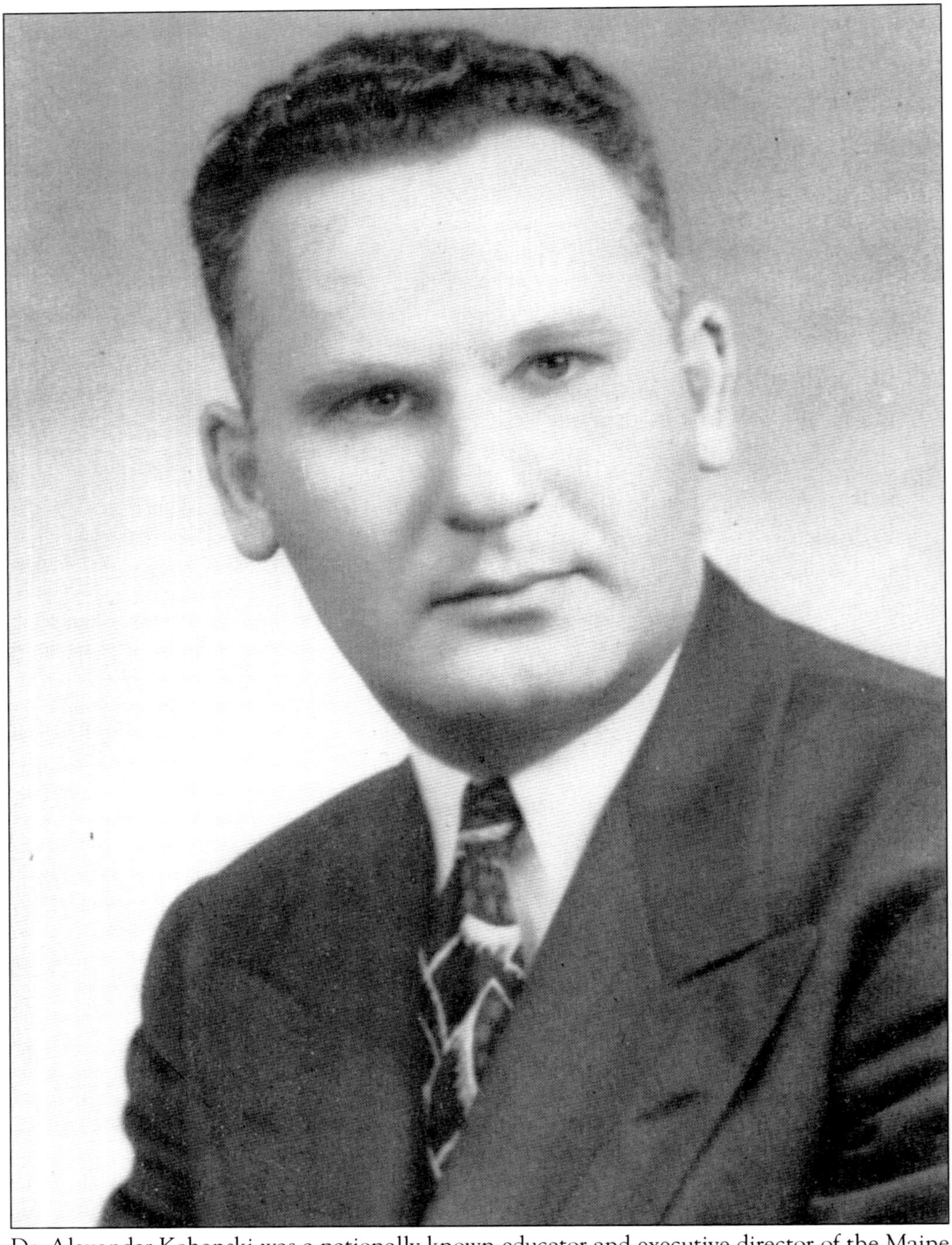

Dr. Alexander Kohanski was a nationally known educator and executive director of the Maine Jewish Council. (Courtesy of the Bangor Public Library.)

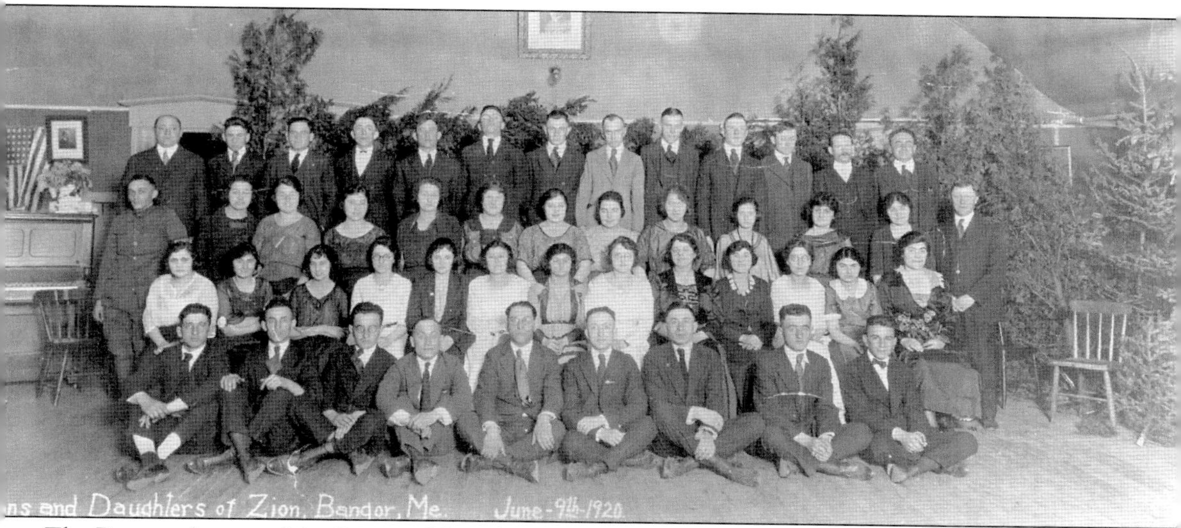

The Bangor chapter of the Sons and Daughters of Zion posed for this picture in 1920. (Courtesy of the Bangor Public Library.)

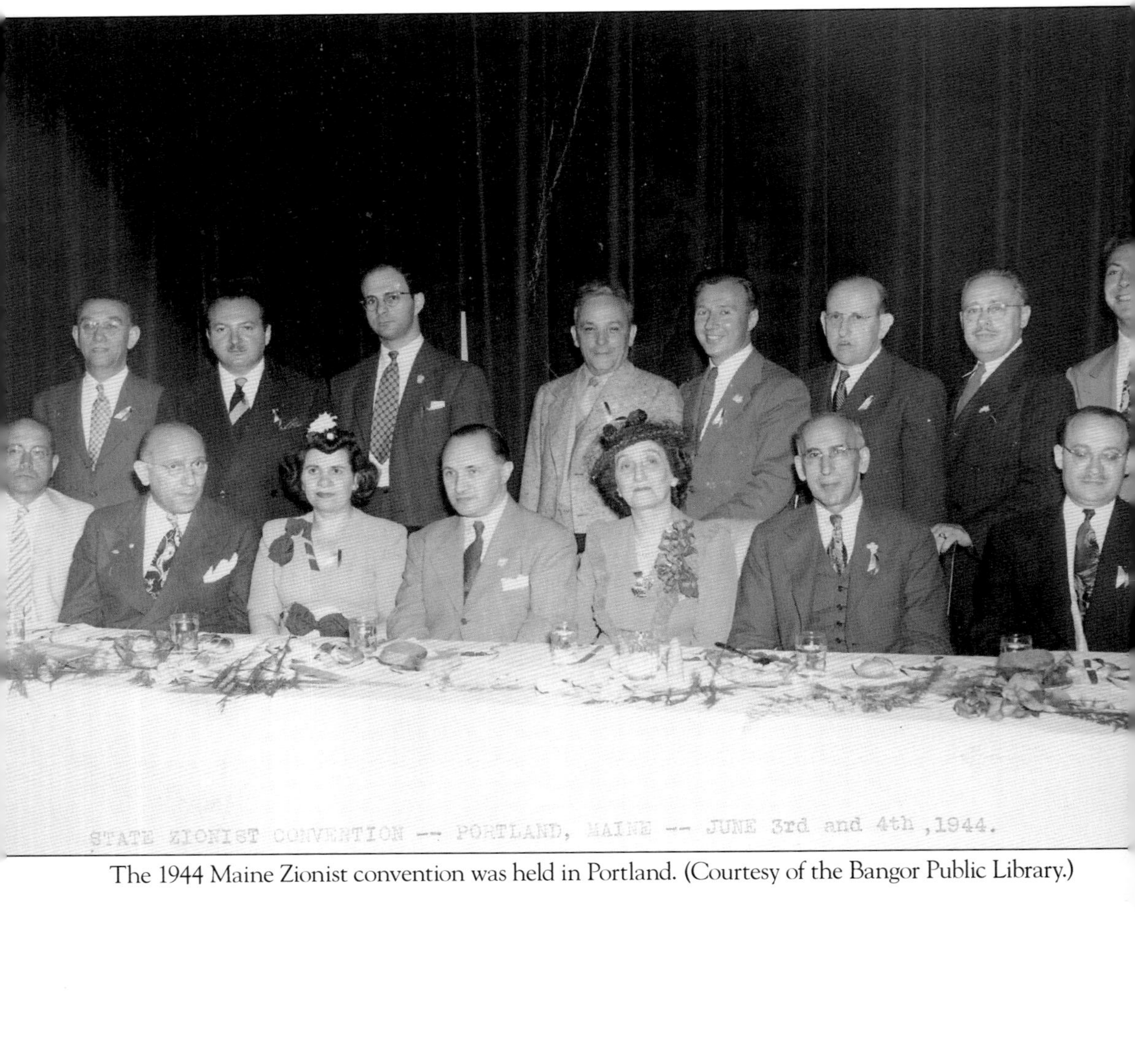

The 1944 Maine Zionist convention was held in Portland. (Courtesy of the Bangor Public Library.)

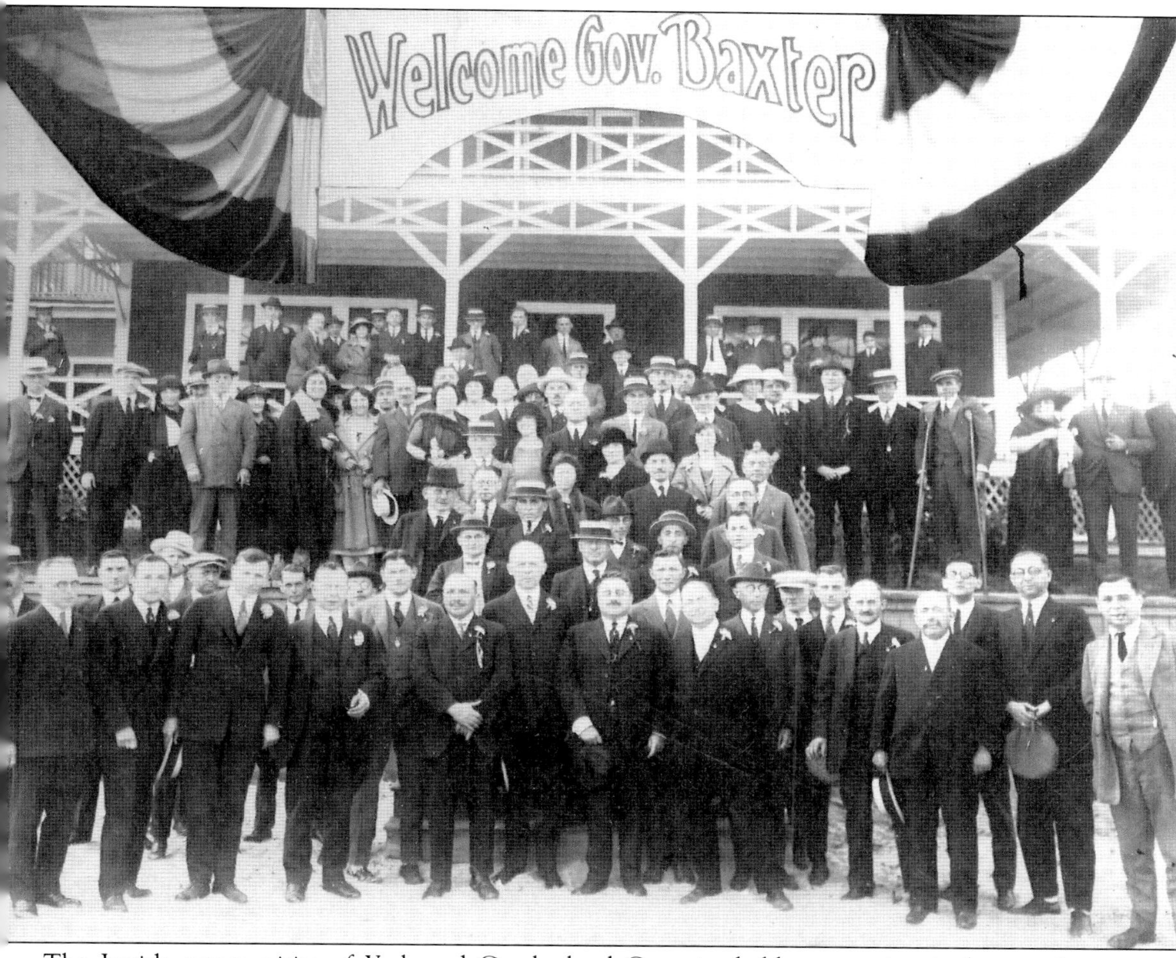

The Jewish communities of York and Cumberland Counties held a reception in honor of Gov. Percival Baxter in September 1922 at the Lafayette Hotel in Old Orchard Beach. (Courtesy of Harold "Babe" Goodkowsky, Old Orchard Beach.)

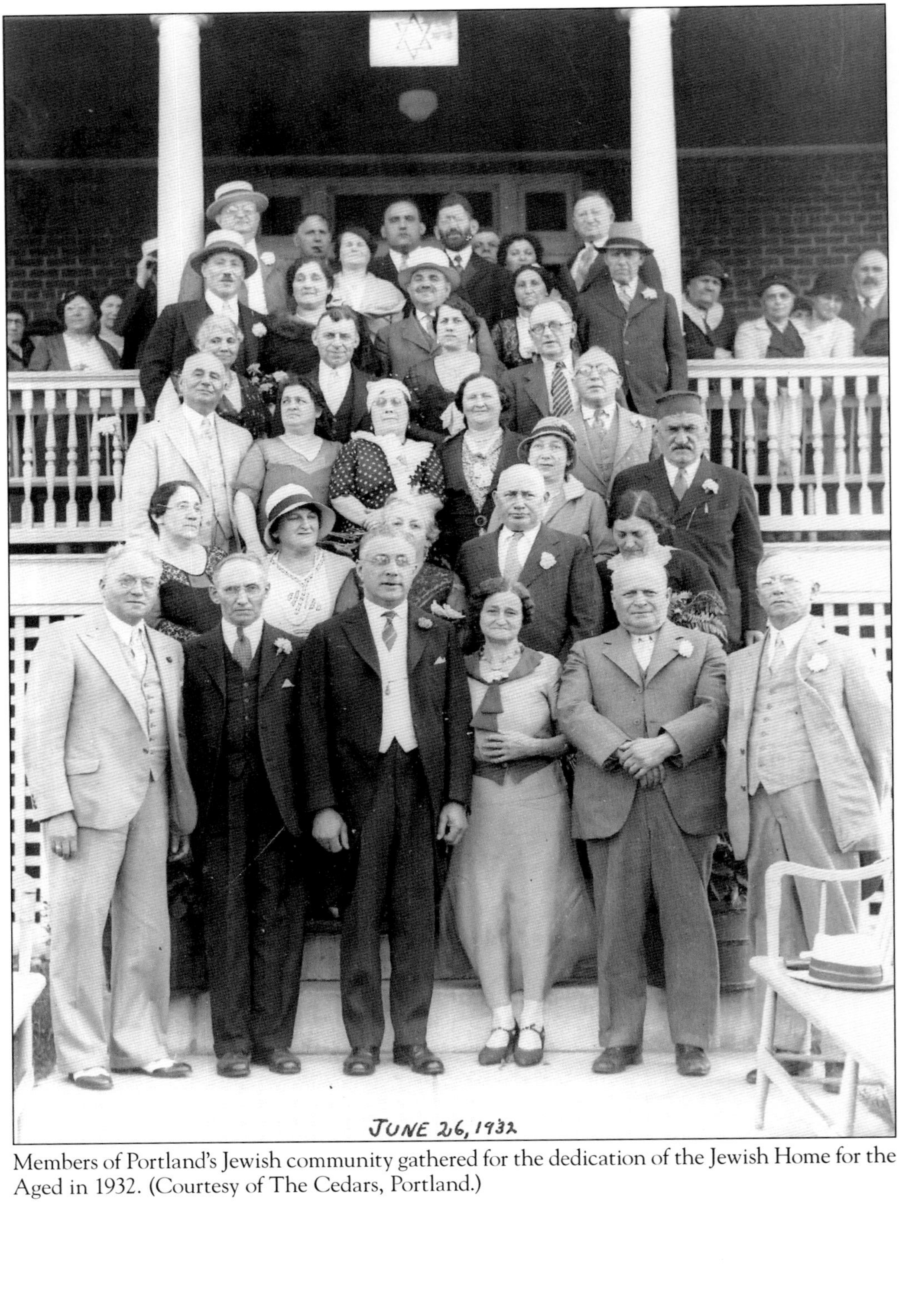

Members of Portland's Jewish community gathered for the dedication of the Jewish Home for the Aged in 1932. (Courtesy of The Cedars, Portland.)

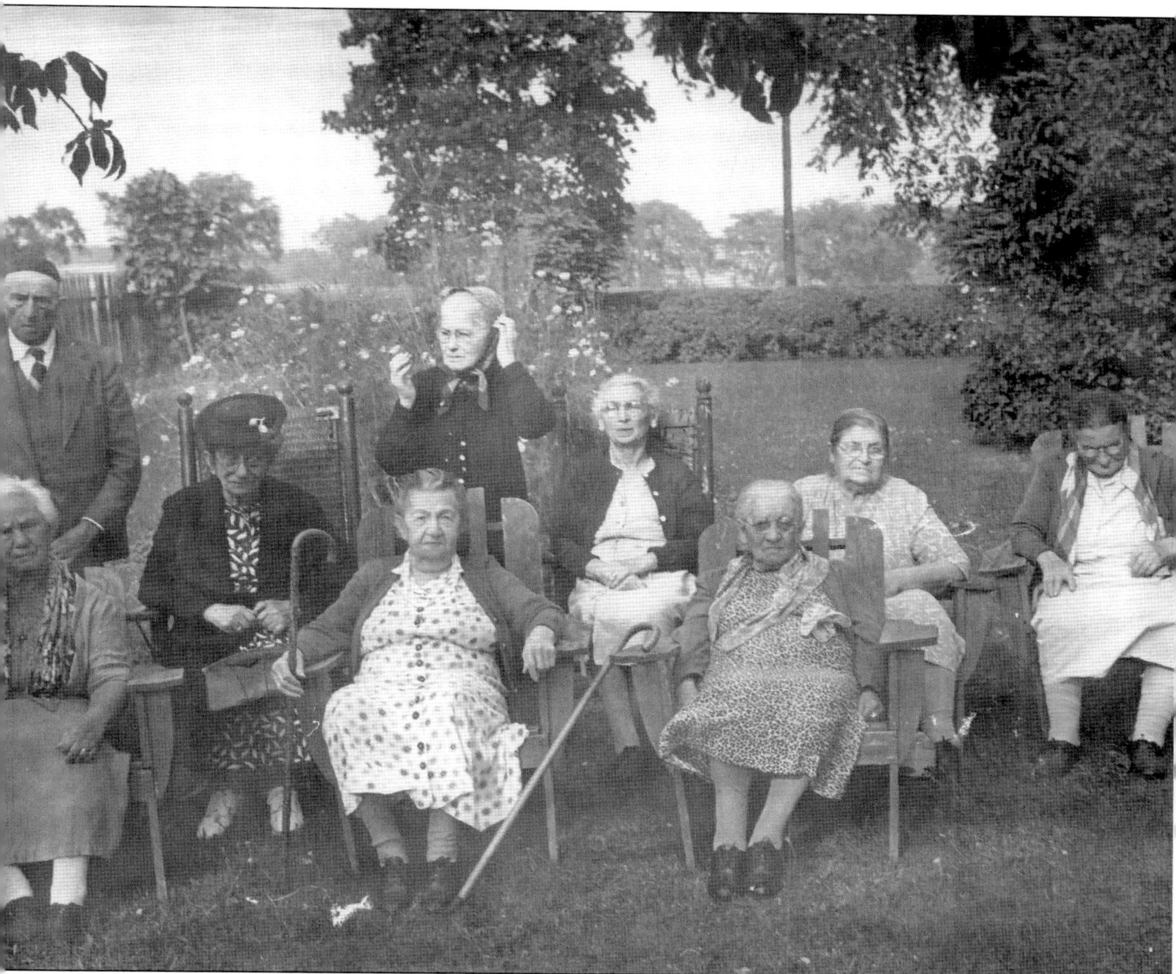

Residents at the Jewish Home for the Aged on Munjoy Hill enjoy the fresh air. (Courtesy of The Cedars, Portland.)

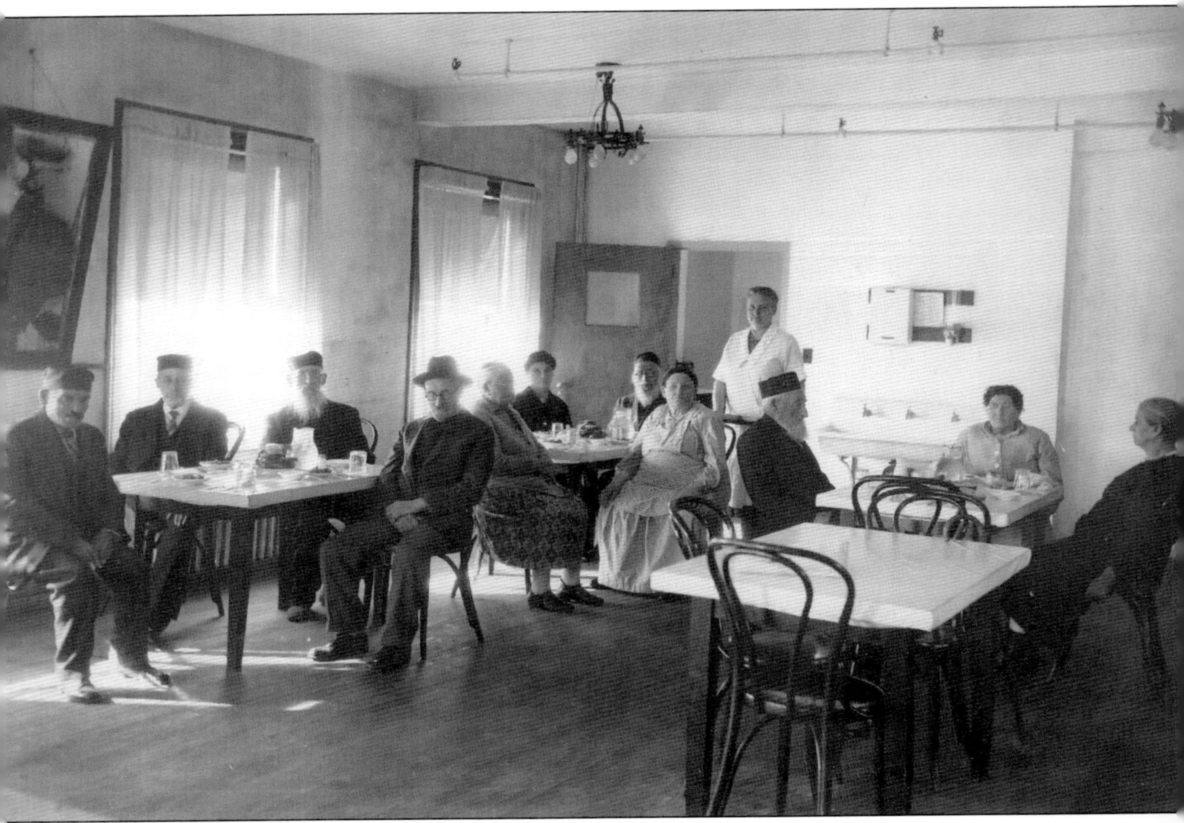

The Jewish Home for the Aged cared for men and women without families to look after them. It did not offer nursing care until the early 1960s. (Courtesy of The Cedars, Portland.)

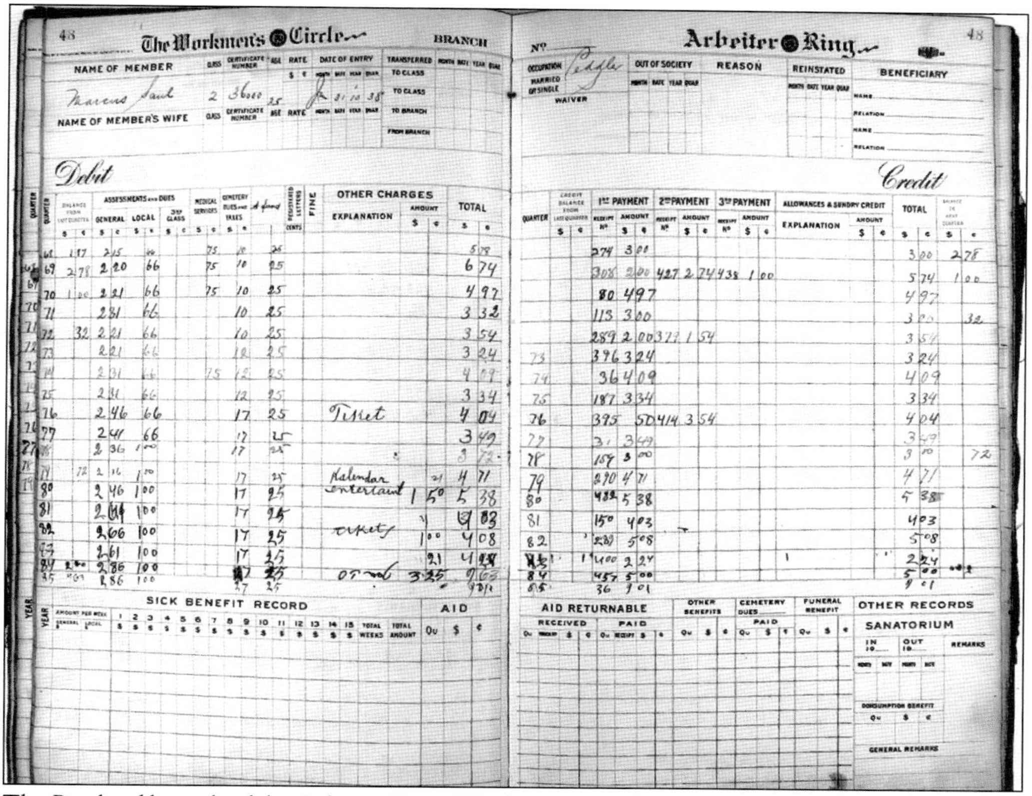

The Portland branch of the Arbeiter Ring (Workman's Circle) kept this ledger in 1910. (Courtesy of the Sampson Center for Diversity, University of Southern Maine.)

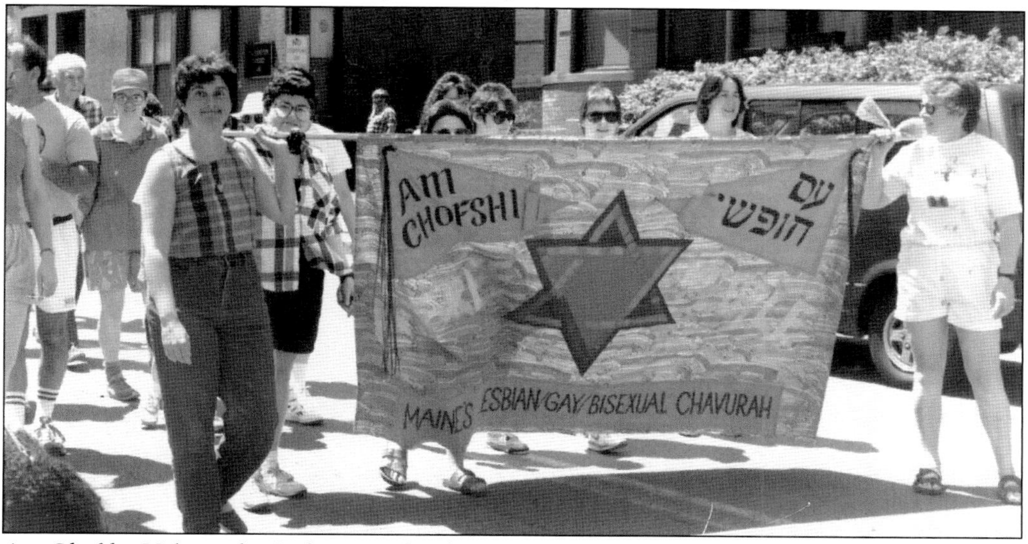

Am Chofshi, Hebrew for "a free people," began in 1989 as a kind of *Chavurah* (community of friends), and soon began holding its own Passover seders and related Jewish community events. It ceased to exist as an organization in 1998 as its gay, lesbian, bisexual, and transgender members found welcoming atmospheres in several Maine congregations.

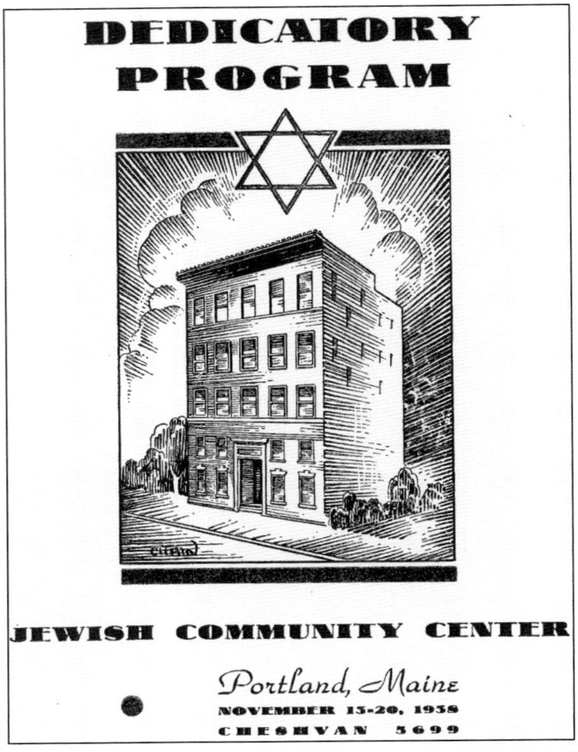

A dedication ceremony was held when the Portland Jewish Community Center (JCC) opened in 1938. (Courtesy of the Portland Jewish Community Alliance.)

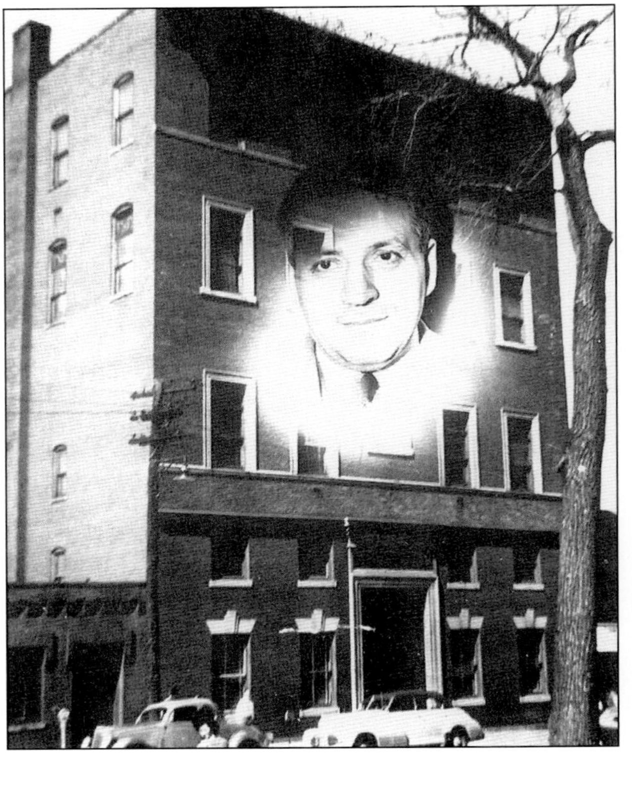

Vic Taylor was a long-time director of the Portland JCC during the middle decades of the 20th century. He knew the name of every member of the center who passed through its doors. (Courtesy of the Jewish Community Alliance, Portland.)

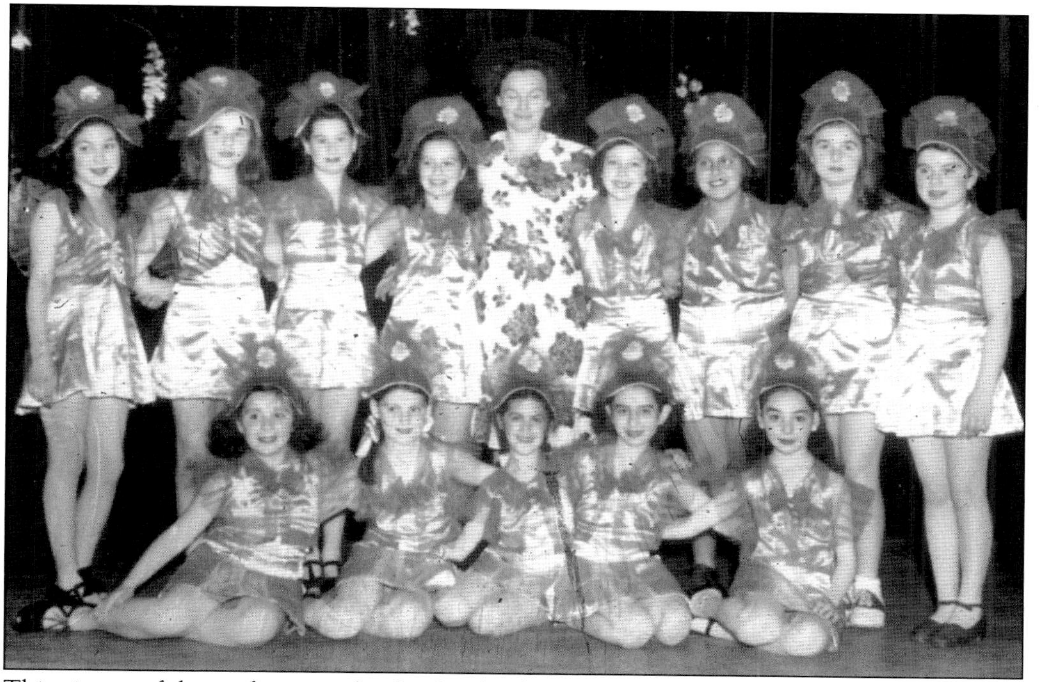

This picture of the performance by this Portland JCC dance troupe, probably in the late 1950s, was one of the many photographs in the collection of the late Dr. Henry Pollard. (Courtesy of Jocelyn Pollard and Jessica Lantos, Portland and Falmouth.)

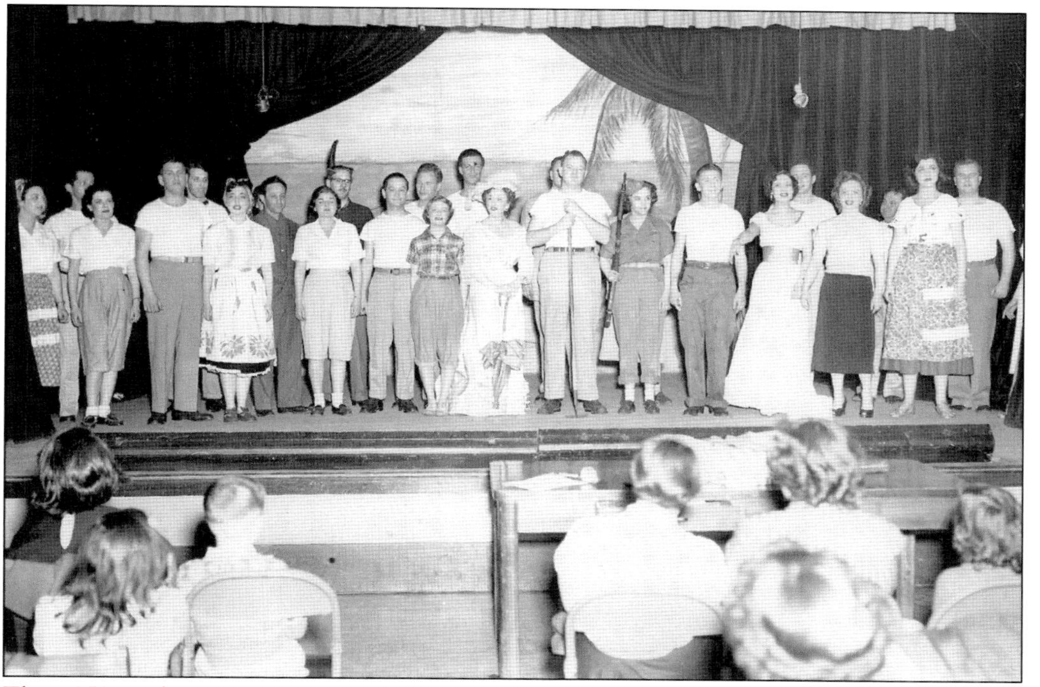

This 1950 production at Portland's JCC made the audience members wonder if they needed to travel to Broadway ever again. (Courtesy of Mark Stern, Portland.)

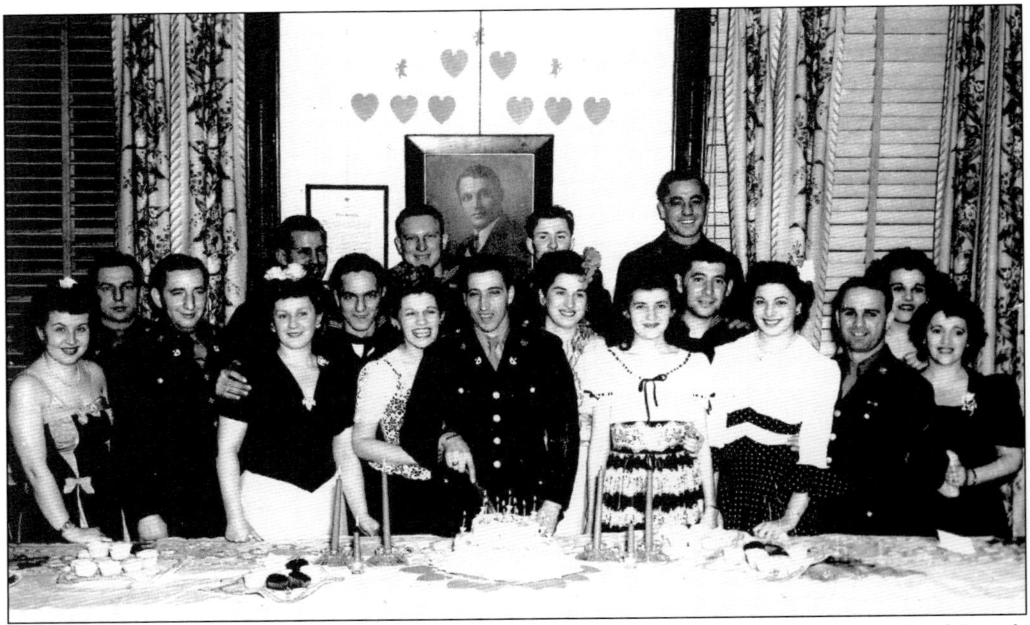

Mildred Glickman (first row, sixth from left) was a pioneer fund-raiser for the Portland Jewish community and a field director for the USO in World War II. Among the other women at the JCC party for the USO were Harriet Kroot Weisman, Gladys Potter, Ruth Karlin Finn, Dorothy Cohen, Ina Schatz Weissman, Annabelle Bornstein Mack, and Rae Modes Wolf. (Courtesy of Judith and Albert Glickman, Portland.)

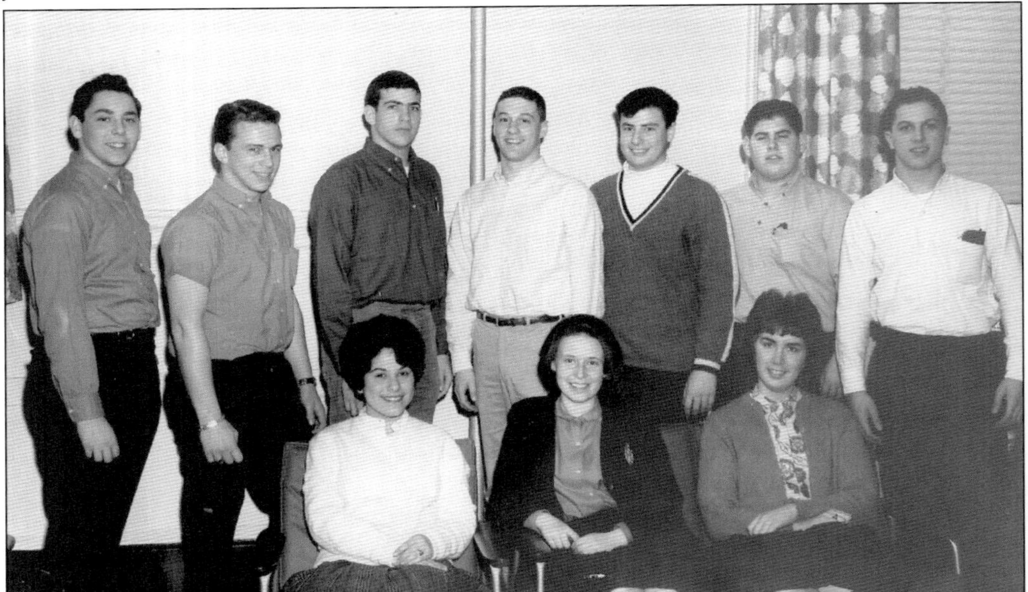

In 1962 or 1963, the Center Youth Organization of the JCC elected these officers, who are, from left to right, (first row) Leiba Pollack, Adele Schwartz, and Gail Zade; (second row) Dick Baker, Barry Glovsky, Richard Blumenthal, Eric Sacknoff, John Gerber, Larry Plavnick, and Steven Glovsky. (Courtesy of John and Sandy Gerber, Portland.)

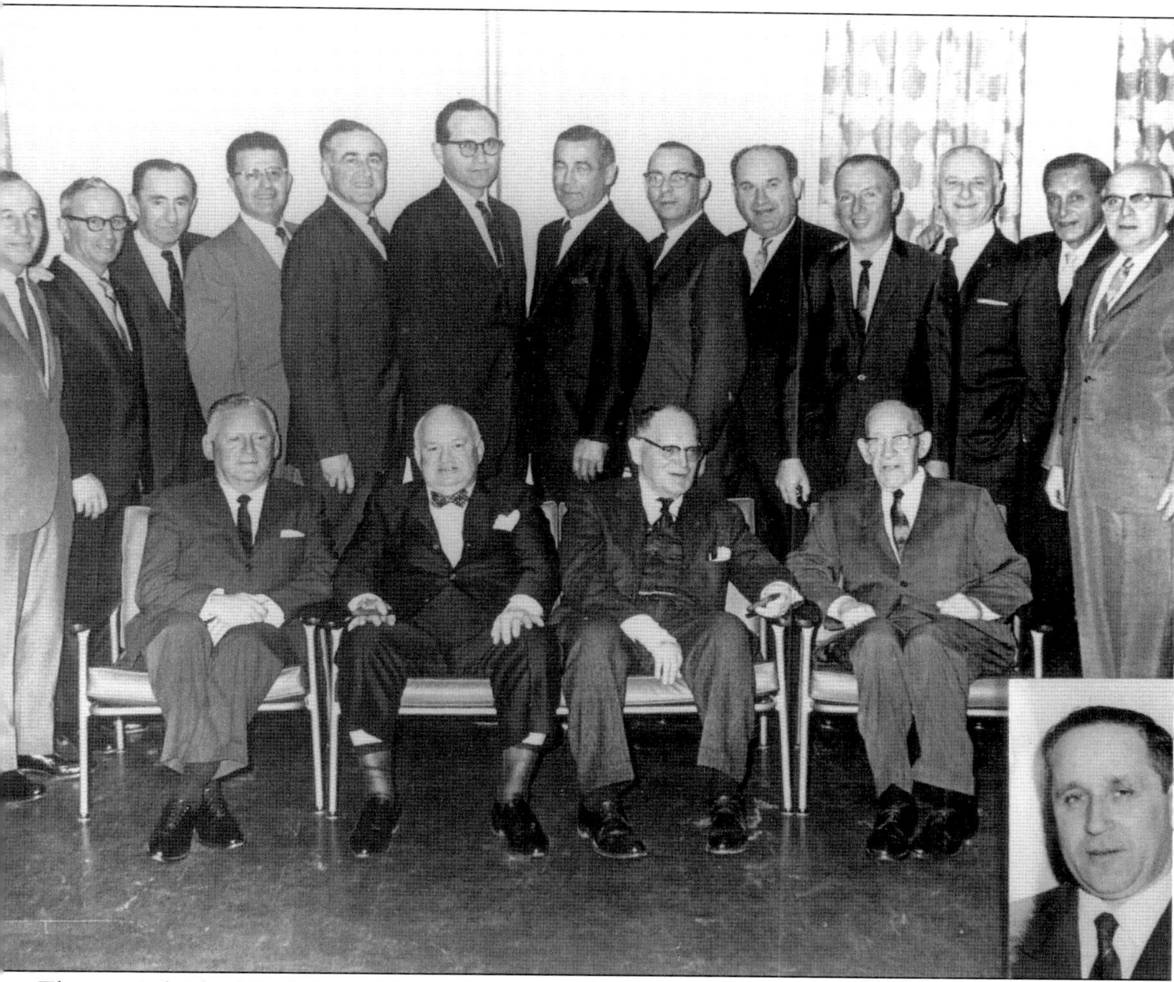

The men's leadership division of Jewish Federation who met at the JCC and posed for this photograph are, from left to right, (first row) Barney Shur, Sidney Davidson, Israel Bernstein, William Goodman, and (insert) George Lewis; (second row) Abie Elowitch, Yudi Elowitch, Jack Agger, Mel Stone, Irving Small, Sumner Bernstein, Bud Kane, Maury Cox, Harmon Hugo, Harold Nelson, Maury Drees, Judge Louis Bernstein, and William Cohen. (Courtesy of the Jewish Community Alliance, Portland.)

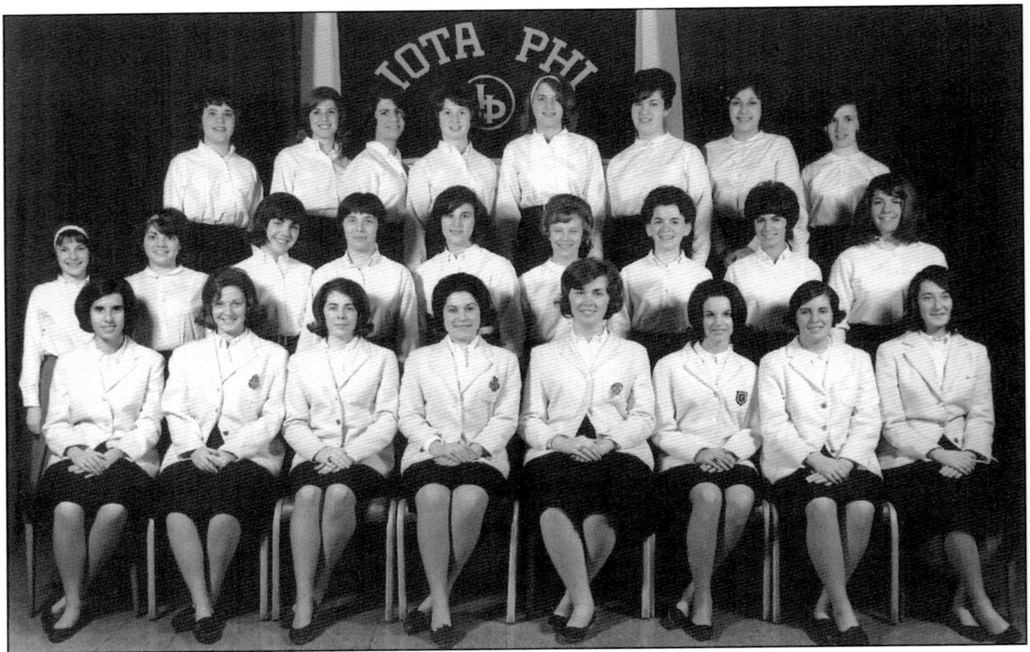

Portland had Jewish sororities, fraternities, and clubs for Jewish high school students, because they were not welcome into the non-Jewish fraternities or clubs at their high schools. This Iota Phi photograph was taken in 1964. (Courtesy of Sherrie Koocher Schatz, Portland.)

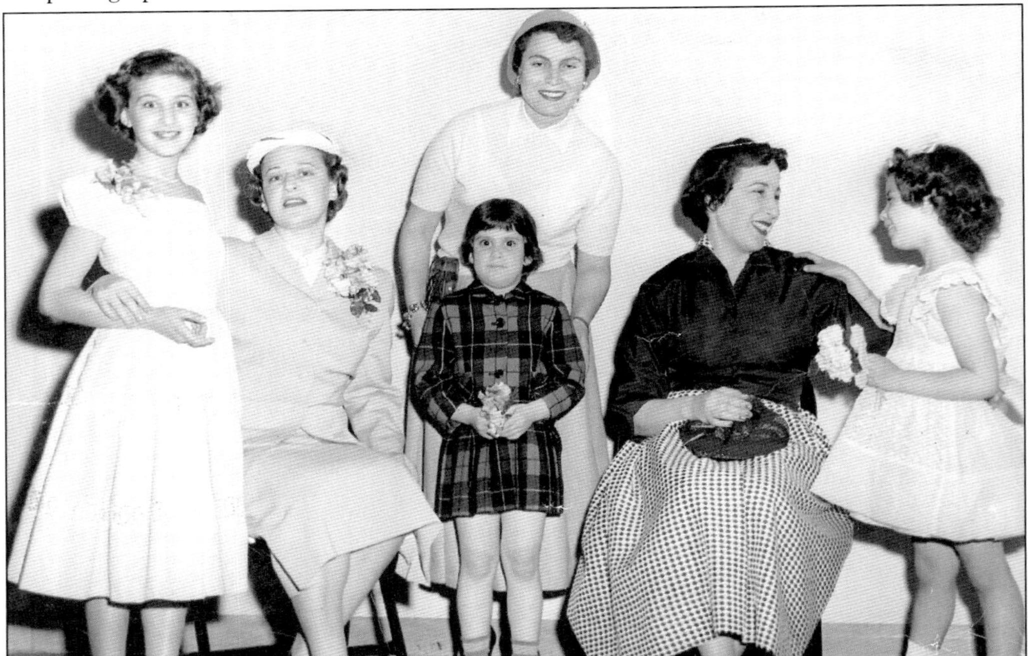

The Temple Beth El Sisterhood in Portland held an annual mother-daughter dinner. Taking part were, from left to right, Cynthia Sacknoff and Eva Sacknoff; Jacqueline Potter and Selma Potter; and Miriam Marcus and Jean Marcus. (Courtesy of Jean M. Peck, Portland.)

Five

OFF TO CAMP

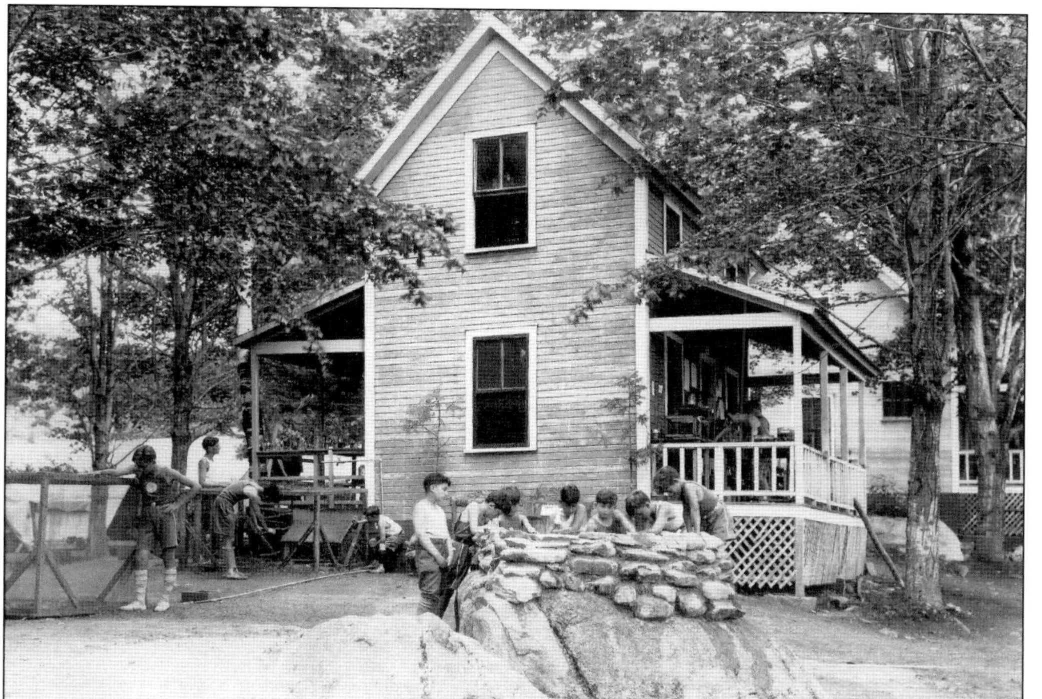

Camp Modin was established in 1922 in the Belgrade Lakes district. It is the oldest Jewish camp in New England. (Courtesy of Camp Modin, Belgrade Lakes.)

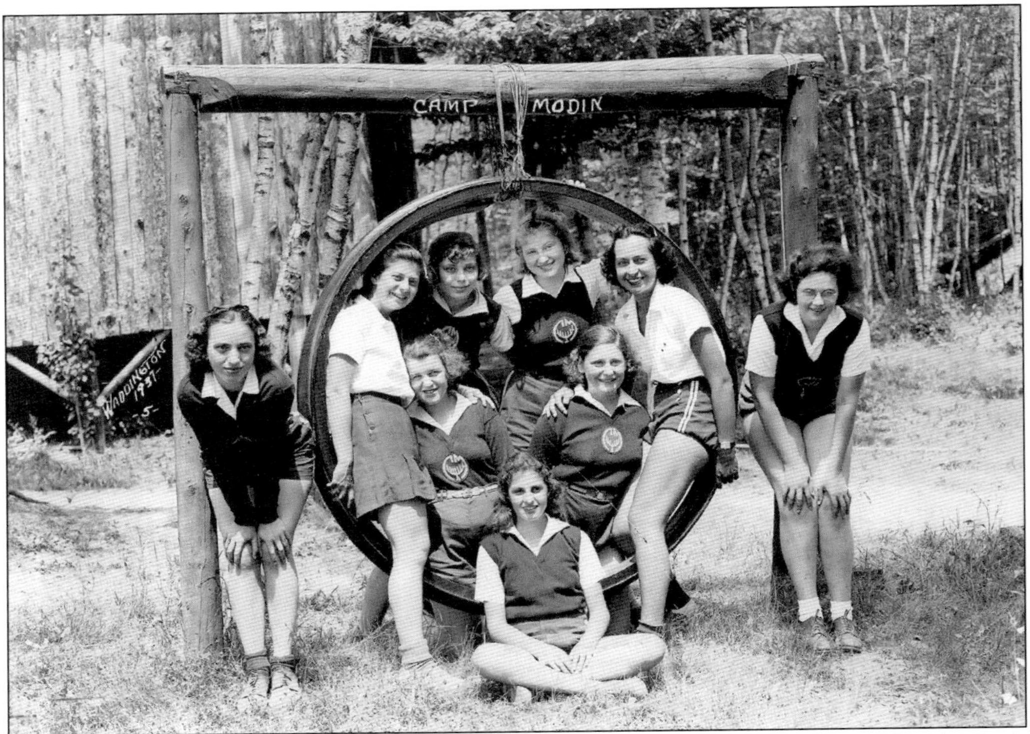

The Camp Modin girls, in an undated picture, came from all over the country for the fresh Maine air. (Courtesy of Camp Modin, Belgrade Lakes.)

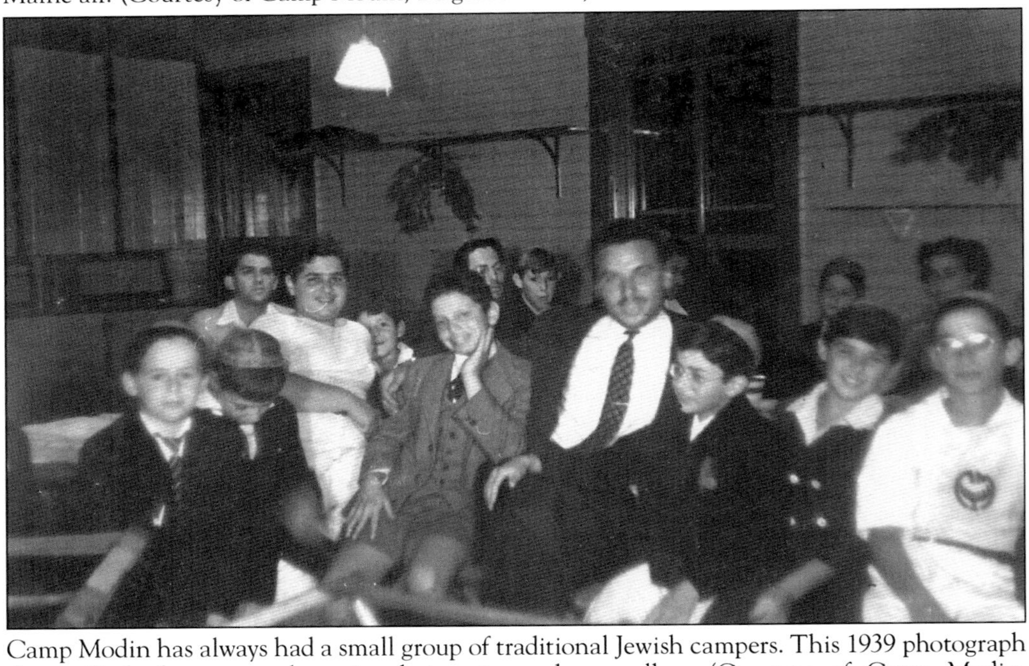

Camp Modin has always had a small group of traditional Jewish campers. This 1939 photograph shows Orthodox young boys in their suits and yarmulkes. (Courtesy of Camp Modin, Belgrade Lakes.)

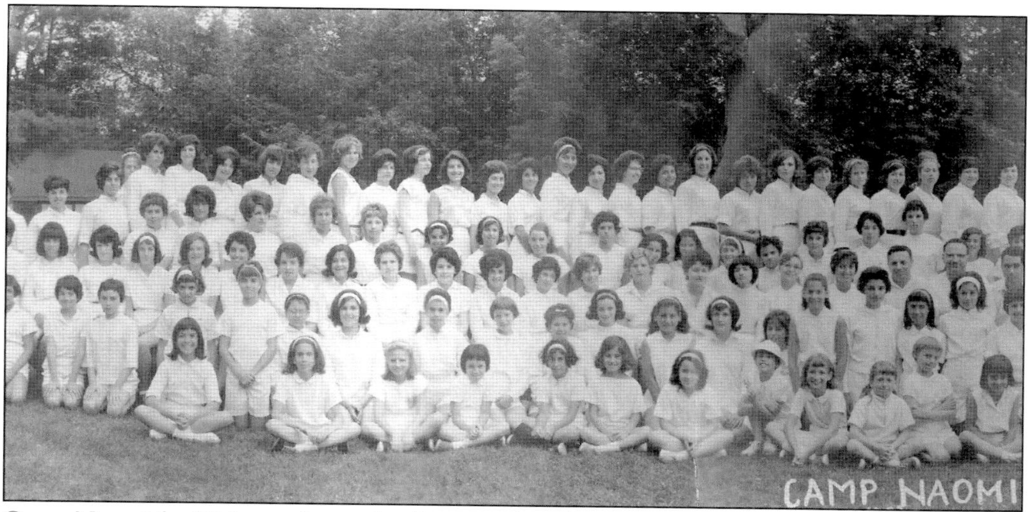

Camp Naomi for Girls was located in Raymond; its brother camp, Camp Joseph was on a lake in nearby Harrison. Both camps were operated by the Jewish Welfare Board of Boston. Camp Naomi closed in 1985. (Courtesy of Jean M. Peck, Portland.)

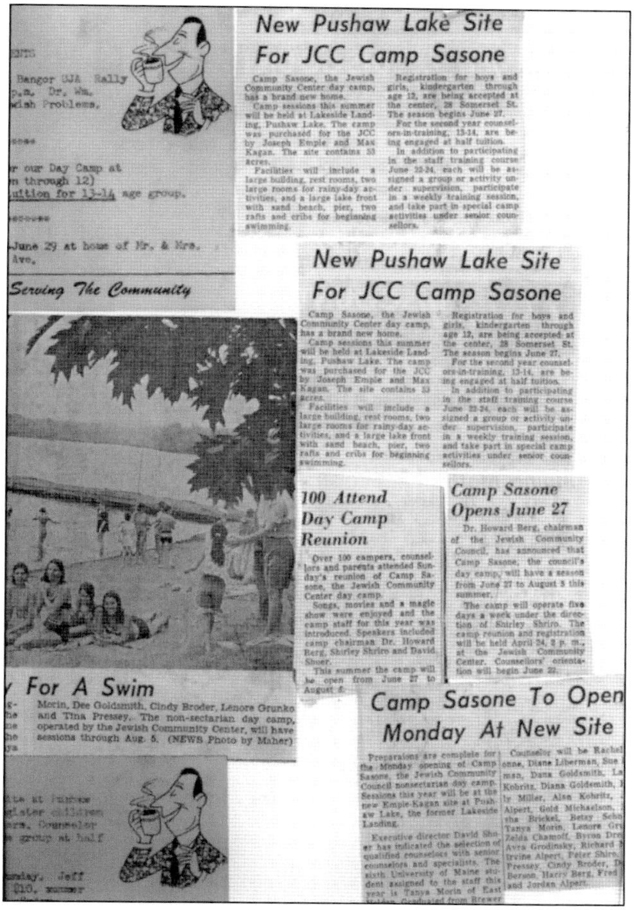

New Pushaw Lake Site For JCC Camp Sasone

Camp Sasone, the Jewish Community Center day camp, has a brand new home.

Camp sessions this summer will be held at Lakeside Landing, Pushaw Lake. The camp was purchased for the JCC by Joseph Emple and Max Kagan. The site contains 53 acres.

Facilities will include a large building, rest rooms, two large rooms for rainy-day activities, and a large lake front with sand beach, pier, two rafts and cribs for beginning swimming.

Registration for boys and girls, kindergarten through age 12, are being accepted at the center, 28 Somerset St. The season begins June 27.

For the second year counselors-in-training, 13-14, are being engaged at half tuition.

In addition to participating in the staff training course June 22-24, each will be assigned a group or activity under supervision, participate in a weekly training session, and take part in special camp activities under senior counsellors.

Serving The Community

New Pushaw Lake Site For JCC Camp Sasone

Camp Sasone, the Jewish Community Center day camp, has a brand new home.

Camp sessions this summer will be held at Lakeside Landing, Pushaw Lake. The camp was purchased for the JCC by Joseph Emple and Max Kagan. The site contains 53 acres.

Facilities will include a large building, rest rooms, two large rooms for rainy-day activities, and a large lake front with sand beach, pier, two rafts and cribs for beginning swimming.

Registration for boys and girls, kindergarten through age 12, are being accepted at the center, 28 Somerset St. The season begins June 27.

For the second year counselors-in-training, 13-14, are being engaged at half tuition.

In addition to participating in the staff training course June 22-24, each will be assigned a group or activity under supervision, participate in a weekly training session, and take part in special camp activities under senior counsellors.

100 Attend Day Camp Reunion

Over 100 campers, counsellors and parents attended Sunday's reunion of Camp Sasone, the Jewish Community Center day camp.

Songs, movies and a magic show were enjoyed and the camp staff for this year was introduced. Speakers included camp chairman Dr. Howard Berg, Shirley Shiro and David Shoer.

This summer the camp will be open from June 27 to August 5.

Camp Sasone Opens June 27

Dr. Howard Berg, chairman of the Jewish Community Council, has announced that Camp Sasone, the council's day camp, will have a season from June 27 to August 5 this summer.

The camp will operate five days a week under the direction of Shirley Shiro. The camp reunion and registration will be held April 24, 2 p. m., at the Jewish Community Center. Counsellors' orientation will begin June 22.

... For A Swim

Morin, Dee Goldsmith, Cindy Broder, Lenore Grunko and Tina Pressey. The non-sectarian day camp, operated by the Jewish Community Center, will have sessions through Aug. 5. (NEWS Photo by Maher)

Camp Sasone To Open Monday At New Site

Preparations are complete for the Monday opening of Camp Sasone, the Jewish Community Council nonsectarian day camp. Sessions this year will be at the new Emple-Kagan site at Pushaw Lake, the former Lakeside Landing.

Executive director David Shoer has indicated the selection of qualified counselors with senior counselors and specialists. The sixth University of Maine student assigned to the staff this year is Tanya Morin of East ...

Counselor will be Rachel ... onne, Diane Liberman, Sue ... man, Dana Goldsmith, La... Kobritz, Diana Goldsmith, ... ly Miller, Alan Kobritz, ... Alpert, Gold Michaelson, ... tha Brickel, Betsy Sch... Tanya Morin, Lenore Gr... Zelda Chamoff, Byron Dr... Avra Grodinsky, Richard ... Irvine Alpert, Peter Shiro, ... Pressey, Cindy Broder, D... Berson, Harry Berg, Fred ... and Jordan Alpert.

Camp Sasone was the Bangor Community Center's day camp. (Courtesy of the Bangor Public Library.)

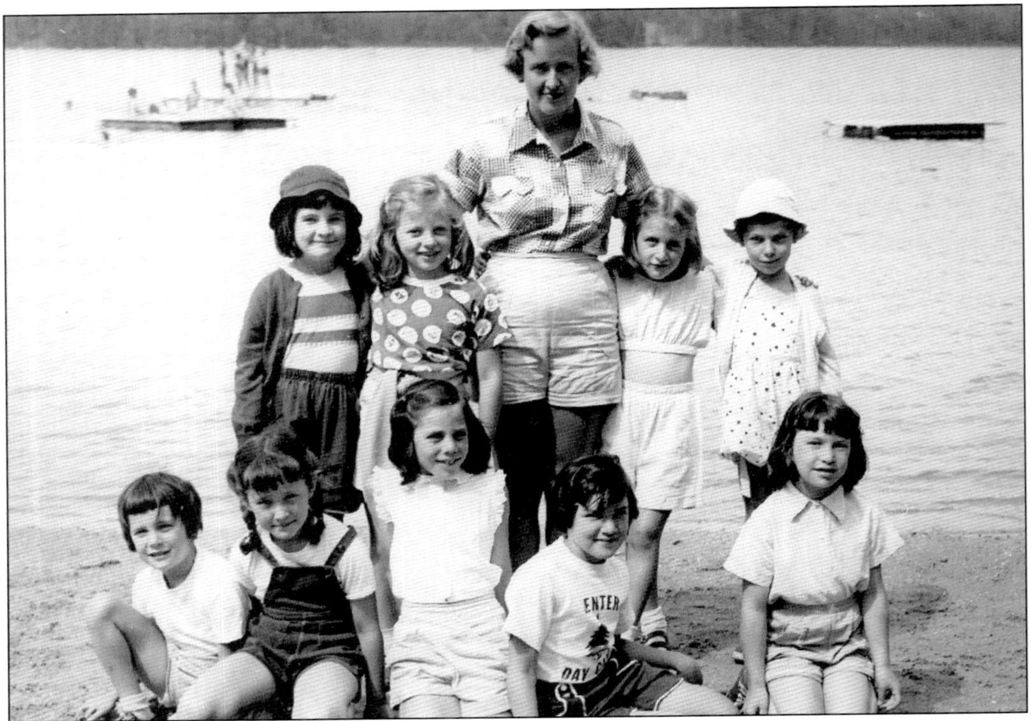

Center Day Camp (CDC) is located on Sebago Lake. In this 1953 or 1954 picture are, from left to right, (first row) Janet Shur, Ellen Lerman, Sandy Burokoff, Nancy Ross, and Sherry Ginsburg; (second row) Lois Fineberg, Dorothy Stern, unidentified, Sharon Taylor, and Ellen Rudek. (Courtesy of Sandy Burokoff Gerber.)

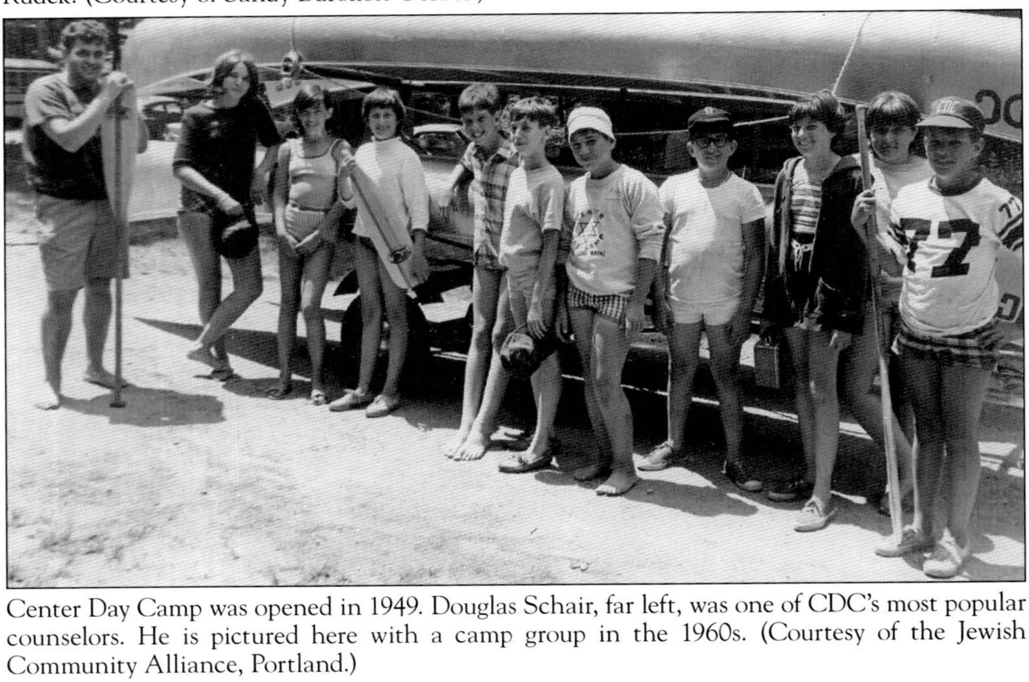

Center Day Camp was opened in 1949. Douglas Schair, far left, was one of CDC's most popular counselors. He is pictured here with a camp group in the 1960s. (Courtesy of the Jewish Community Alliance, Portland.)

Six

Friends and Family

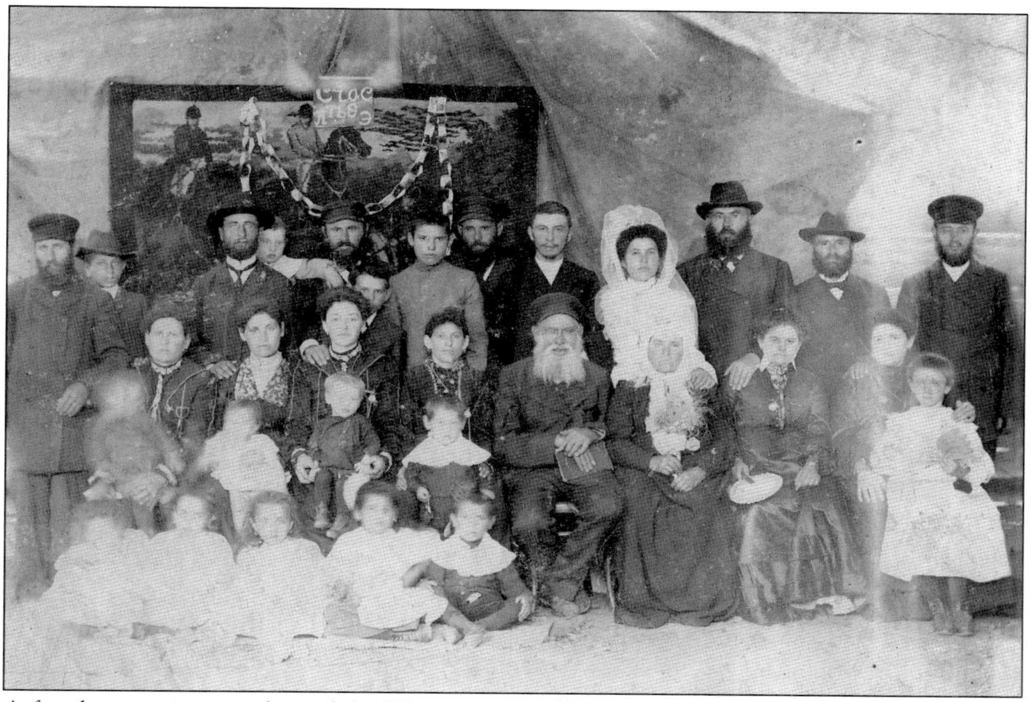

A family portrait was taken of the Weinstein, Coolberg, and Wishnetski families of Rorbakh, Ukraine. One of the girls in the front row was the matriarch of Portland's Gerber family. (Courtesy of John Gerber, Portland.)

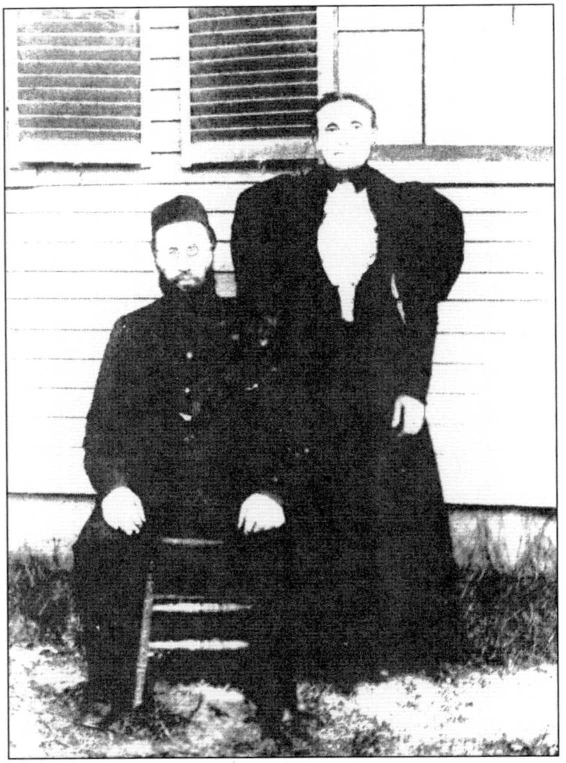

Nathan and Rose Cohen were prominent citizens of Bangor. (Courtesy of the Bangor Public Library.)

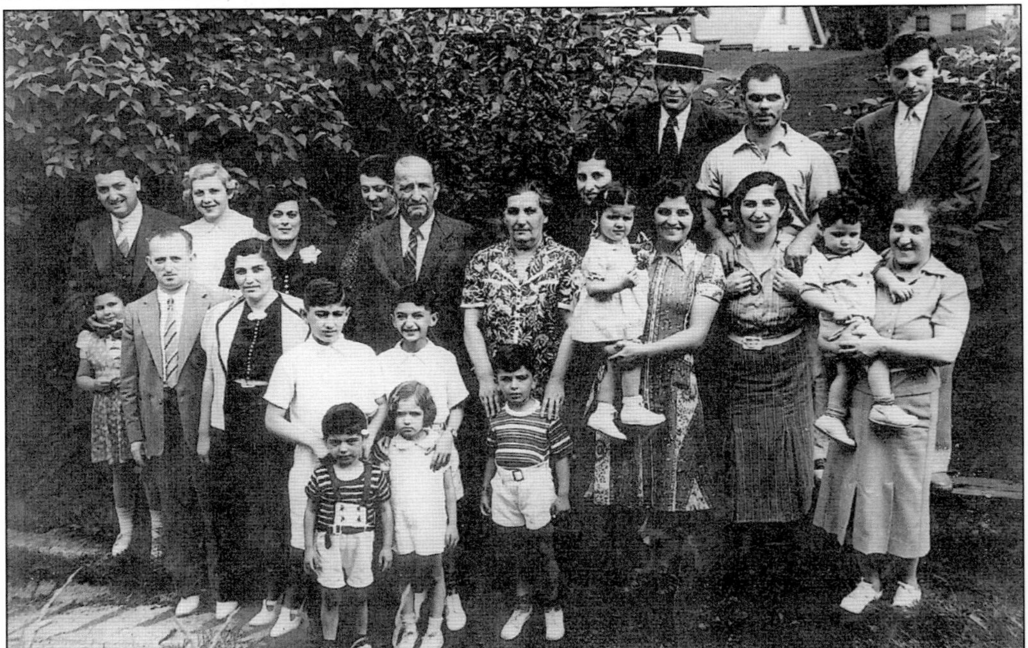

The Share, Miller, Striar, Hartstone, and Seiden families pose on Bangor's Pine Street for this 1938 photograph. (Courtesy Bangor Public Library).

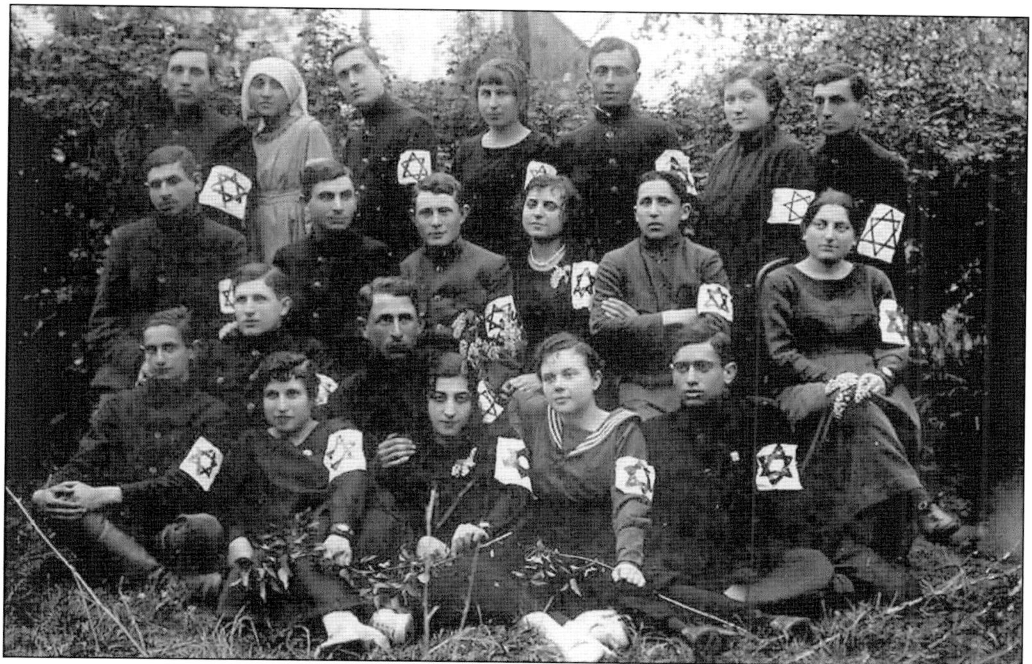

Before George Lewis (second row, fifth from the left) immigrated to Portland in 1922, he was a Zionist in Kossovo, Poland. (Courtesy of David Lewis and Peter Lewis, Portland.)

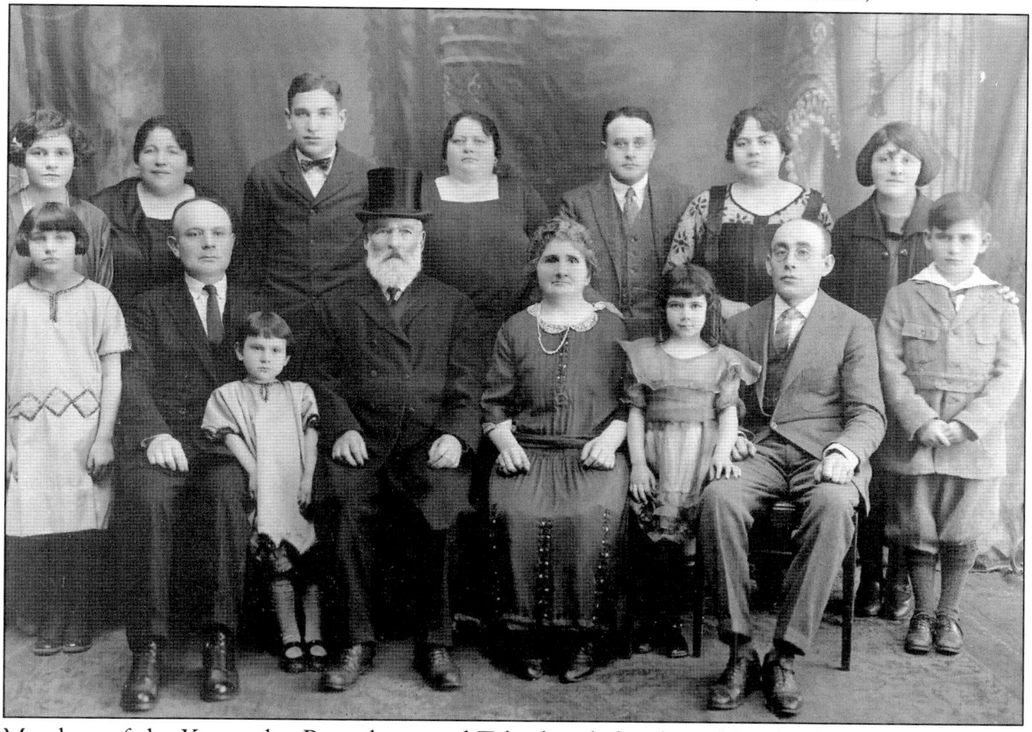

Members of the Kornetsky, Rosenberg, and Tabachnick families of Portland sit for this picture during the early years of the 20th century. (Courtesy of Karen Kornetsky Levine.)

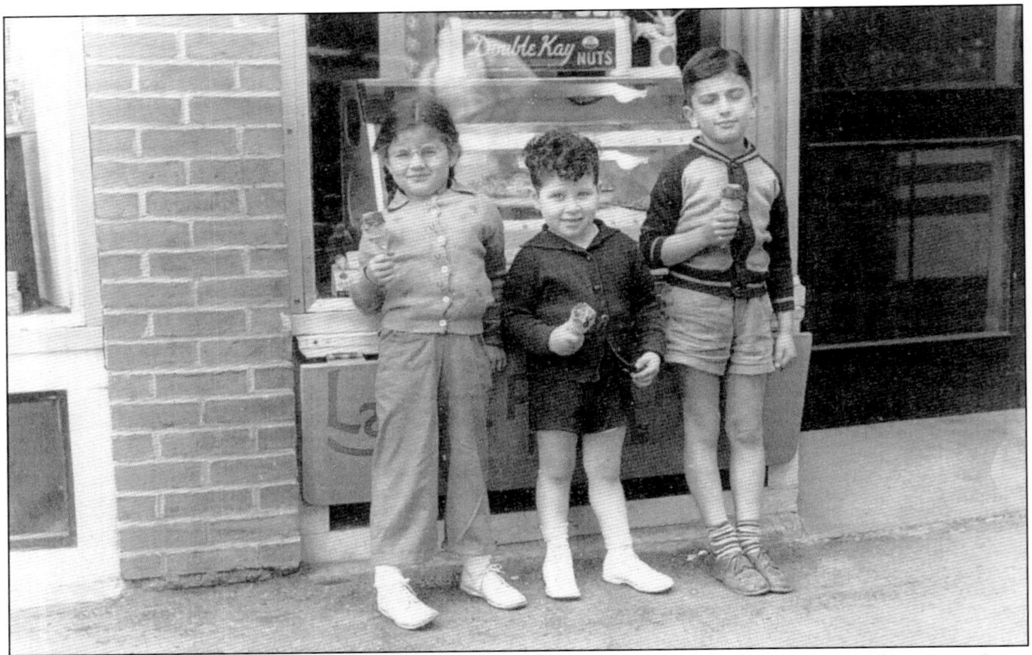

Three Bangor children pose with ice cream in front of Miller's Variety Store. Seen here are, from left to right, Naita "Sybil" Miller, Robert Miller, and Bernard Miller. (Courtesy of the Bangor Public Library.)

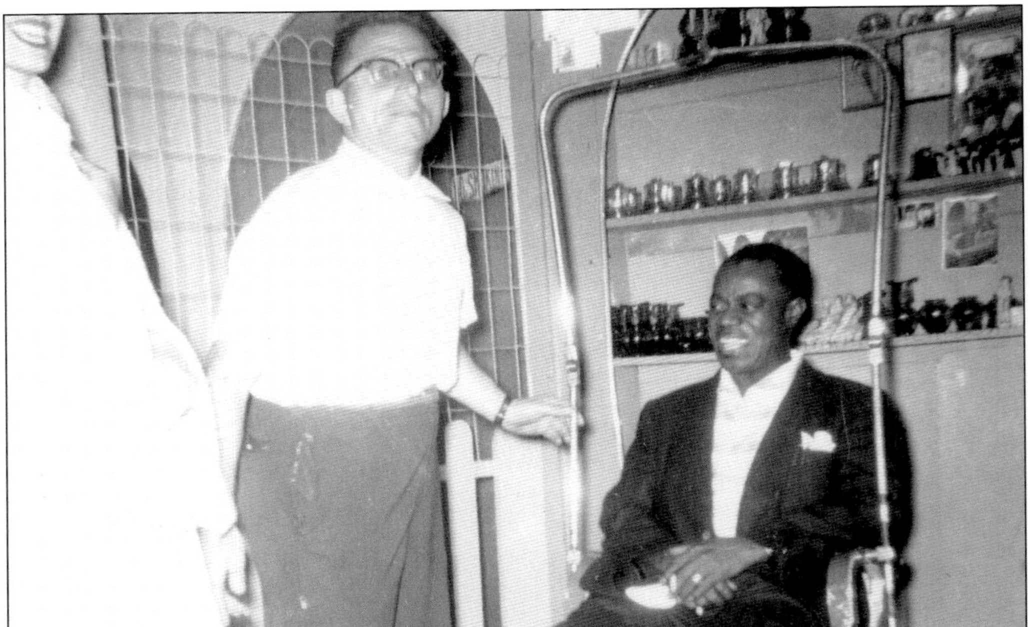

Dave "the Guesser" Glovsky guesses Louis Armstrong's weight during a break from one of "Satchmo's" musical performances at the Old Orchard Beach pier. For years, Glovsky was a fixture at the Old Orchard Beach amusement park, guessing the weight and age of his customers. (Courtesy of Adeline Glovsky Hale, California.)

Maurice Charles Miller, a well-known Maine guide and former boxer, helps train youngsters at the Pine Tree Camp for Crippled Children in Rome, Maine. (Courtesy of the Bangor Public Library.)

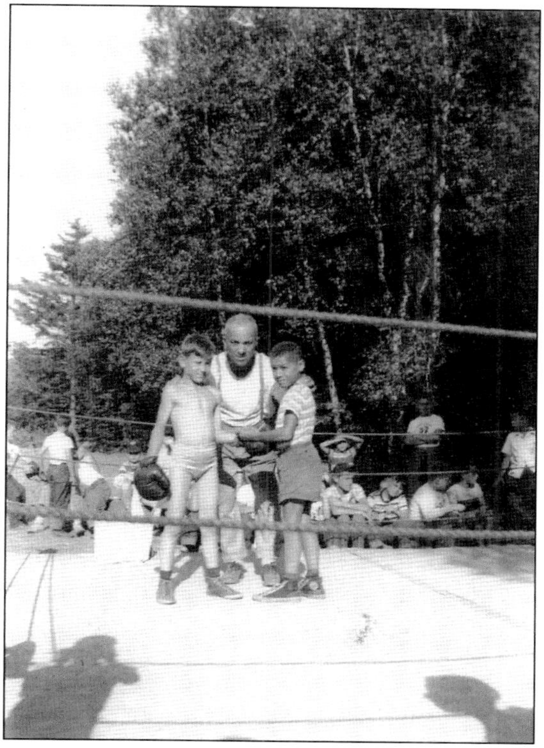

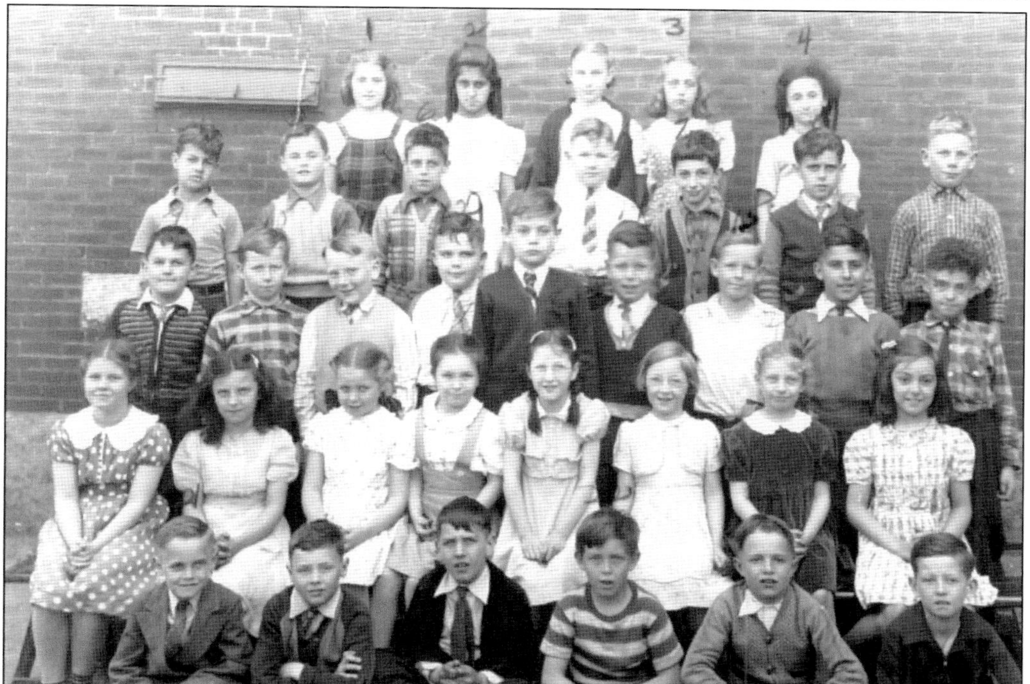

In Portland's Monument School's 1941 photograph, Judy Venner is seated in the second row, second from the right. (Courtesy of Judy Venner Halpert, Portland.)

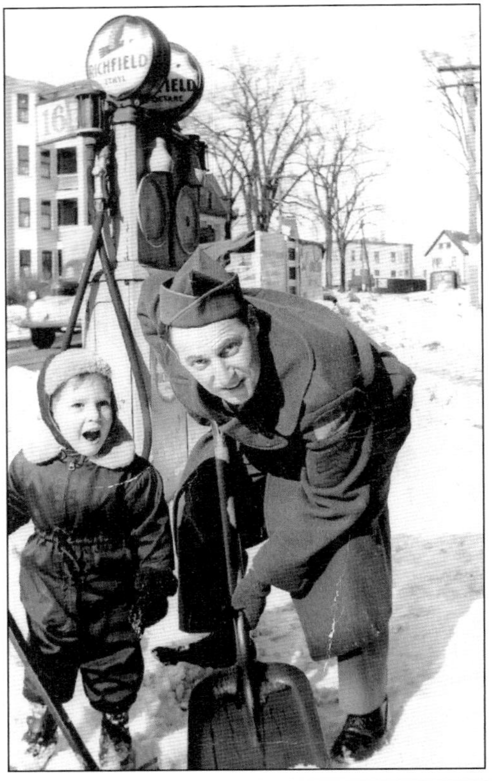

Mark Stern and his father, Herbert Stern, shovel out in this 1946 photograph. (Courtesy of Mark Stern, Portland.)

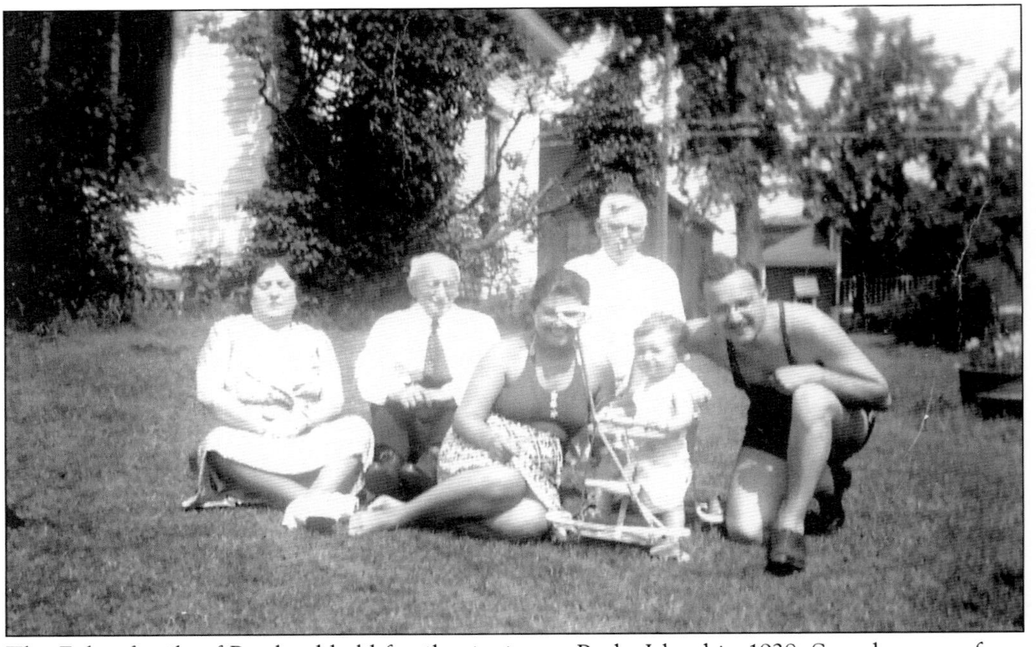

The Zolov family of Portland held family picnics on Peaks Island in 1938. Seen here are, from left to right, Sadie Tabachnick Zolov, unidentified, Edith Zolov, Samuel Zolov, David Zolov, and Benjamin Zolov. (Courtesy of Mark Stern.)

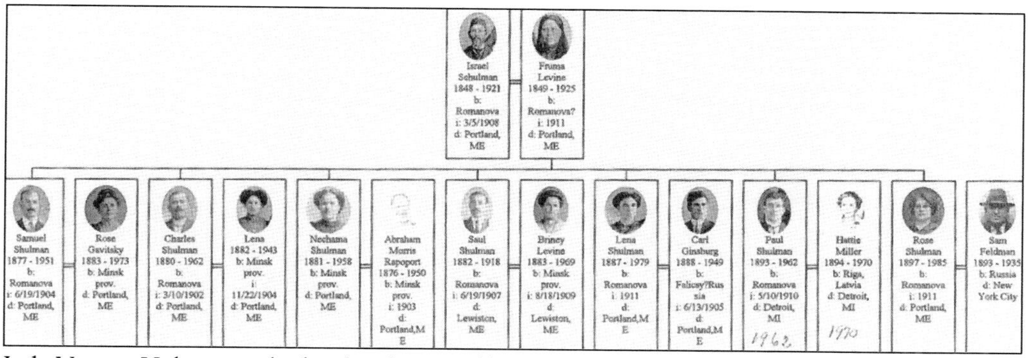

Judy Venner Halpert made this family tree of her maternal grandfather's family, the Schulman's. (Courtesy of Judy Venner Halpert, Portland.)

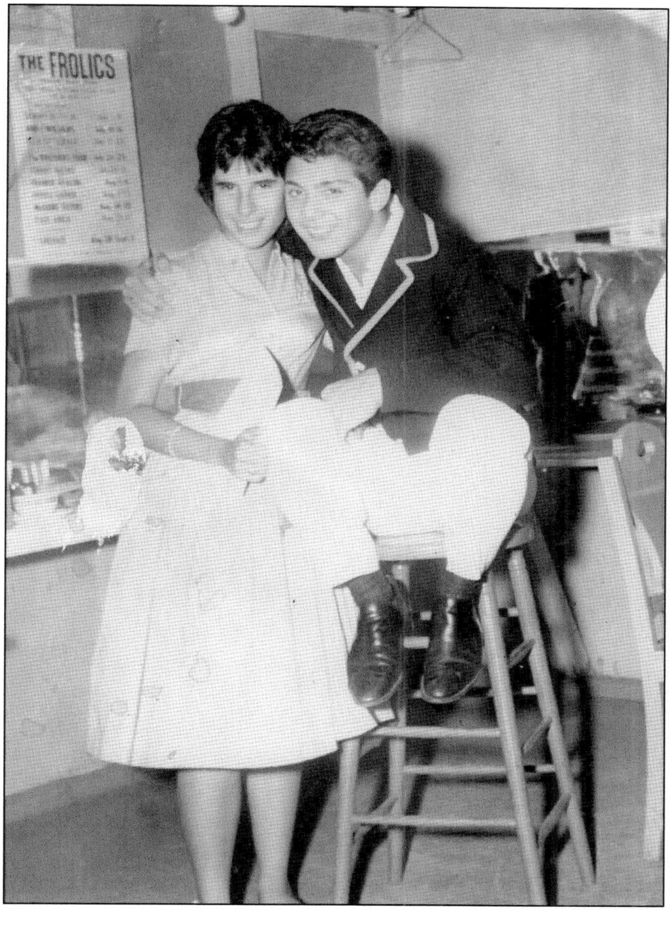

Karen Kornestsky poses with singer Paul Anka after one of his performances in the early 1960s. (Courtesy of Karen Kornetsky Levine.)

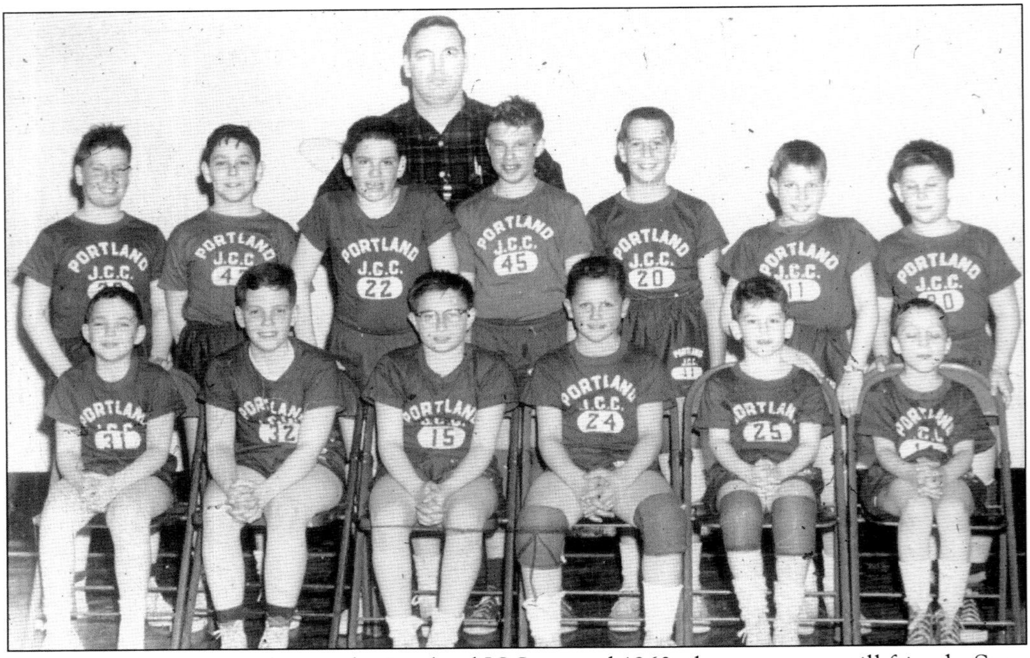

After this picture was taken at the Portland JCC around 1960, these guys are still friends. Seen here are, from left to right, (first row) David Ross, Jimmy Bress, Harvey Silverman, Steven Glovsky, Alan Zimmerman, Mark Finkelstein; (second row) Johnny Gerber, Dick Baker, Gary Taylor, coach Jim Connolly, Bruce Fenton, Myles Goodman, Stanley Sax, and Stanley Turetsky. (Courtesy of Jocelyn Pollard and Jessica Lantos, Portland and Falmouth.)

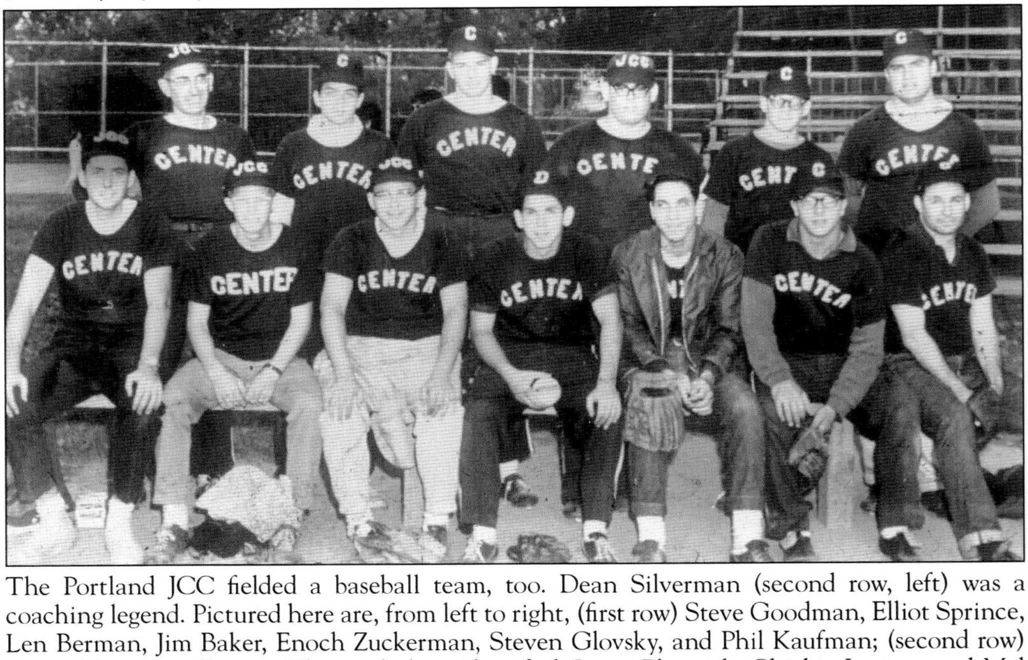

The Portland JCC fielded a baseball team, too. Dean Silverman (second row, left) was a coaching legend. Pictured here are, from left to right, (first row) Steve Goodman, Elliot Sprince, Len Berman, Jim Baker, Enoch Zuckerman, Steven Glovsky, and Phil Kaufman; (second row) Dean Silverman, Ronnie Blumenthal, unidentified, Larry Plavnick, Chickie Levine, and Mel Zimelman. (Courtesy of Jocelyn Pollard and Jessica Lantos, Portland and Falmouth.)

Seven

Some Who Made A Difference

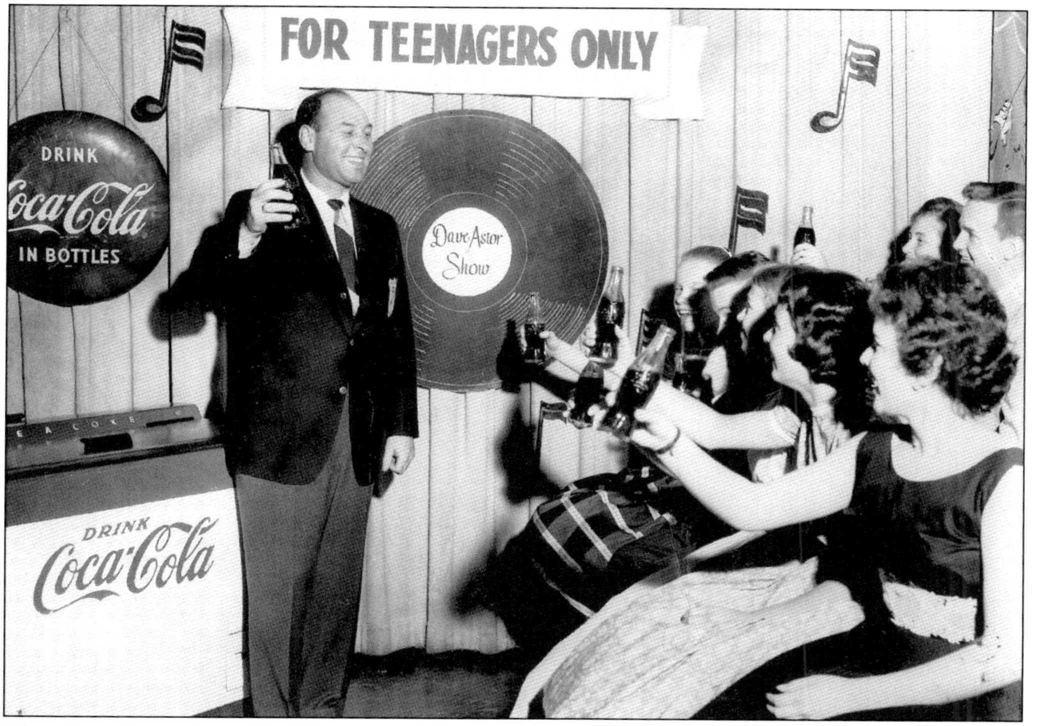

The Dave Astor show, *For Teenagers Only*, was Maine's version of American Bandstand. Astor invited students from Maine high schools to be part of the weekly audience and participate along with his troupe of lip-synching regulars. The show ran from 1956 to 1971. (Courtesy of Dave Astor.)

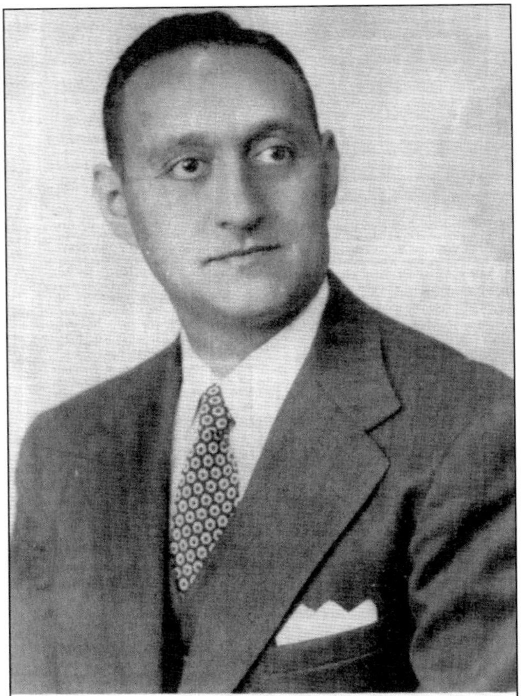

NORMAN I. GODFREY
JUNE 6, 1910–JANUARY 24, 1947

Norman Godfrey was the beloved first executive director of Portland's modern JCC. He died at the age of 37 after nearly a decade of leadership.

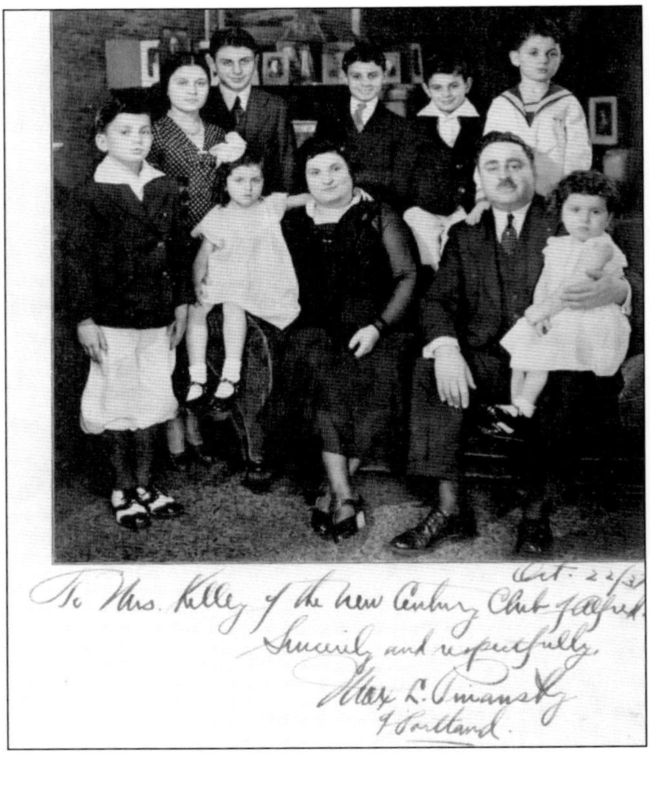

Judge Max Pinansky, in front, holding the little girl on his lap in this 1937 photograph, was a prominent member of Portland's legal community as well as the founder of Portland's interracial and interreligious association. (Courtesy of the Maine Historical Society, Portland.)

Israel Bernstein began his practice of law in Portland in 1915 with his brother Louis. He was a founder of Portland's Jewish Federation as well as the law firm that is now Bernstein, Shur, Sawyer and Nelson. (Courtesy of Bernstein, Shur, Sawyer and Nelson.)

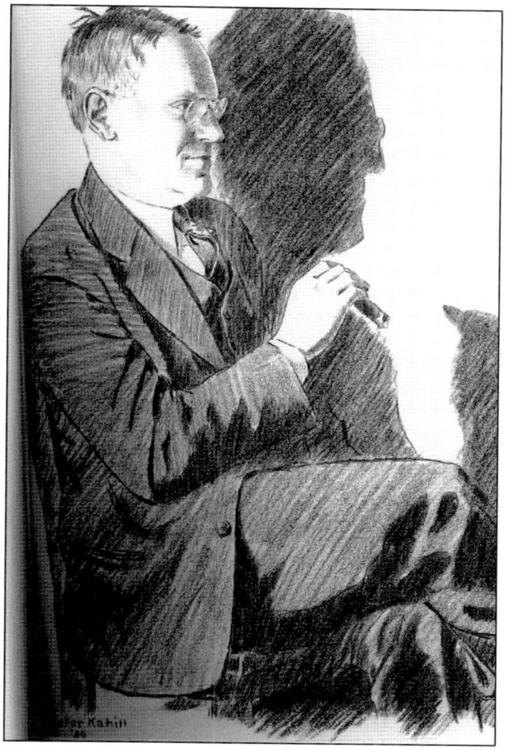

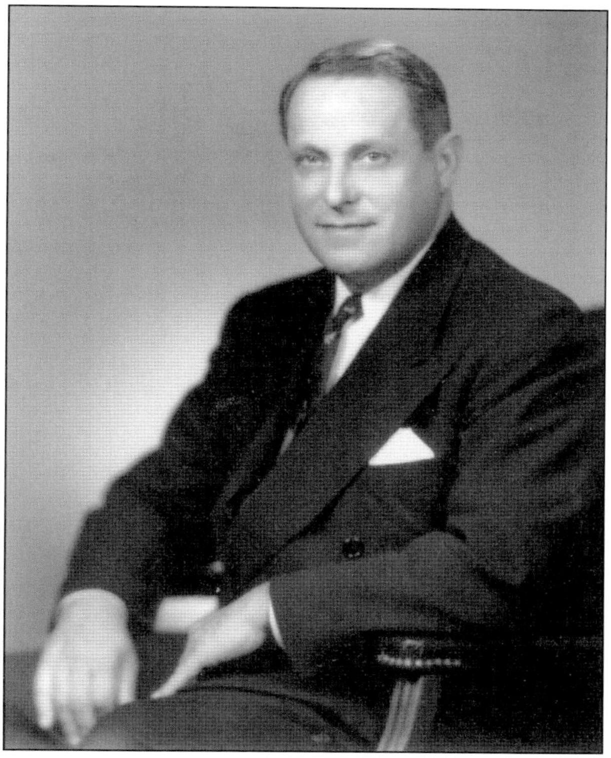

Judge Louis Bernstein, with his brother Israel, founded the law firm that is now Bernstein, Shur, Sawyer and Nelson. Judge Bernstein was a founder of the JCC and served as the first Jewish head of Bowdoin's Board of Overseers. (Courtesy of Bernstein, Shur, Sawyer and Nelson.)

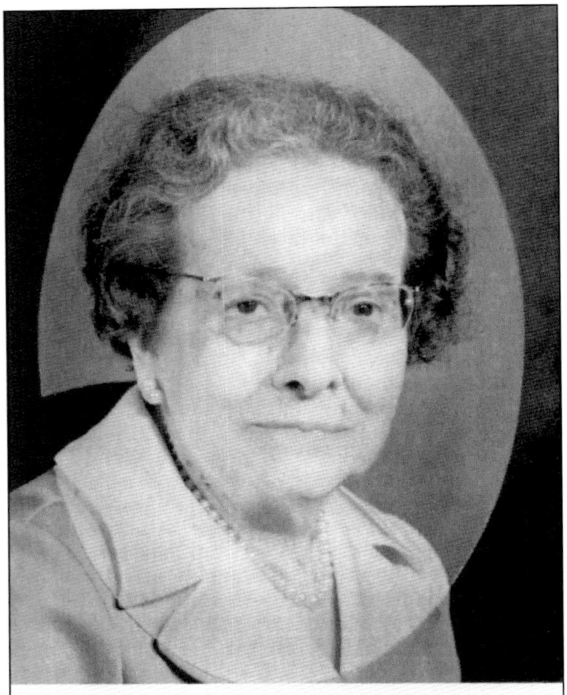

Peggy Bernstein

Affectionately known as "the conscience of Portland Jewry," Rebecca "Peggy" Bernstein was an attorney like her husband Israel, who considered her his "full and equal partner." She was a local, regional, and national officer in the National Council of Jewish Women, first vice president of Portland's Jewish Federation, and a member of the board of directors of Portland's United Fund.

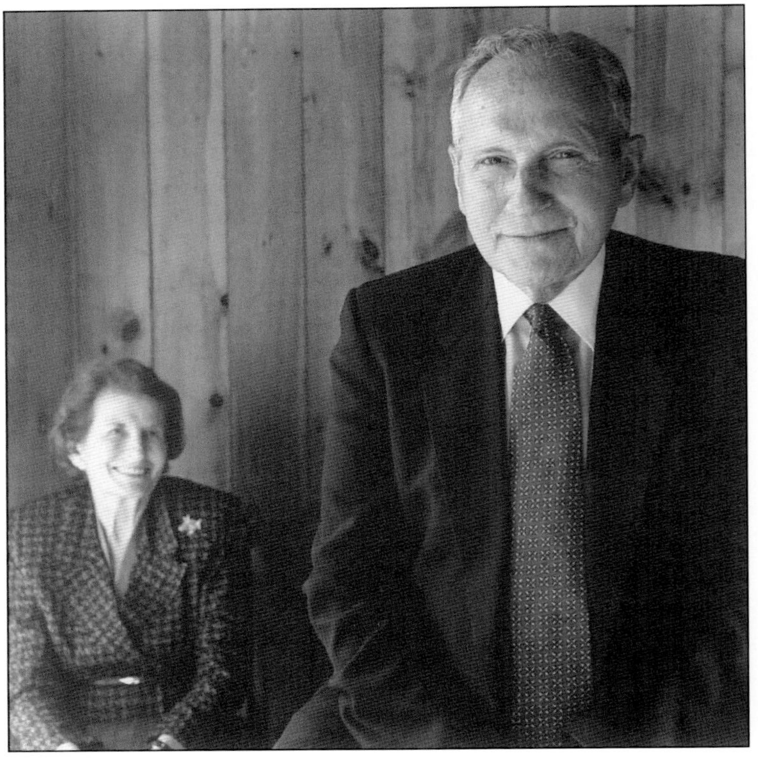

Rosalyne and Sumner Bernstein both played prominent roles in Portland's Jewish community and the community at large. A member of the law firm founded by his father and uncle, Sumner Bernstein was also president of the board of governors of the Maine State Bar Association and a member of the Portland City Council. Rosalyne Bernstein, also a lawyer, was chair of the board of visitors of the University of Southern Maine.

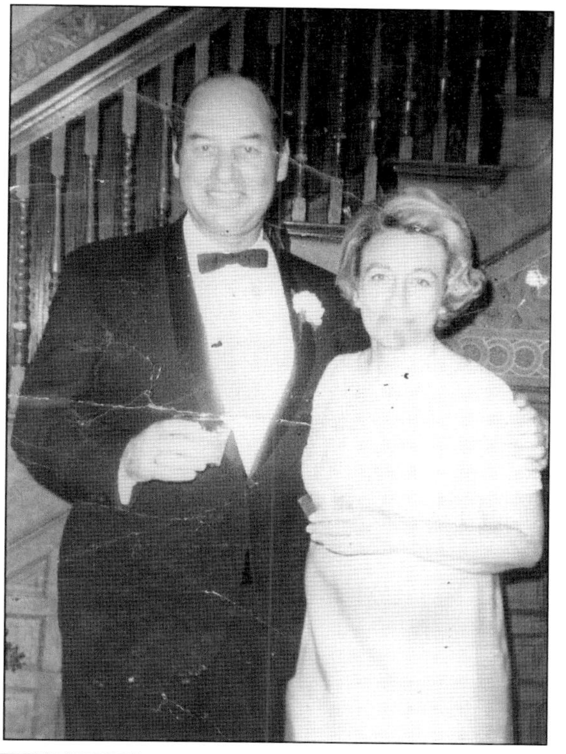

In addition to Dave Astor's huge success in Portland television, he was also on the boards of the JCC and The Cedars. Esta Astor was the long-time librarian of the Maine Historical Society. Many area teenagers considered Dave and Esta their mentors. (Courtesy of Dave Astor, Falmouth.)

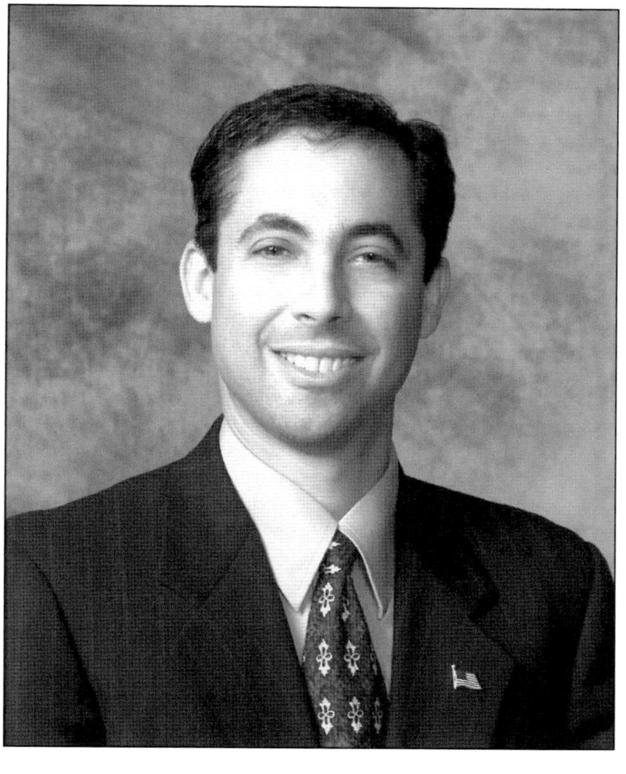

Jim Cohen has been a member of the Portland City Council since 2002, and currently serves as Portland's mayor. (Courtesy, Jim Cohen, Portland.)

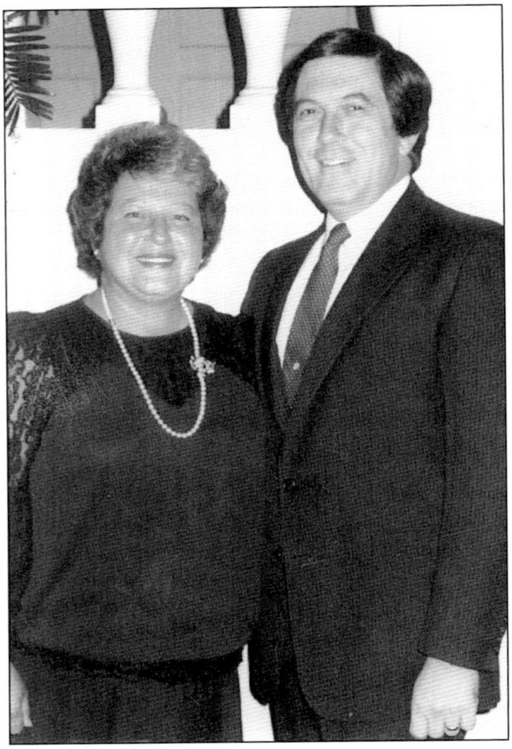

Linda and Joel Abromson of Portland were active in the Jewish community and in local, state, and national affairs. Linda was the first Jewish woman mayor of Portland, and Joel was a well-respected member of the Maine State Legislature. The Joel and Linda Abromson Community Education Center is located on the Portland campus of the University of Southern Maine. (Courtesy of Linda Elowitch Abromson, Portland.)

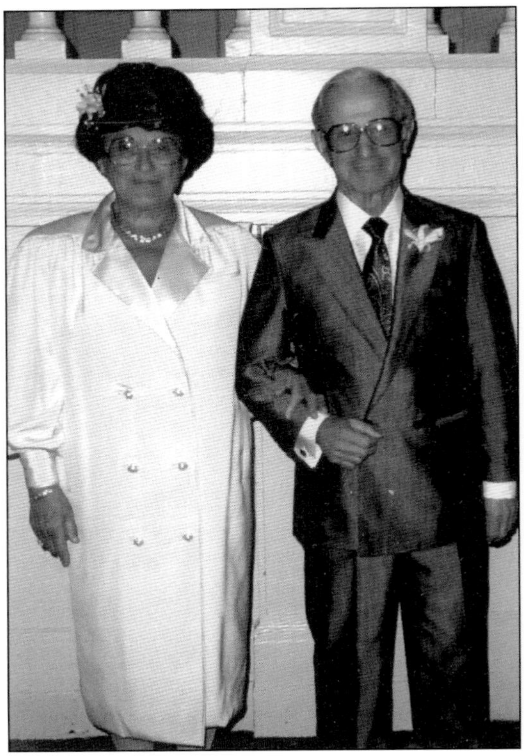

Frances and Yudy Elowitch were long-time supporters of the Portland Jewish community. Yudy, a three-sport athlete at Portland High School, went on to establish Yudy's Tires with stores in Maine and New Hampshire. He was also the founder, in 1971, of the Fitzpatrick Award, given annually to the state's outstanding high school football player. (Courtesy of Linda Elowitch Abromson.)

Robert Elowitch, co-owner of Portland's Barridoff Galleries with his wife, Annette, practices another art, too; as Robbie Ellis, he continues to maintain an active schedule on the pro-wrestling tour. (Courtesy of Robert Elowitch.)

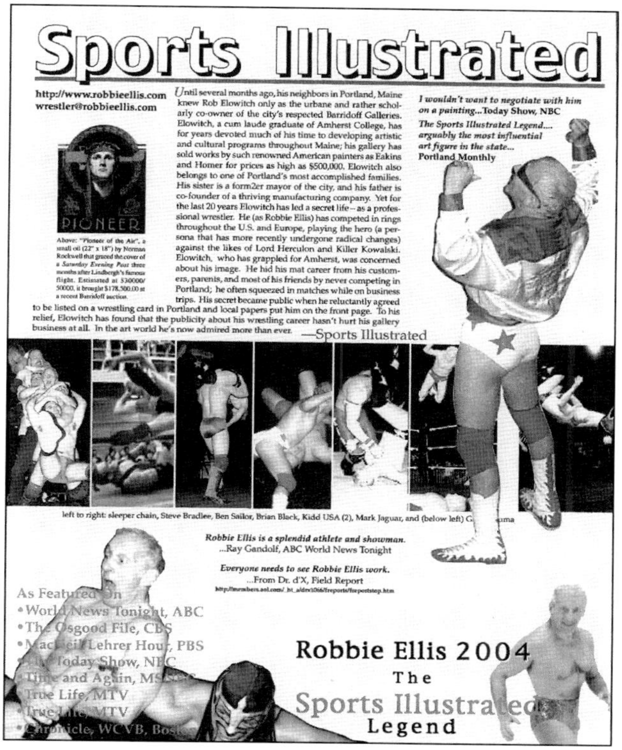

Sports Illustrated

http://www.robbieellis.com
wrestler@robbieellis.com

Above: "Pioneer of the Air", a small oil (22" x 18") by Norman Rockwell that graced the cover of a *Saturday Evening Post* three months after Lindbergh's famous flight. Estimated at $30000/50000, it brought $178,500.00 at a recent Barridoff auction.

Until several months ago, his neighbors in Portland, Maine knew Rob Elowitch only as the urbane and rather scholarly co-owner of the city's respected Barridoff Galleries. Elowitch, a cum laude graduate of Amherst College, has for years devoted much of his time to developing artistic and cultural programs throughout Maine; his gallery has sold works by such renowned American painters as Eakins and Homer for prices as high as $500,000. Elowitch also belongs to one of Portland's most accomplished families. His sister is a form2er mayor of the city, and his father is co-founder of a thriving manufacturing company. Yet for the last 20 years Elowitch has led a secret life -- as a professional wrestler. He (as Robbie Ellis) has competed in rings throughout the U.S. and Europe, playing the hero (a persona that has more recently undergone radical changes) against the likes of Lord Herculon and Killer Kowalski. Elowitch, who has grappled for Amherst, was concerned about his image. He hid his mat career from his customers, parents, and most of his friends by never competing in Portland; he often squeezed in matches while on business trips. His secret became public when he reluctantly agreed to be listed on a wrestling card in Portland and local papers put him on the front page. To his relief, Elowitch has found that the publicity about his wrestling career hasn't hurt his gallery business at all. In the art world he's now admired more than ever. —Sports Illustrated

I wouldn't want to negotiate with him on a painting...Today Show, NBC

The Sports Illustrated Legend.... arguably the most influential art figure in the state...
Portland Monthly

left to right: sleeper chain, Steve Bradlee, Ben Sailor, Brian Black, Kidd USA (2), Mark Jaguar, and (below left) G[illegible]uma

Robbie Ellis is a splendid athlete and showman.
...Ray Gandolf, ABC World News Tonight

Everyone needs to see Robbie Ellis work.
...From Dr. d'X, Field Report
http://members.aol.com/_ht_a/drx1066/freports/freportstop.htm

As Featured On
- World News Tonight, ABC
- True Life, MTV

Robbie Ellis 2004
The
Sports Illustrated
Legend

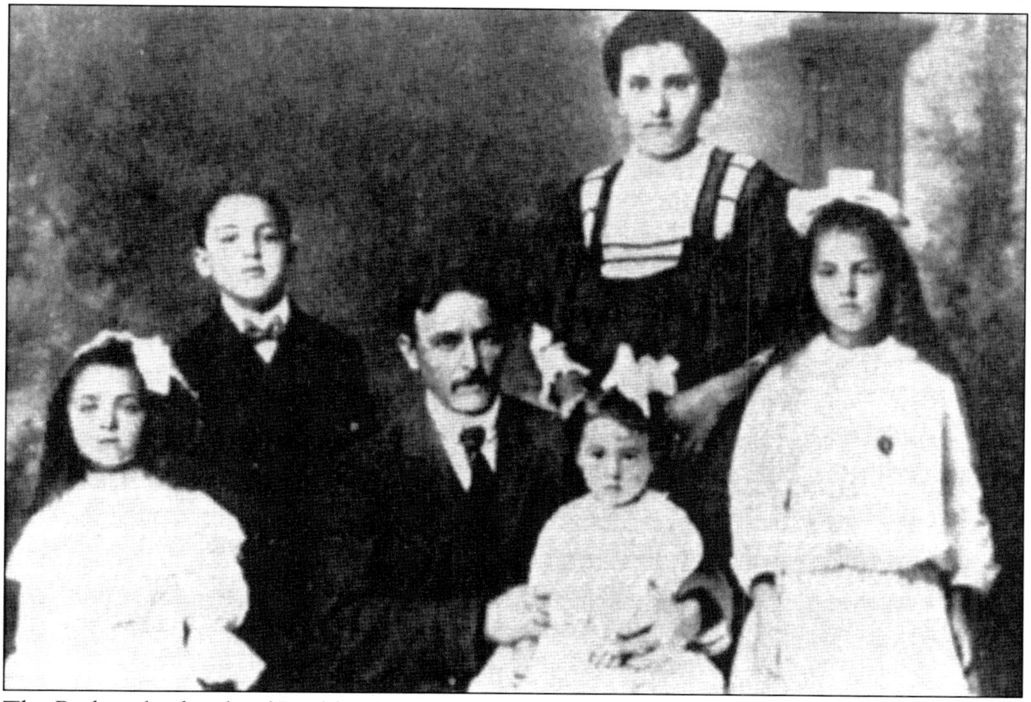

The Berliawsky family of Rockland posed for this picture in the early 20th century. The young girl at far right is the artist Louise Nevelson.

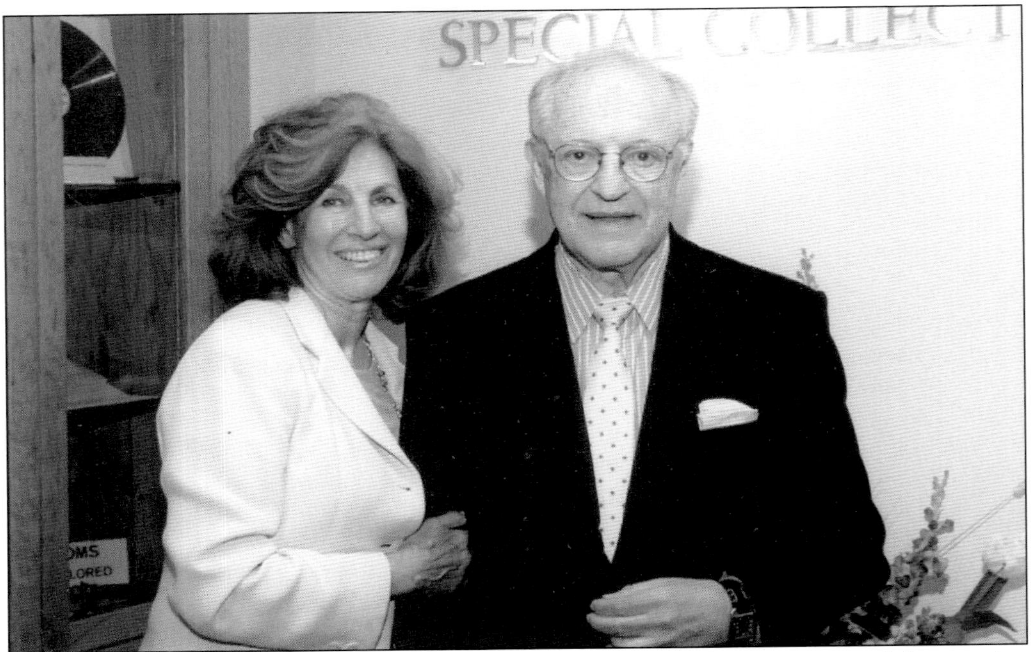

Judy and Albert Glickman, two of Portland's most generous benefactors, supported the creation of the Albert Brenner Glickman Family Library and the Glickman Family Collection of Interreligious Studies on the Portland campus of the University of Southern Maine. (Courtesy of the University of Southern Maine, photograph by Dan Courter.)

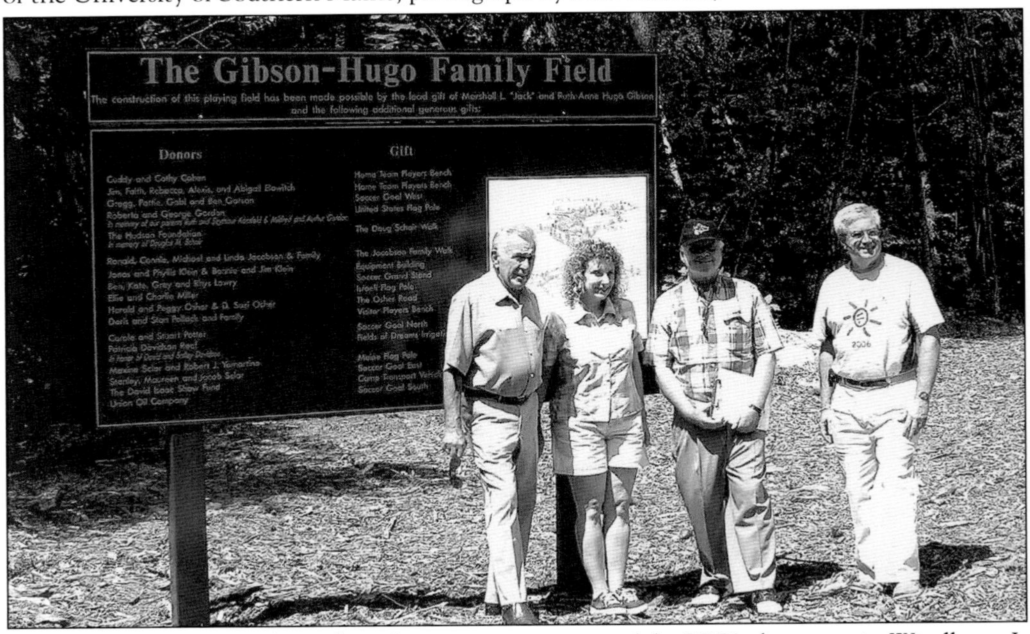

Kenny Nelson and David Small are long-time supporters of the JCC's day camp in Windham. It was their fund-raising abilities and vision that led to the successful creation of the Gibson-Hugo Family Field at the camp. In this photograph are, from left to right, Marshall L. "Jack" Gibson, Ruth-Anne Hugo, Kenny Nelson, and David Small. (Courtesy of Kenny Nelson.)

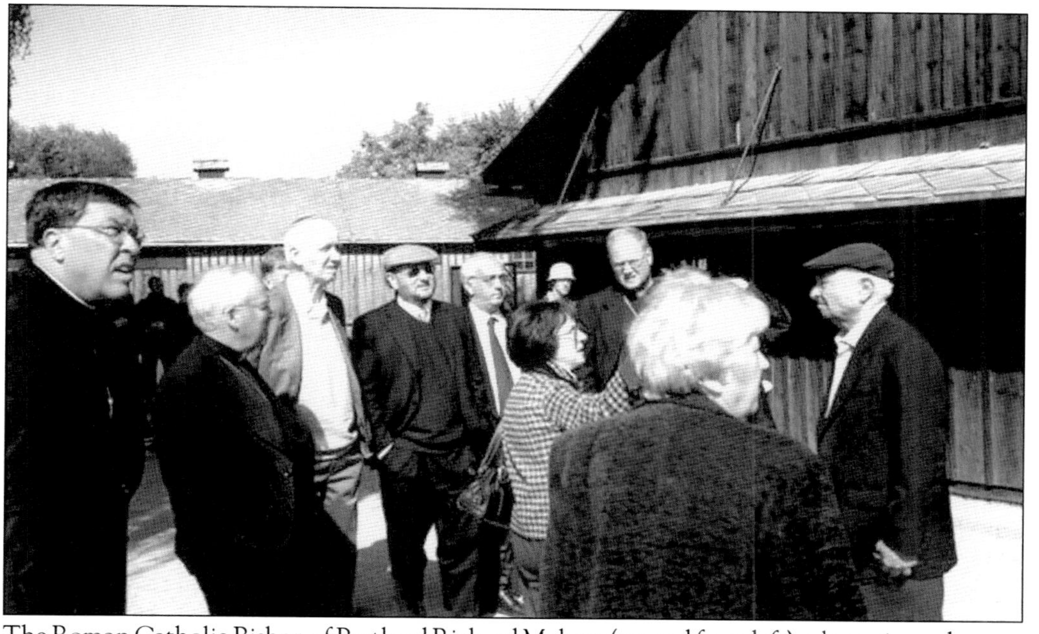

The Roman Catholic Bishop of Portland Richard Malone (second from left), a long-time advocate of Catholic-Jewish dialog, stands at the Auschwitz death camp in Poland in the summer of 2005. Next to Bishop Malone, third from left, is the noted American Jewish theologian Rabbi Irving "Yitz" Greenberg. (Courtesy of Bishop Richard Malone, Portland.)

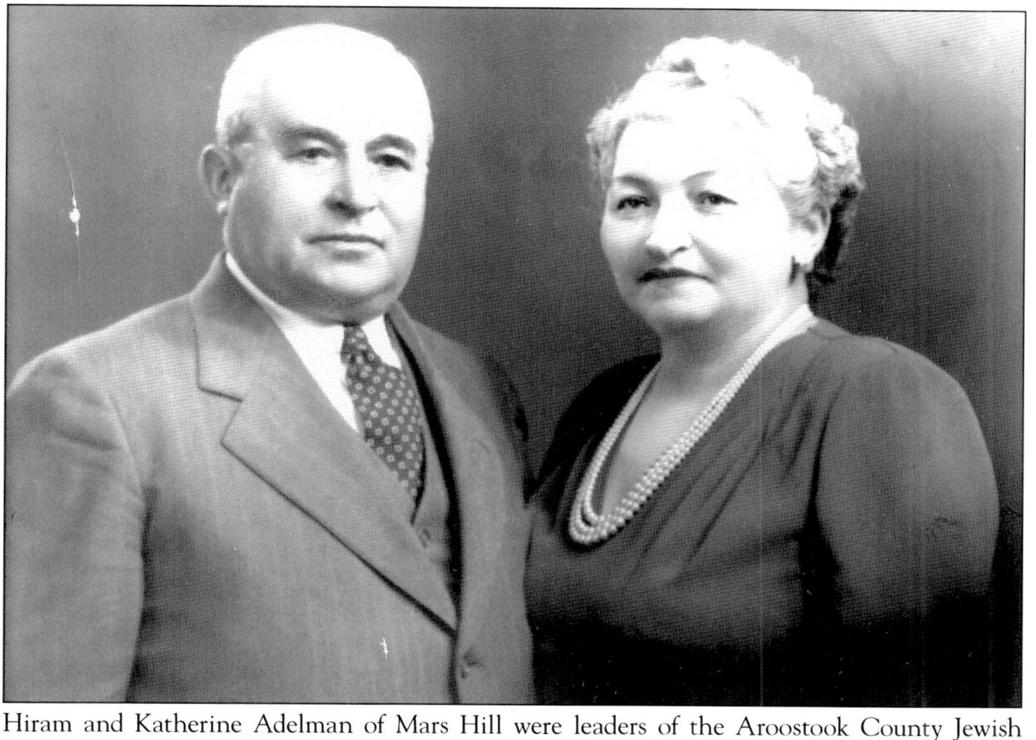

Hiram and Katherine Adelman of Mars Hill were leaders of the Aroostook County Jewish community. (Courtesy of Milton Adelman, Mars Hill.)

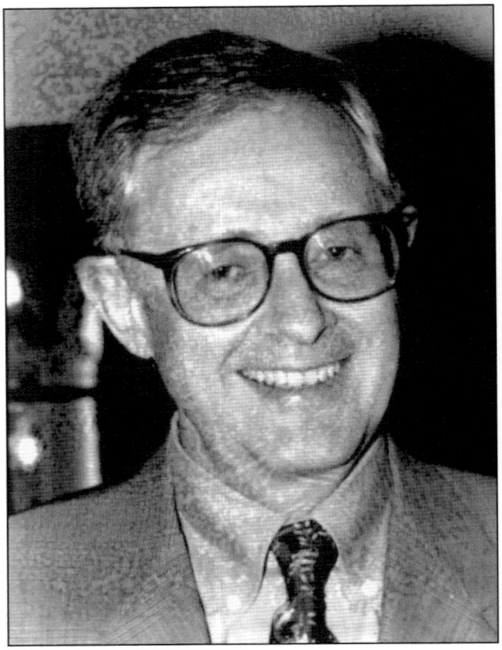
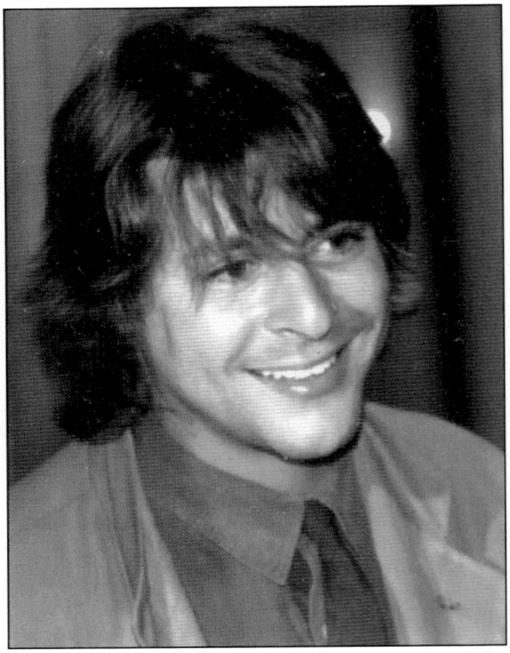

The Nelson family has made outstanding contributions in many facets of community life. Leonard Nelson (seen above left) has played a leadership role in representing the Jewish community in the cultural life of Maine. He was the first Jewish president of the Portland Symphony Orchestra (1963–1966) and used his position to publicize restrictions against Jewish membership in various Portland clubs and organizations. Merle Nelson (seen below) is a former member of the Maine legislature and took a leading role in the support of Otisfield, Maine's Seeds of Peace camp. Their son, Judd Nelson (seen above right), is a stage, screen, and television actor who has appeared in memorable roles in *The Breakfast Club* and *St. Elmo's Fire*. (Courtesy of Merle Nelson, Falmouth.)

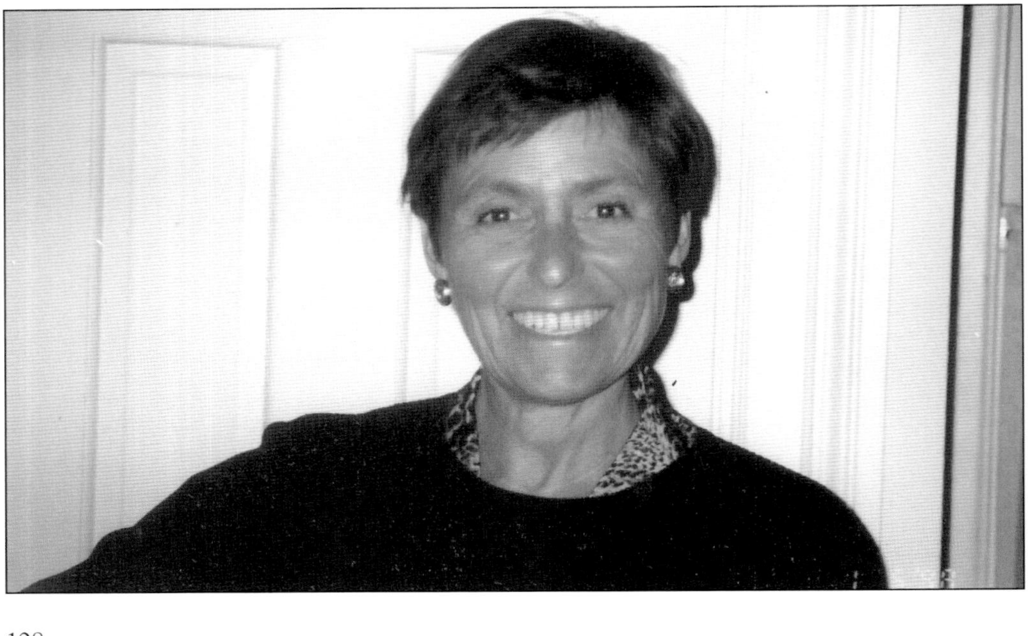

Portland-born Linda Lavin began her acting career at the Jewish Community Center. The Tony Award–winning actress has appeared in many Broadway performances and had a starring role in the television series *Alice*. (Courtesy of Bill Westmoreland.)

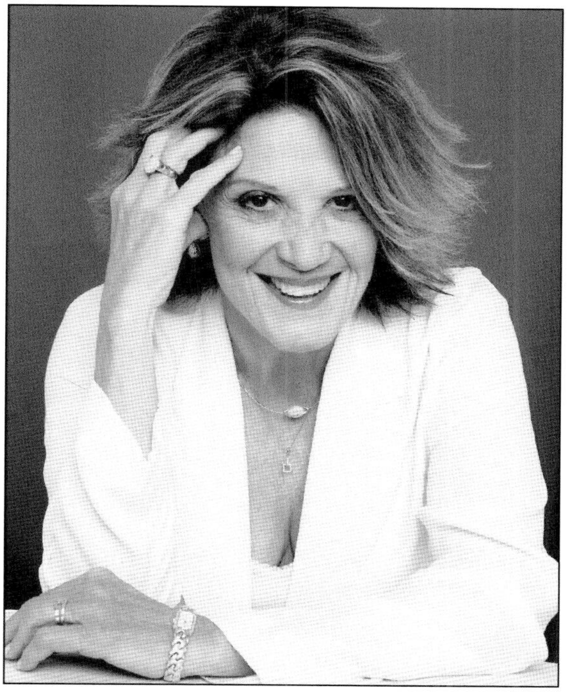

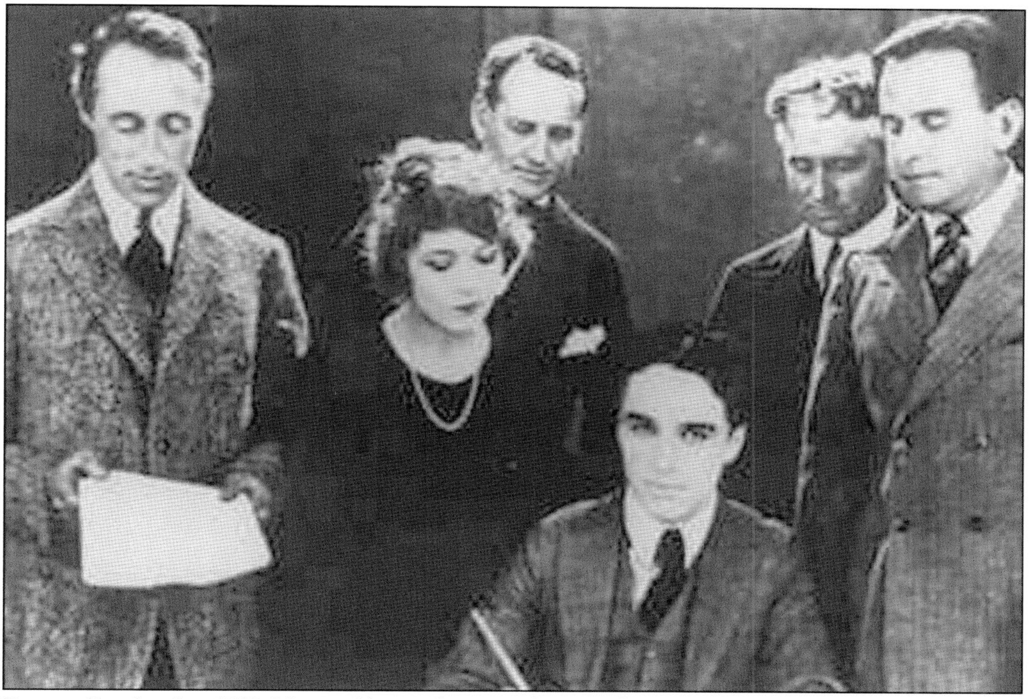

Born in Portland in 1878, Hiram Abrams became the president of Paramount Pictures and formed United Artists, two of the biggest Hollywood studios. Looking on while Douglas Fairbanks signs a contract are, from left to right, D. W. Griffith, Mary Pickford, Hiram Abrams, Charlie Chaplin, and Dennis O'Brien. (Courtesy of Bruce Torrence, Hollywood Photography Collection.)

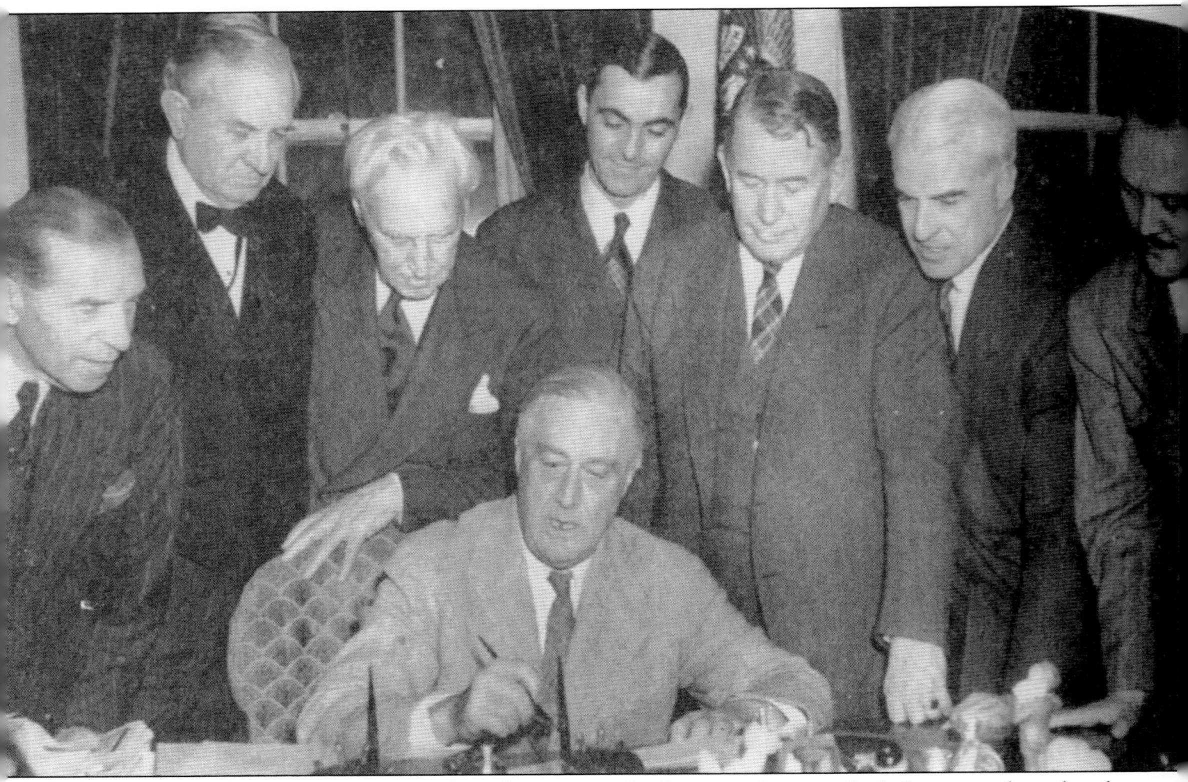

Portland-born Oscar Cox was best known as the lawyer who supplied the precedent for the drafting of the Lend-Lease Act. He is the fourth from the left, standing right behind Pres. Franklin Roosevelt.

Dr. Henry Pollard was the first and only Jew named to the presidency of the Portland United Charity, a forerunner of United Way. He also photographed many activities of the JCC. (Courtesy of Jocelyn Pollard and Jessica Lantos, Portland and Falmouth.)

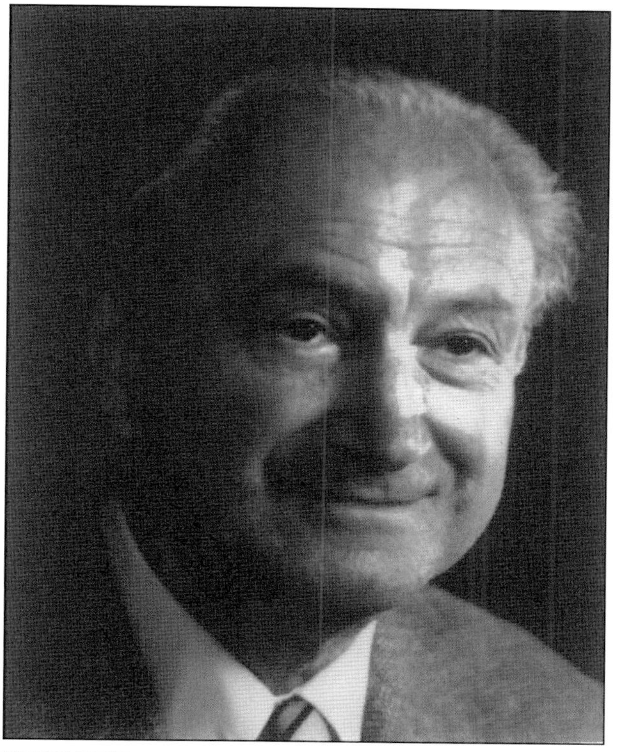

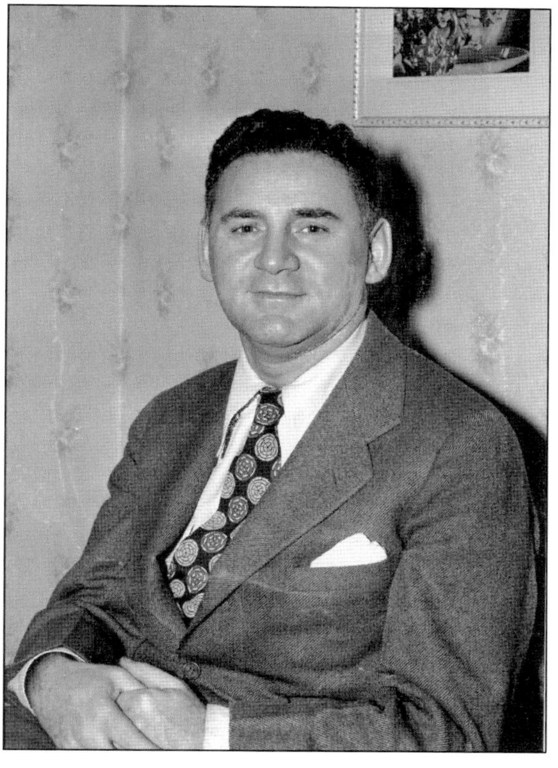

Barnett Shur served as Portland's corporation counsel for 25 years as well as a turn as acting city manager. Shur was active in Portland's Jewish community affairs for more than four decades. (Courtesy of Janet Shur, Belmont, Massachusetts.)

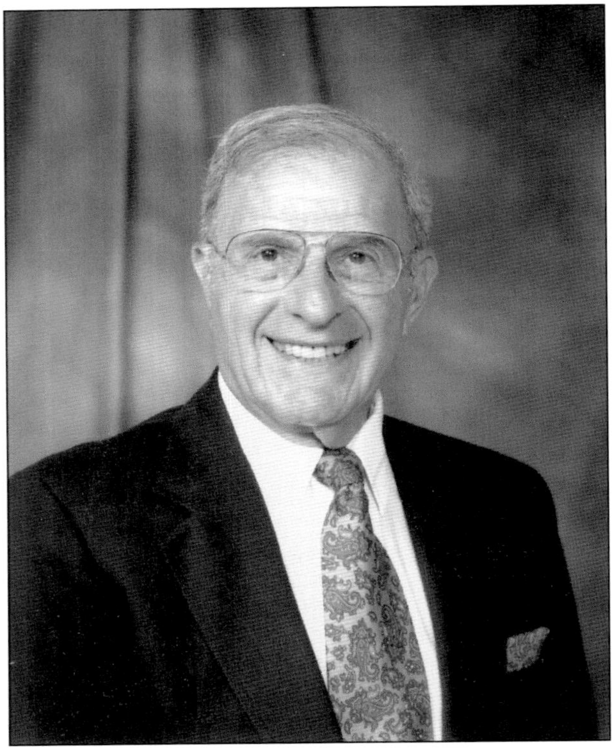

Melvin Stone of Portland was a pioneer in Maine broadcasting and owned several radio stations in the state. He continues to serve the Cedars on the board of directors. (Courtesy of Mel Stone.)

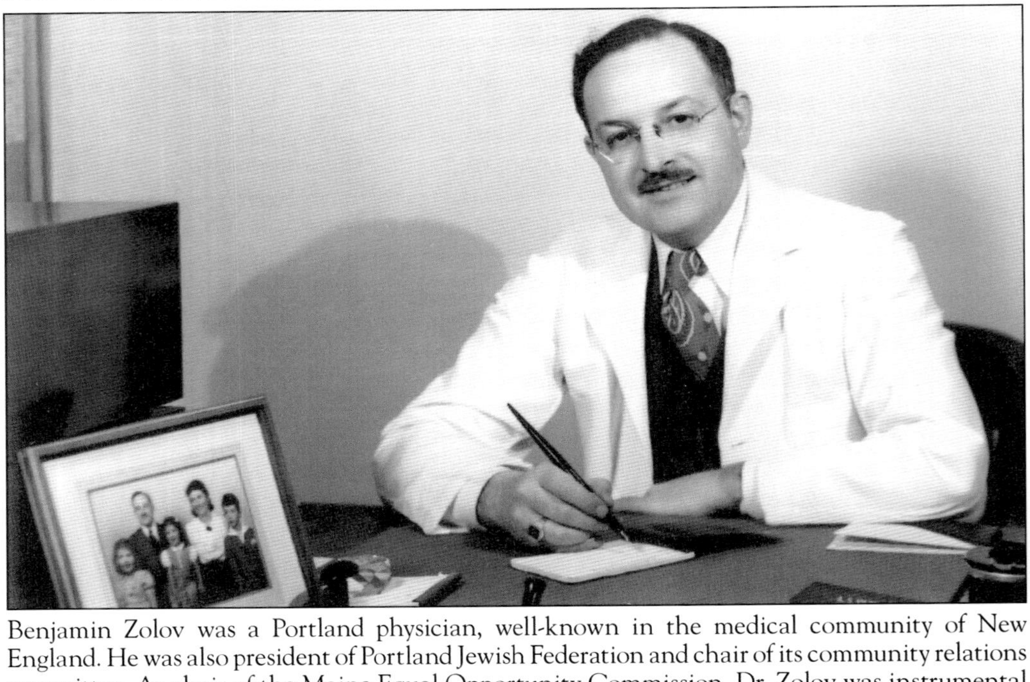

Benjamin Zolov was a Portland physician, well-known in the medical community of New England. He was also president of Portland Jewish Federation and chair of its community relations committee. As chair of the Maine Equal Opportunity Commission, Dr. Zolov was instrumental in obtaining passage of a bill by the Maine State Legislature that barred discrimination by hotels and resorts on the basis of race, color, or creed. (Courtesy of Mark Stern, Portland.)

Charles Allen was a non-Jewish member of Portland City Council who threatened to pull the liquor licenses of some local Portland clubs and organizations if they did not give up their discriminatory practices against African Americans and Jews. Ultimately this act initiated by Allen led to the breakdown of minority exclusion. (Courtesy of Congressman Tom and Diana Allen, Portland.)

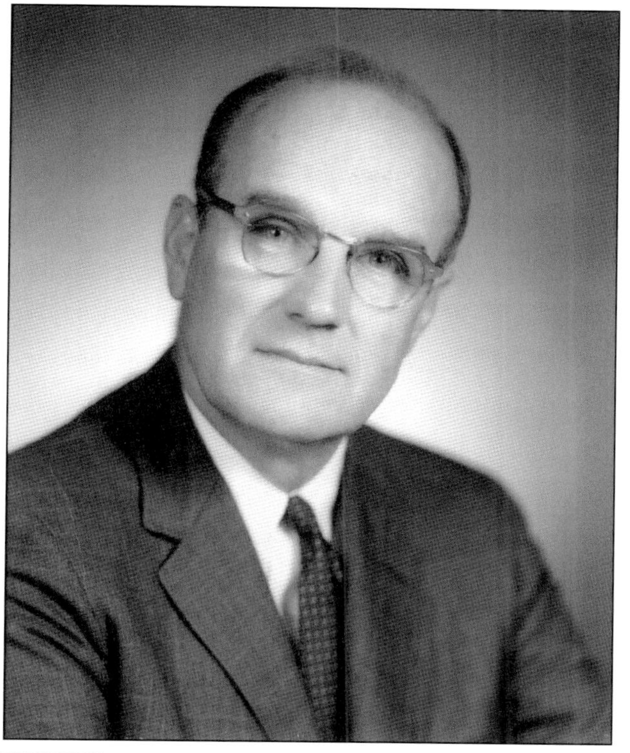

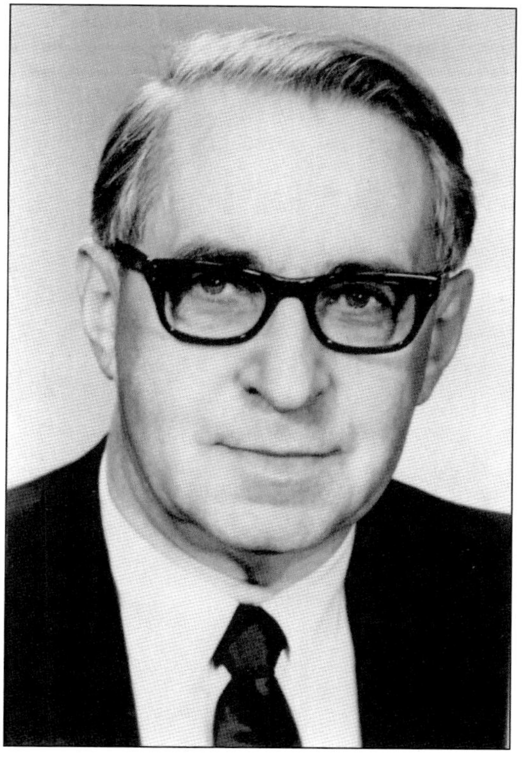

Albert "Jim" Abrahamson of Portland was the first Jew hired to teach at Bowdoin College, his alma mater. Professor Abrahamson taught economics at Bowdoin for nearly 50 years. In addition, he also held many government appointments, including WPA administrator for Maine, special assistant to the United States secretary of labor, and deputy director of the War Refugee Board, created by Pres. Franklin Roosevelt, the only official government organization with a responsibility to rescue Jews from Nazi Europe. (Courtesy of George J. Mitchell Department of Special Collections and Archives, Bowdoin College Library, Brunswick.)

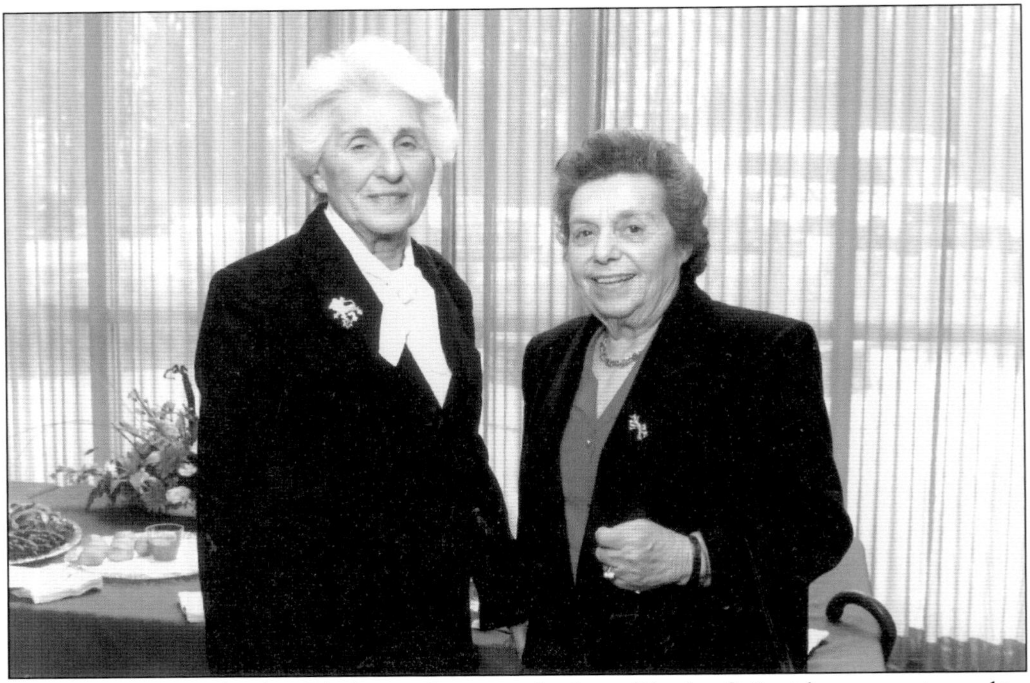

Rita Willis (left) and Selma Black were long-time leaders of Portland's Jewish community and its activities. (Courtesy of the Cedars, Portland.)

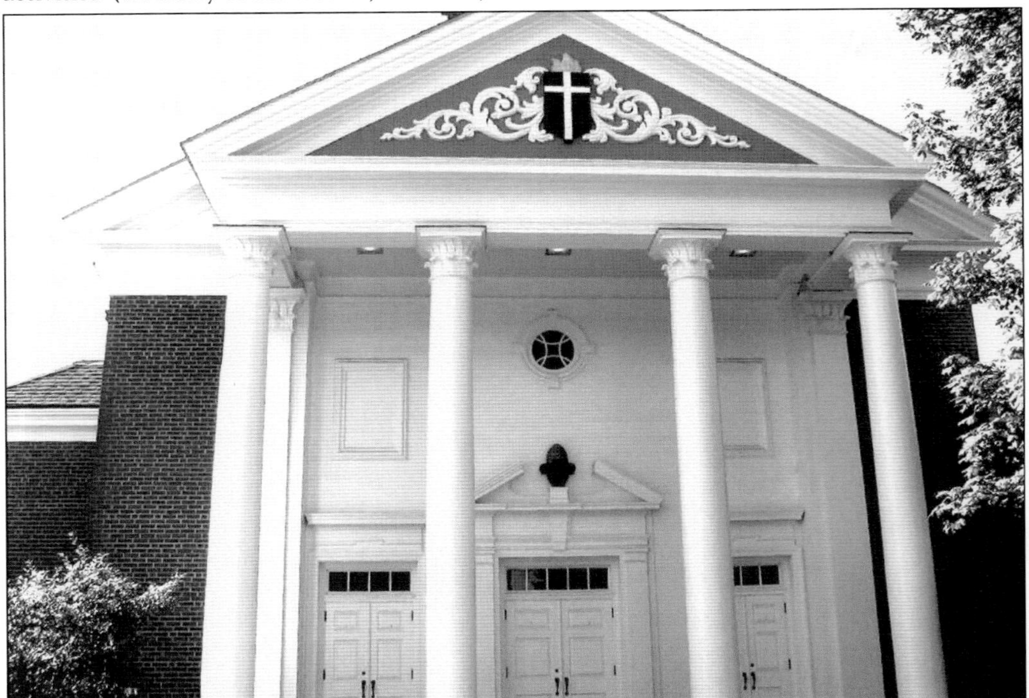

The Woodfords Congregational Church, Portland, has hosted High Holiday services for Temple Beth El and Congregation Bet Ha'am.

Philip Lown of Auburn was a philanthropist and a founder of Camp Lown, a Jewish camp in Oakland. He was also president of the Maine Jewish Council.

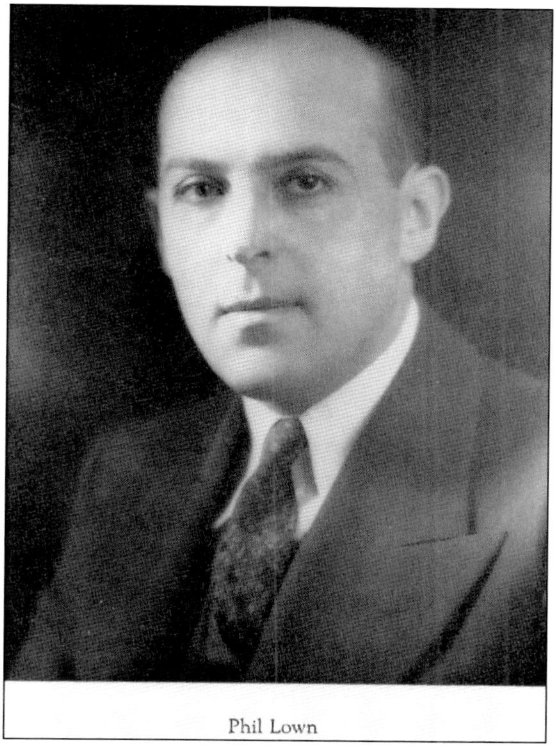

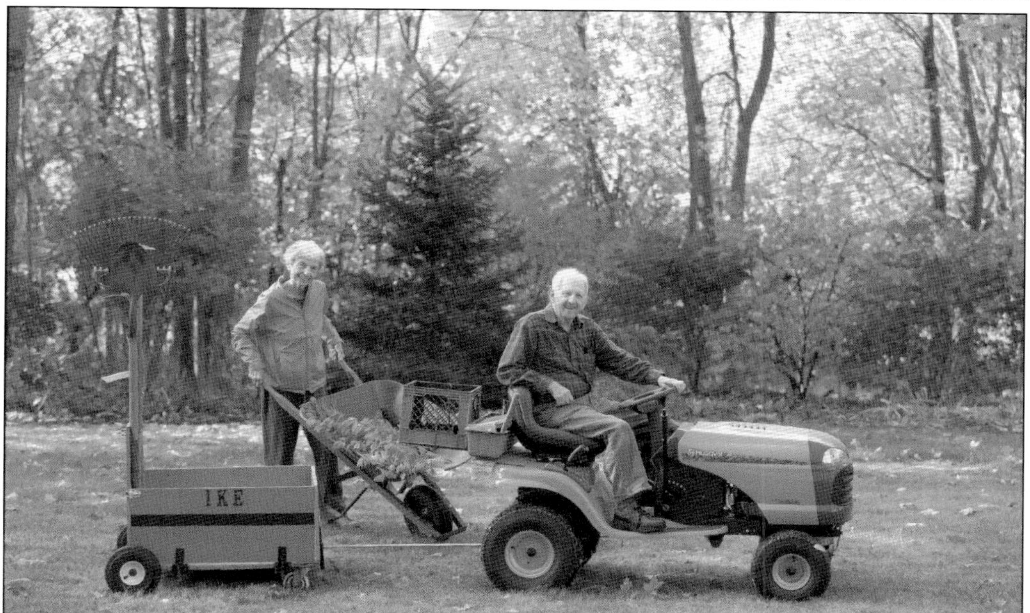

Judith Isaacson, a survivor of Auschwitz, wrote one of the most important Holocaust memoirs, *Seed of Sarah*. For many years, she served as a dean at Bates College. Irving Isaacson was a Lewiston lawyer who also worked as that city's corporation counsel. (Courtesy of Phyllis Graber Jensen, Lewiston.)

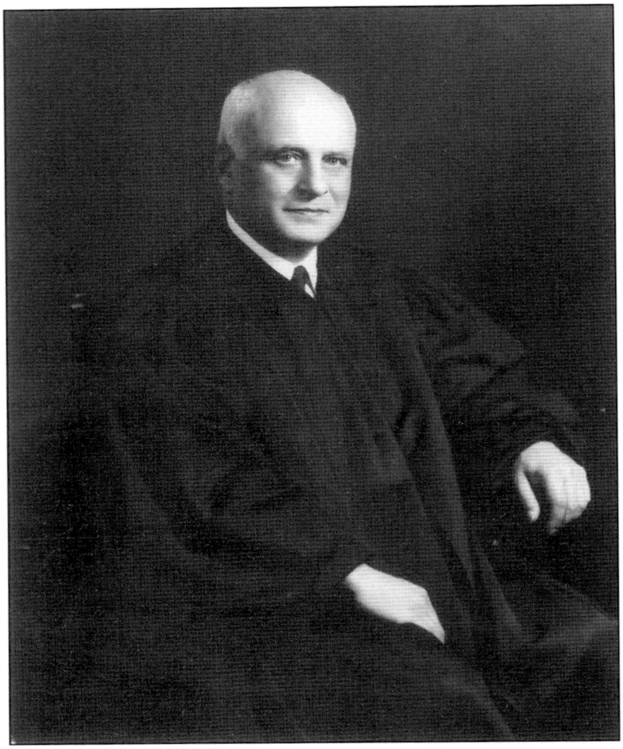

Abraham Rudman founded a Bangor law firm in 1917, now called Rudman and Winchell. In 1954, he became a justice of the Maine Superior Court, and in 1965 was appointed as the first Jewish justice of the Maine Supreme Court. In 1991, his son, Paul Rudman, was also appointed a justice of the Maine Supreme Court. (Courtesy of the Bangor Public Library.)

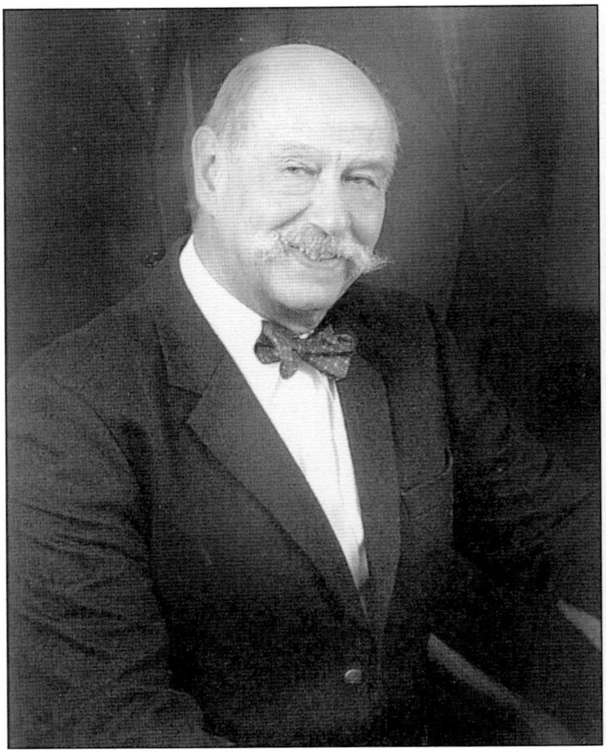

Norman Minsky is a historian of the Bangor Jewish experience and is deeply committed to the University of Maine. (Courtesy of Norman Minsky, Bangor.)

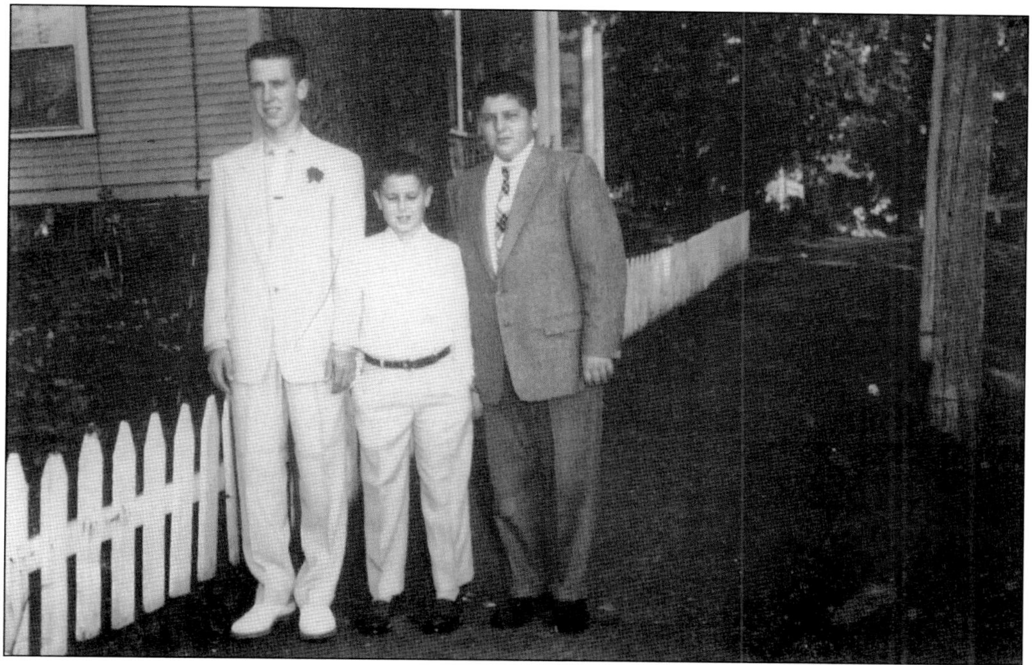

Future United States senator from Maine and secretary of defense William Cohen of Bangor (left), with his brother, Robert "Bobby" Cohen (center) and Maxwell "Mickey" Miller, pose for a photograph in 1954, on the occasion of Miller's bar mitzvah. (Courtesy of the Bangor Public Library.)

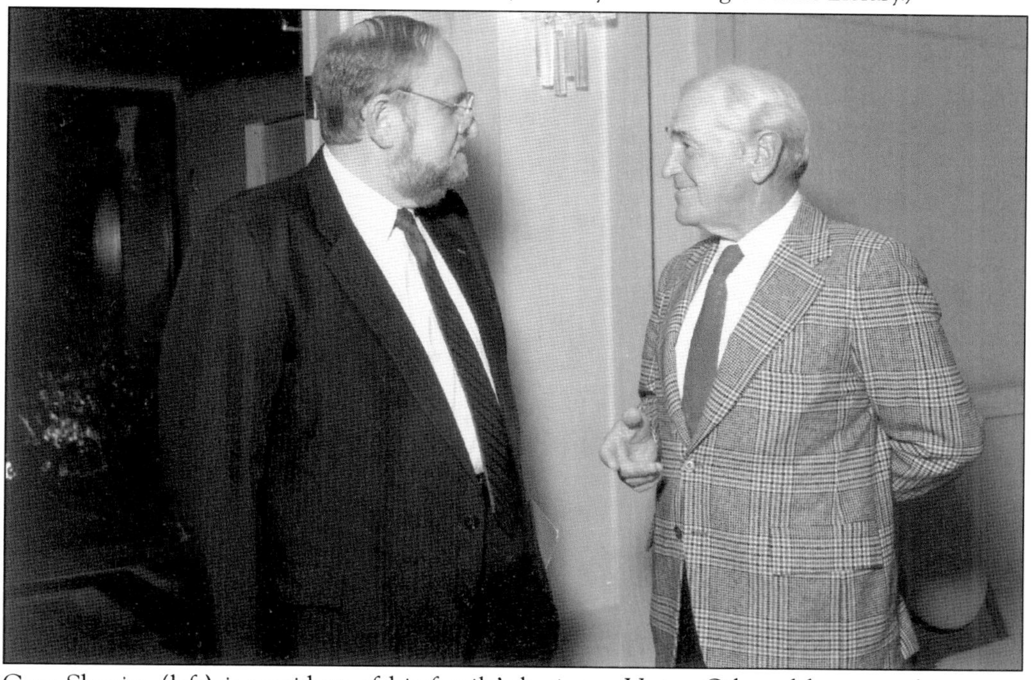

Greg Shapiro (left) is president of his family's business, Union Oil, and has served in many capacities at the Jewish Home for Aged, now the Cedars. In this picture, he is conferring with Joe Stillman, a former president of Temple Beth El.

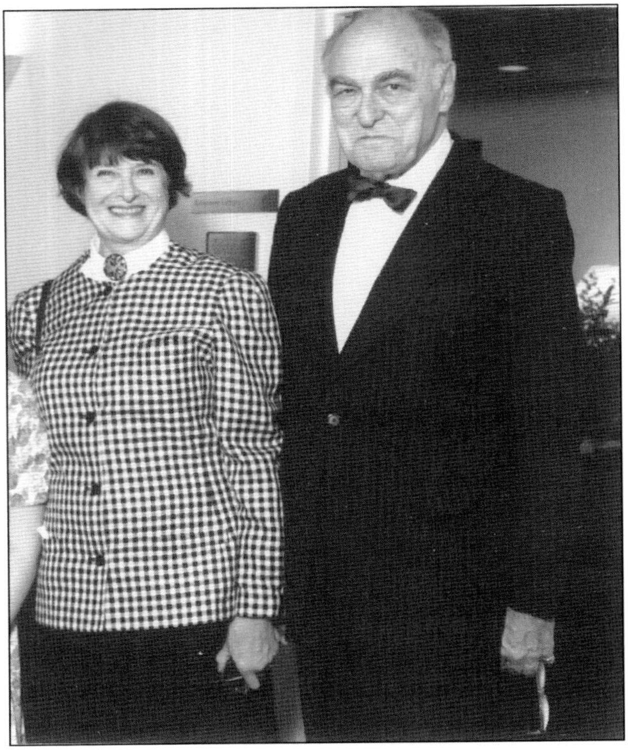

Al Aranson, at right, was the first Jewish chief of medicine at the Maine Medical Center, the state's leading hospital, and also served as a president of Temple Beth El. In 1991, he escorted his wife Golde to the Cedars's opening gala. (Courtesy of the Cedars.)

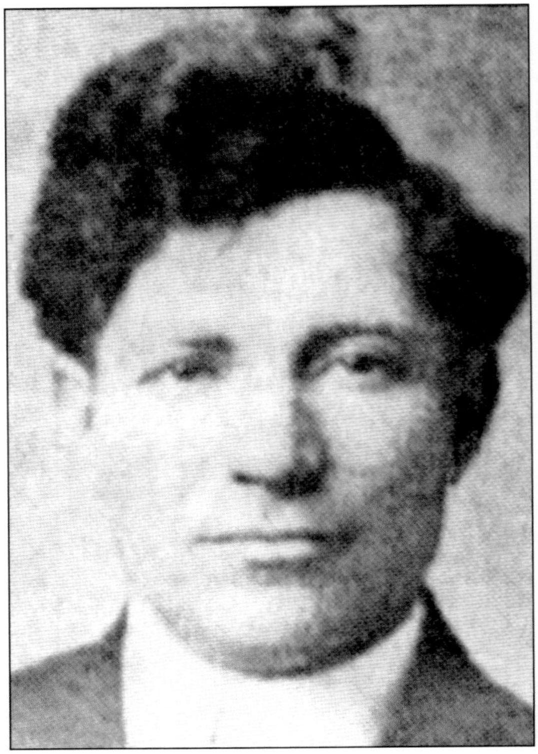

Benjamin Stern, born in Lithuania in 1885, was a New Deal Democratic legislator in the Maine House of Representatives in the 1930s. A resident of Biddeford and a long-time champion for social justice, Stern helped to create laws for child labor, workers' rights and safety initiatives, and old-age pensions. (Courtesy of the Maine Historical Society, Portland.)

Cantor Kurt Messerschmidt and his wife, Sonya, both survivors of Auschwitz, came to Portland in 1951, where Kurt served as the cantor of the Temple Beth El until he retired in 1985. Many of his former colleagues and students were on hand in 2004 to celebrate his 90th birthday. (Courtesy of the Messerschmidt family, Portland.)

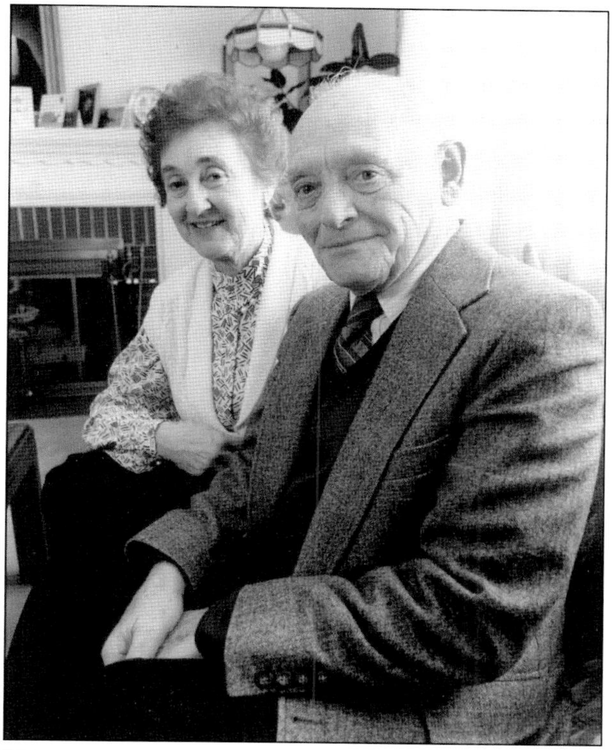

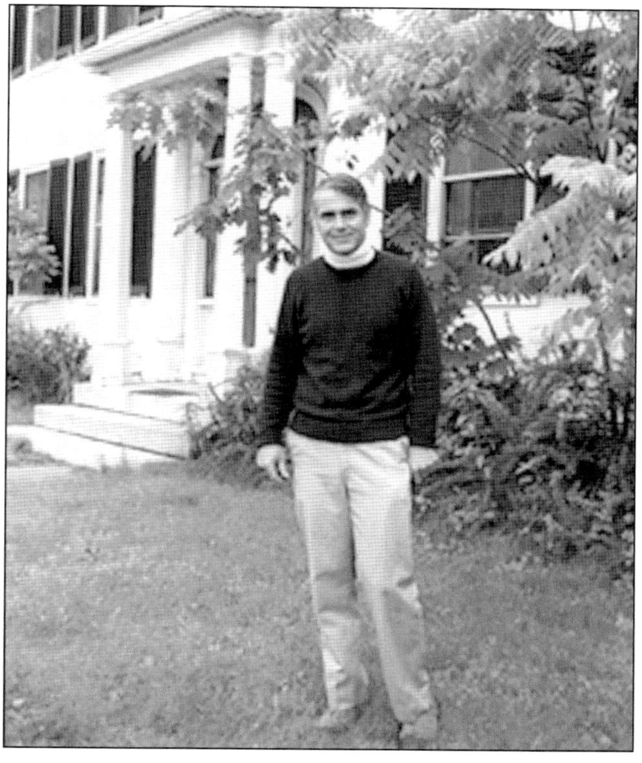

Peter Cox of Topsham, the son of Oscar Cox (see photograph on page 110), was a cofounder of the *Maine Times*, one of the earliest papers to report on the environment and social justice in Maine. (Courtesy of the Boston Phoenix.)

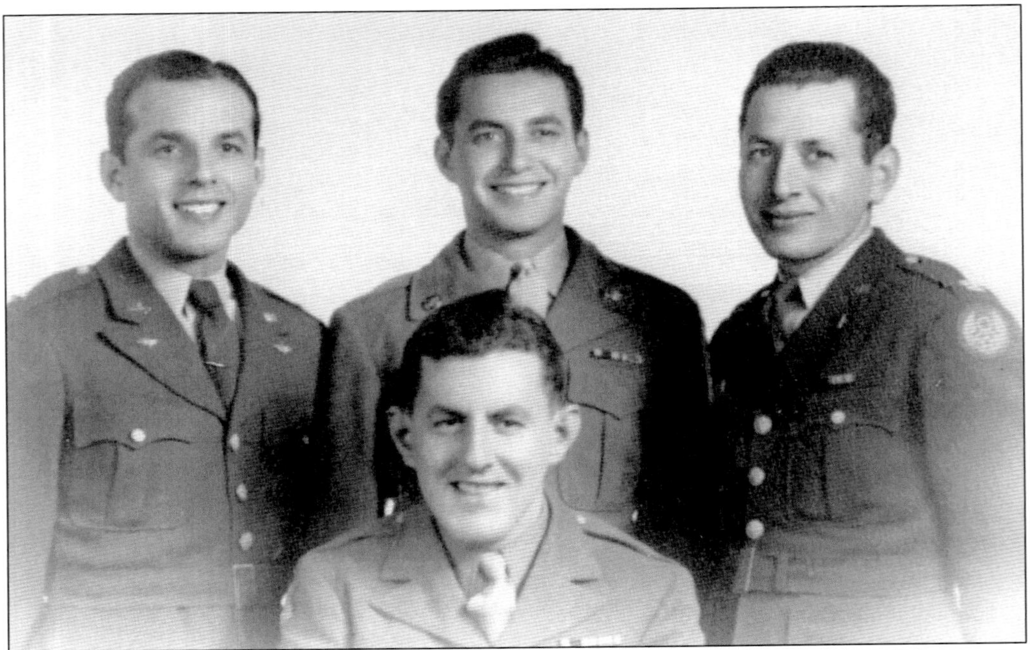

The Cohen brothers, all in uniform, were Biddeford businessmen. They are, from left to right, (first row) George; (second row) Sam, Lester, and Bernard. (Courtesy of Bea Cohen Espovich, Newburyport, Massachusetts.)

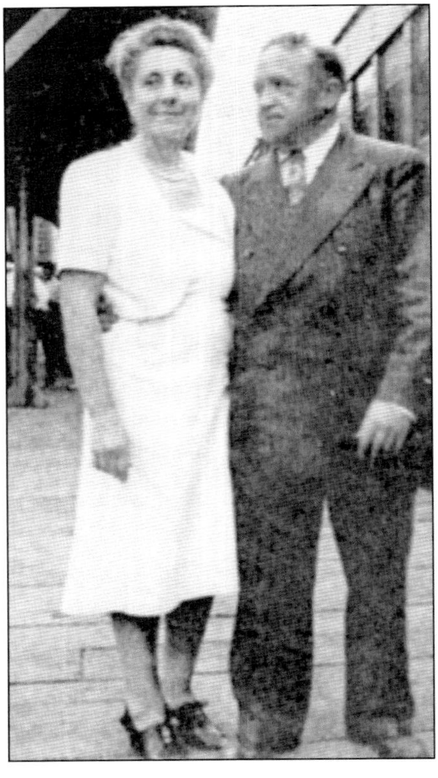

Lillian and Arthur Unobskey were leaders in the Calais business and Jewish communities.

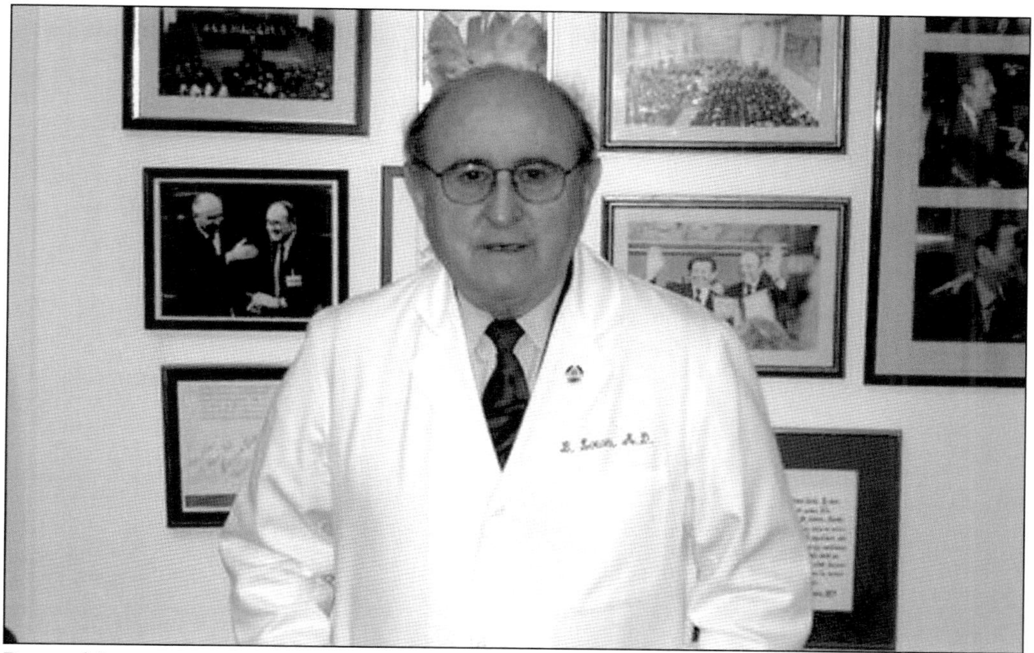

Bernard Lown grew up in Lewiston and is a cardiologist of world renown. He is the inventor of the direct current defibrillator. In 1985, Dr. Lown, as cofounder of the Physicians for the Prevention of Nuclear War, was the corecipient of the Nobel Peace Prize. (Courtesy of Dr. Bernard Lown, Brookline.)

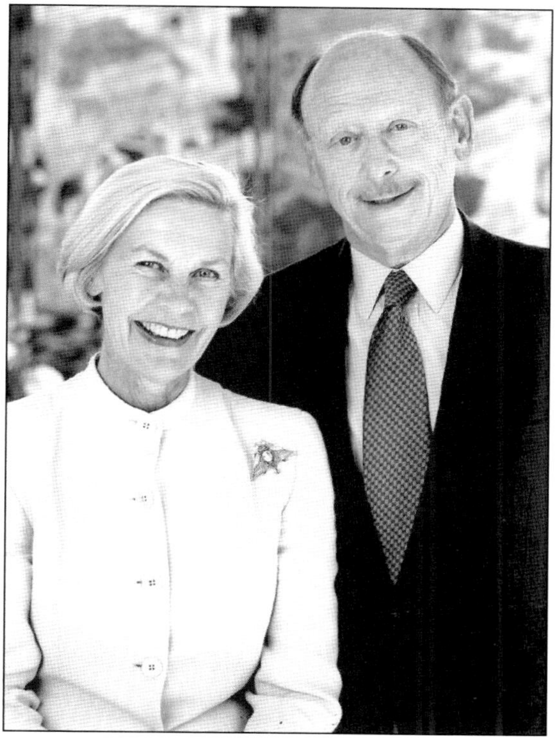

Born in Biddeford, Barney Osher is a nationally known philanthropist who endowed the Osher Lifelong Learning Institute at the University of Southern Maine. He is pictured with his wife, Barbro. (Courtesy of the Osher Lifelong Learning Institute, University of Southern Maine.)

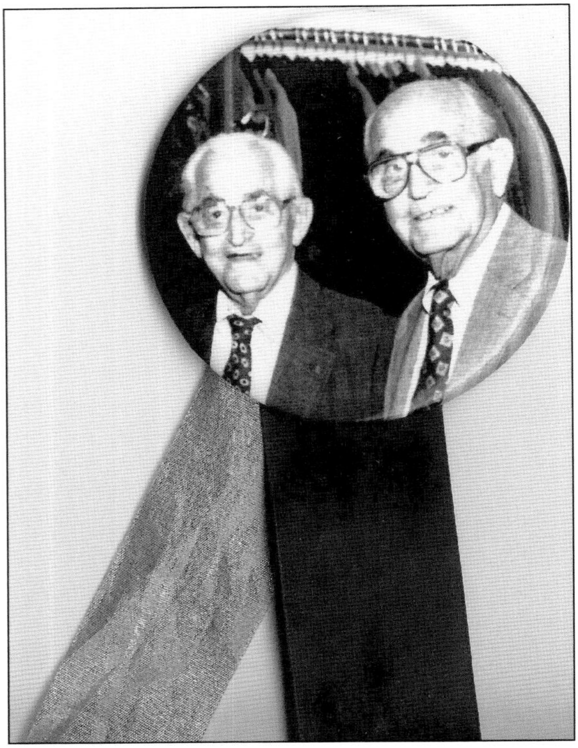

Ludy (left) and Pacy Levine were the owners of Levine's Clothing Store in Waterville, which was open for business for 105 years. (Courtesy of Daniel Pearl, Falmouth.)

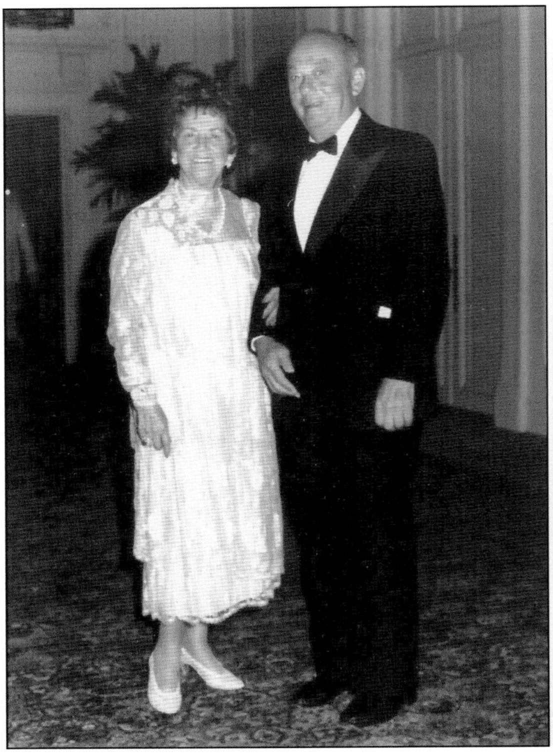

Dorothy "Bibby" Alfond was the last living child of William Levine, the founder of Levine's Clothing Store in Waterville. Harold Alfond is a major Maine philanthropist who founded the Dexter Shoe Company and the first private foundation in the state of Maine, the Harold Alfond Foundation. (Courtesy of Daniel Pearl, Falmouth.)

Henry Roth, a native of New York, wrote the great American Jewish novel, *Call It Sleep*, published in 1934. Roth and his wife, Muriel, moved to Maine in 1946 and eventually bought a farm where they bred ducks and geese. (Courtesy of the American Jewish Archives, Cincinnati.)

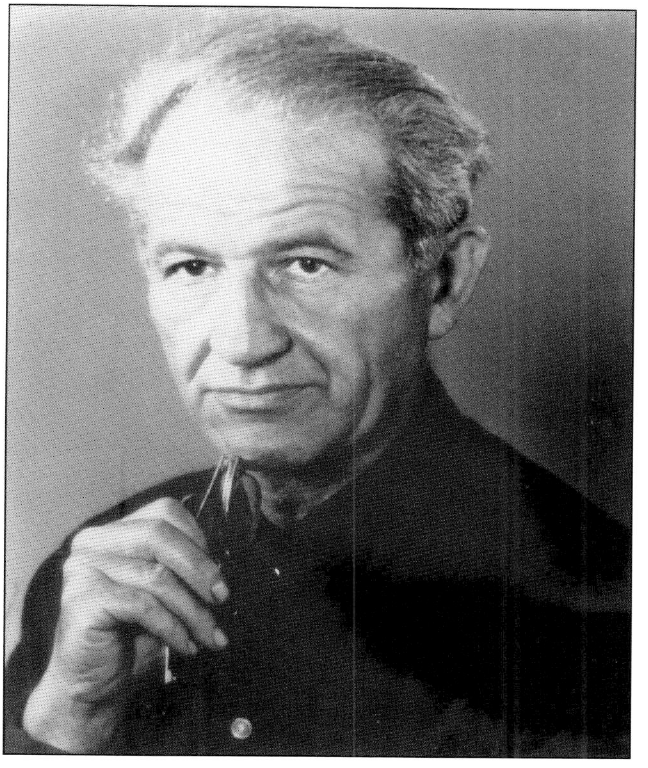

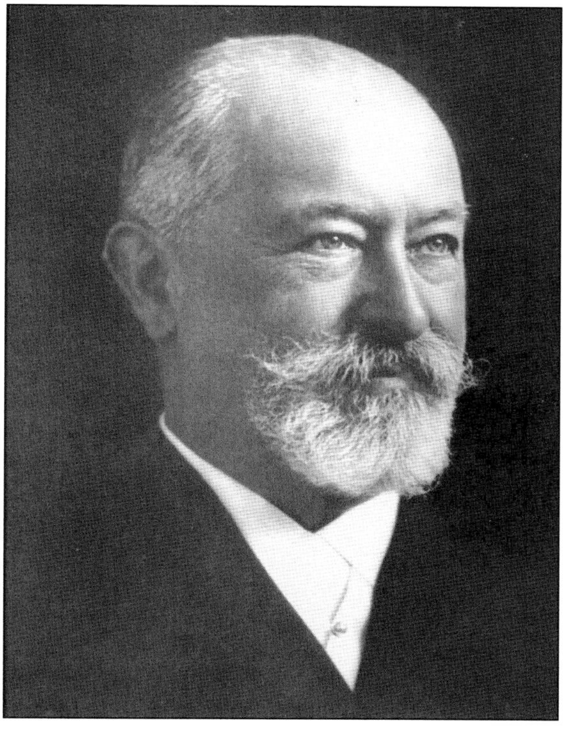

The famous philanthropist and Jewish communal leader Jacob Schiff and his wife Therese spent summers on Mount Desert Island. (Courtesy of the American Jewish Archives, Cincinnati.)

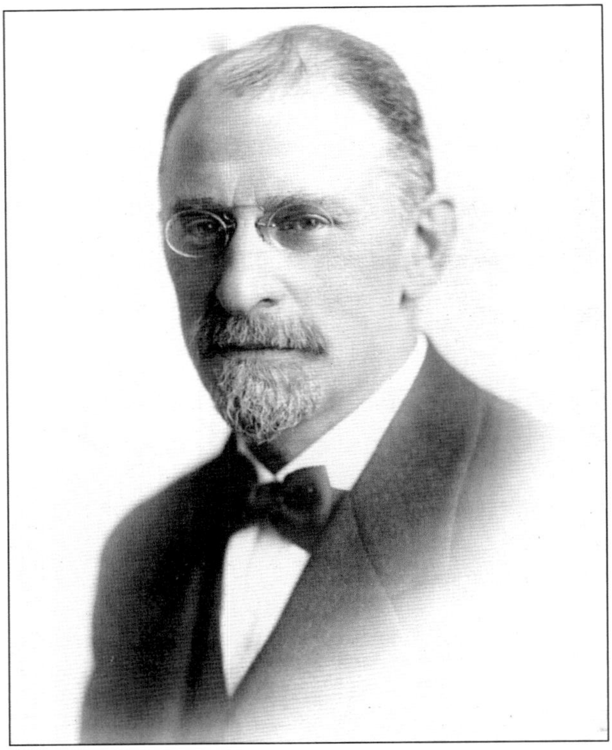

Henry Morgenthau Sr. was the ambassador to Turkey in 1915 who alerted the world to the murder of 1.5 million Armenians in Turkey. He and his wife Josephine summered on Mount Desert Island. (Courtesy of the American Jewish Archives, Cincinnati.)

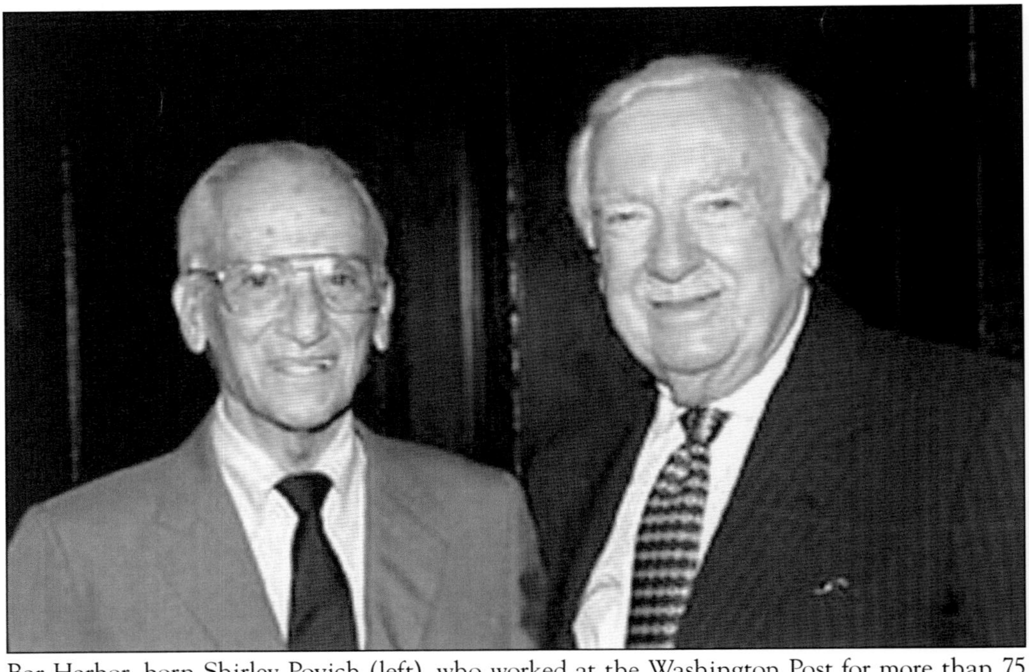

Bar Harbor–born Shirley Povich (left), who worked at the Washington Post for more than 75 years, was one of the greatest sportswriters of his generation. He is pictured here with Walter Cronkite. (Courtesy of the National Press Club, Washington, D.C.)

Wilhelm Reich, a controversial psychoanalyst, was a student of Sigmund Freud in Vienna. He moved to Maine in 1940 and ultimately bought several acres in the Rangeley Lakes area in order to build a research facility for his work on human sexuality.

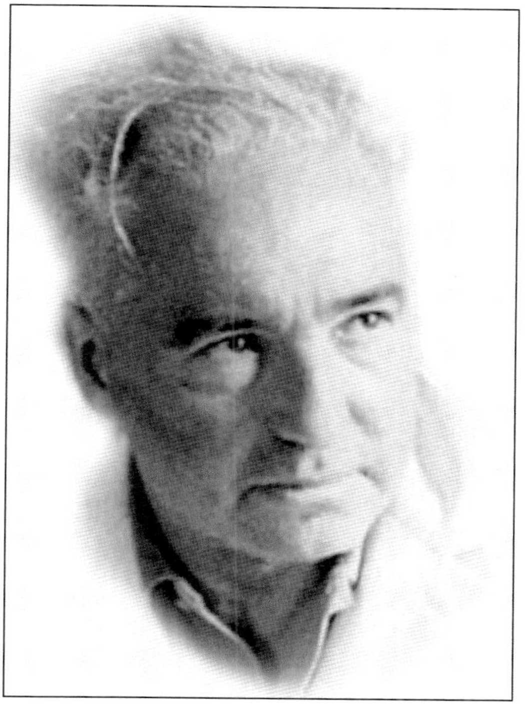

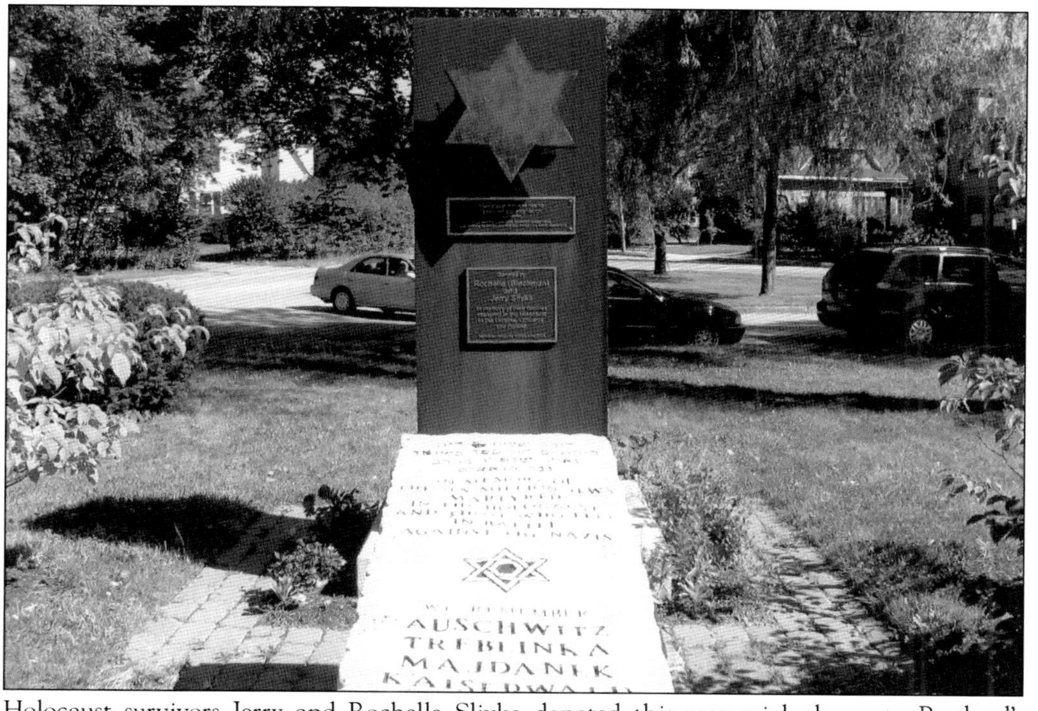

Holocaust survivors Jerry and Rochelle Slivka donated this memorial plaque to Portland's Temple Beth El, where it is displayed on the grounds. It is the only Holocaust memorial plaque in Maine.

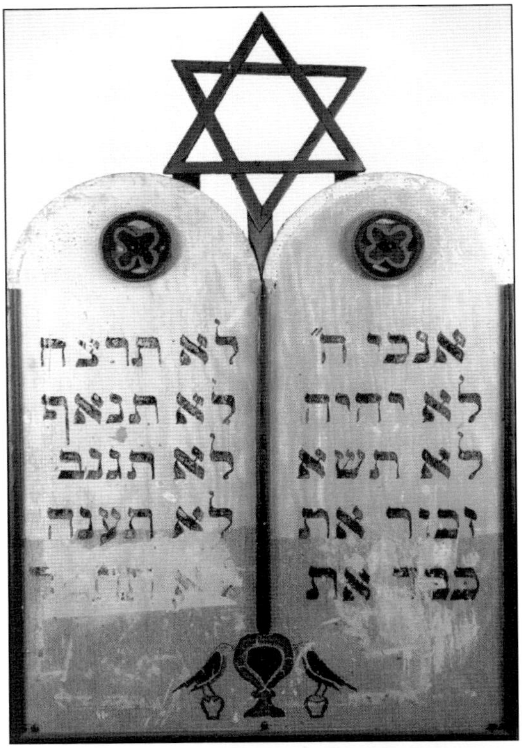

These Ten Commandments, where Maine's Jewish heritage began, once hung in the now inactive Gardiner synagogue. (Courtesy of Bruce and Nancy Schatz, Augusta.)

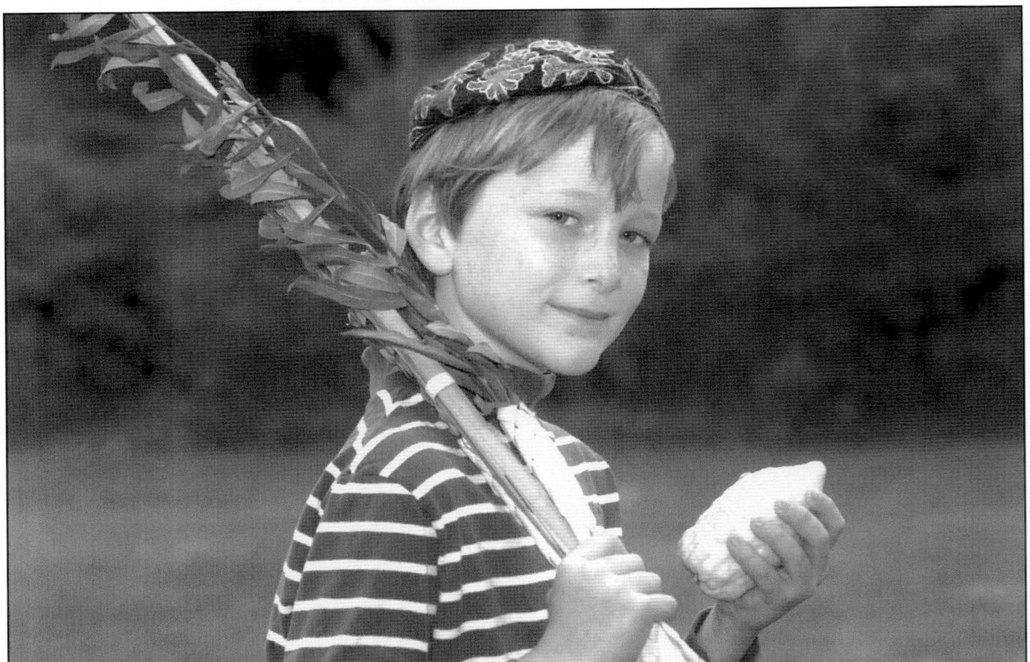

Zachary Olstein, a symbol of Maine's Jewish future, celebrated Sukkot at Temple Shalom Synagogue-Center in Auburn. (Courtesy of Phyllis Graber Jensen, Lewiston.)

BIBLIOGRAPHY

Band, Benjamin. *Portland Jewry: Its Growth and Development.* Portland: Jewish Historical Society, 1955.

Cohen, Michael. "Jerusalem of the North: An Analysis of Religious Modernization in Portland, Maine's Jewish Community." Honors thesis, Brown University, 2000.

Epstein, Howard. *Jews in Small Towns: Legends and Legacies.* Santa Rosa, California: Vision Book International, 1997.

Goldstein, Judith S. *Crossing Lines: Histories of Jews and Gentiles in Three Communities.* New York: Morrow, 1992.

Hoberman, Michael. *How Strange It Seems: An Oral History of Jewish Cultural Life in Small Town New England.* Amherst: University of Massachusetts Press, forthcoming.

Lipez, Julia. "A Time to Build Up and A Time to Break Down. The Jewish Secular Institutions of Portland, Maine." Honors thesis, Amherst College, 2002.

Risen, Celia C. *Some Jewels of Maine: Jewish Maine Pioneers.* Pittsburgh: Dorrance Publishing Company, 1997.

Weissbach, Lee Shai. *Jewish Life in Small Town America: A History.* New Haven: Yale University Press, 2005.